THE WINTER OLYMPICS

THE WINTER OLYMPICS

AN INSIDER'S GUIDE TO THE LEGENDS, THE LORE, AND THE GAMES

VANCOUVER EDITION

RON C. JUDD

THE MOUNTAINEERS BOOKS

THE MOUNTAINEERS BOOKS
is the nonprofit publishing arm of The Mountaineers Club, an organization founded in 1906 and dedicated to the exploration, preservation, and enjoyment of outdoor and wilderness areas.

1001 SW Klickitat Way, Suite 201, Seattle, WA 98134

Manufactured in China

Copy Editor: Rebecca Pepper
Book Design: Mayumi Thompson
Cartography: Pease Press

Photographs on the following pages are by Dean Rutz/ © *The Seattle Times* and are used with permission:
2, 10, 13, 16, 19, 38, 42, 55, 64, 72, 76, 88, 91, 96, 99, 102, 105, 112, 118, 121, 125, 129, 133, 134, 142, 146, 153, 154, 159, 160, 165, 167, 182, 183, 212, 214, 226, 235, 242, 243
Photographs on page 17 and 20 are © Dean Rutz
Photographs on the following pages are © Getty Images: 24, 32, 34, 74, 92, 100, 101, 104, 108, 114, 116, 135, 144, 170, 176, 180, 189, 194, 207, 236, 238.
Photograph on page 81 (U.S. men's curling team at Turin) and 228 (Birger Ruud statue) thanks to commons.wikimedia.org.
Photograph of Sandra Schmirler on page 84 courtesy of the Sandra Schmirler Foundation.
Photograph on page 175 of Jean Claude Killy reprinted from Library of Congress Prints & Photographs Division, Look Magazine Photograph Collection Call number: LOOK-Job 67-3544
All other photographs are by the author.

Library of Congress Cataloging-in-Publication Data
Judd, Ron C.
  The Winter Olympics : an insider's guide to the legends, the lore, and the game : Vancouver edition / by Ron C. Judd. — 1st ed.
      p. cm.
  Includes index.
  ISBN-13: 978-1-59485-063-9
  ISBN-10: 1-59485-063-1
  1. Winter Olympics. I. Title.
  GV841.5.J83 2008
  796.98—dc22
                        2008038796

CONTENTS

Introduction   9

Roots: A Brief History of the Winter Games   18
Vancouver Edition: The Sea to Sky Games   40

PART ONE: ICE SPORTS

Bobsled, Luge, Skeleton   58
Curling   79
Figure Skating   87
Ice Hockey   110
Speedskating   128
Short-Track Speedskating   151

PART TWO: SNOW SPORTS

Alpine Skiing   166
Cross-Country Skiing and Biathlon   188
Freestyle Skiing   206
Ski Jumping and Nordic Combined   218
Snowboarding   233

Further Reading   245
Acknowledgments   247
Index   249

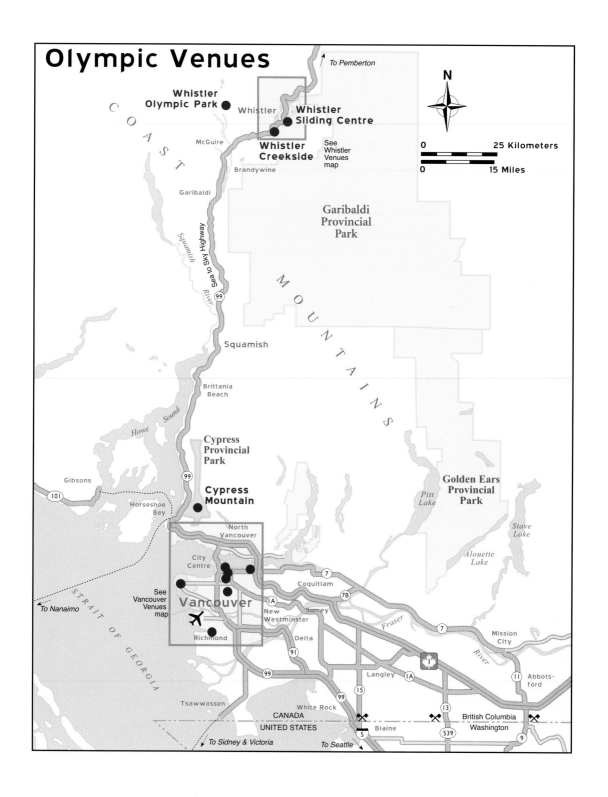

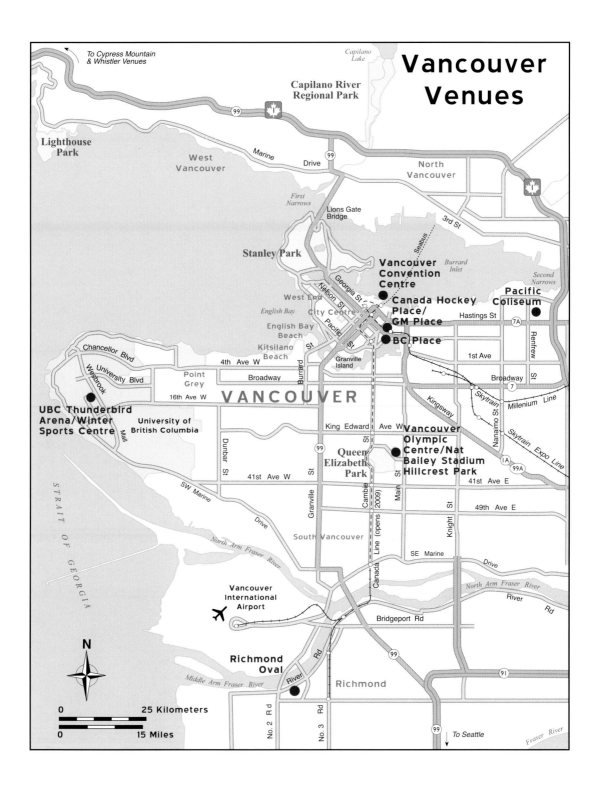

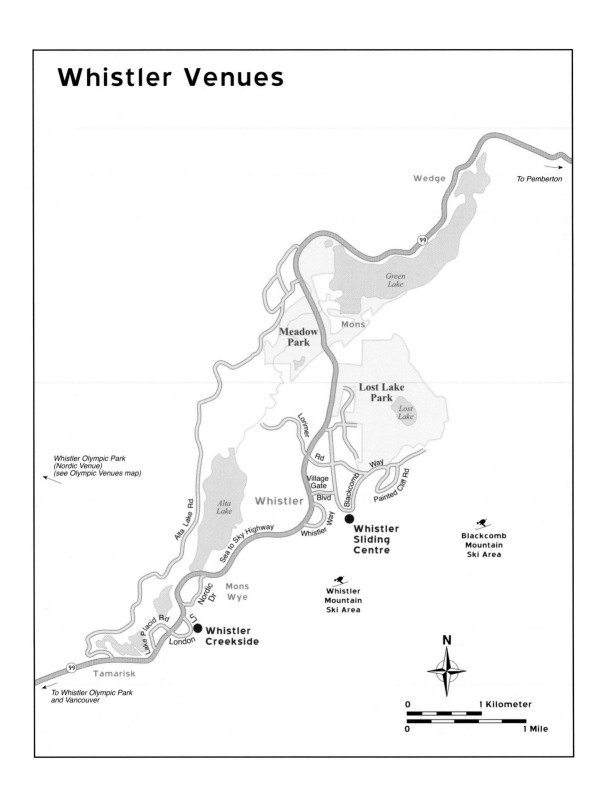

INTRODUCTION

❄ ❄ ❄ ❄ ❄

It's 5 AM, and the sun has not yet risen on Nagano, Japan.

I'm half asleep, which is a good thing, because full consciousness would only amplify the searing pain in my knees, wedged into the seatback in front of me on a bus designed for fourth graders.

It's mid-February, 1998—almost halfway through the Nagano Olympic Games. I'm sick, having been assailed by some feverish bug that always seems to rage through the Olympic Village and media center at every such global gathering of tens of thousands of people working too long, sleeping too little, and stressing too much. I'm tired, having boarded this same bus four times in the past week to undertake the winding, three-hour journey to Hakuba, in the Japanese Alps, to cover a ski race that, in every instance, was canceled because of excess snow.

And I'm grumpy, fully immersed in the mid-Olympics fog that overtakes all Olympics journalists after more than a week of 20-hour days, nonstop deadlines, unsympathetic editors, and—let's just come right out and say it—the entire European media corps, every member of which seems to be a chain smoker.

Amidst all this, the idling bus, parked next to the apartment building serving as media housing, offers a rare cocoon of calm. Five or six dozen "ringheads," as Olympic journalists call themselves, are sitting there, backpacks in their laps, trying to catch a few winks and silently wondering how those poor saps who boarded late are going to be able to stand in that skinny center aisle for the next three hours without dropping dead.

Breaking the silence, from the front row comes the surprisingly loud *pshhht!* of an aluminum can tab being pulled, then pushed back. Followed by a noisy, pronounced sluuuurp, the way someone might thirstily sip tea. And a glurg-glurg swallowing, capped off by a hefty sigh.

"Aaaah. Nothing like a hot can of coffee in the morning," the faceless canned-coffee drinker deadpans to no one in particular.

At which point we all bust up, right there, on that cramped, smelly bus, parked in a rain squall in Nagano, in the middle of Japan, where you can, and

Crowded buses, like this one in Nagano, Japan, are a fact of life for Olympic journalists, athletes, and officials.

often must, buy everything—*everything*—including your favorite piping-hot coffee drink, from a vending machine.

It was a moment of great levity, because in our journalistic stupor we all realized that each of us had been on the business end of the same can of coffee more times than we could count in the past days—and probably at many Olympics past. And with that small, shared indignity, a sense of camaraderie spread through the bus like roasted garlic wafting from an Italian restaurant. It made us all feel just a little bit more okay.

In my case, a whole lot of Olympic memories include public transport—the effectiveness of which, when you come right down to it, is really what defines the success or failure of any given

Olympics. In simple terms: If you want to get up close and personal with Olympic glory, you've got to be able to get to the ice rink.

"What's it like to cover the Games?" friends, colleagues, and students sometimes ask. "You ride a lot of buses," I'll say.

The truth is, however, that covering the Olympics is any good journalist's dream assignment. The palette of possible stories laid out before you every day is broad, diverse, and occasionally even magical. Good journalism, for all its acknowledged faults, is little more than good storytelling. And good stories are rife with drama. Few other assignments, short of war, perhaps, afford a dramatic stage as brightly lit as an Olympic Games.

Mixed in with that dream job, however, are

frequent bouts of nightmare. Yes, great stories are there for the taking, any day and every day. But where do you start? You start the night before with the following day's schedule, which you're usually poring over with some colleagues, trying to do some basic triage. What to cover? If I take the bus to Hakuba to watch Hermann Maier ski the downhill, will I be back in time to watch Michelle Kwan skate? (Answer: No. I stayed in town—and missed Maier's legendary ascent into orbit before he crashed spectacularly after flying 60 feet into the cold, thin air above Hakuba.)

Often, coverage choices are dictated by simple logistics. The daily challenge goes something like this: (1) Pick a sport, any sport. (2) Figure out how in the world you will get there under the constraints of the Olympics' byzantine, baffling, and all-too-often ineffectual bus system. (3) Strategize about just how early you need to be at the chosen venue to get a decent seat in its cramped, overrun, temporary press center and hook your laptop up to AC power and internet connections before they're all taken by someone else. (4) Make a test run and compile a mental map of a route from the arena, where the game or event is taking place, to the bowels of the venue to find the "mix zone," a fenced-off area where competitors are interviewed, and then back into the press center to write and file your story or photos, usually on a tight deadline. (5) Pace yourself, knowing that you must get back to the main press center, regroup, and do it all over again—as many as three or four times a day, for the three-week duration of most Olympics.

If you play this game successfully, of course, the payoff can be tremendous. It is almost a given that, sooner or later, you're going to see something great—perhaps even transcendent. The flip side? You're going to miss about five other similarly grand moments, simply because you can be in only one place at one time—and most of us, about half the time, choose the wrong one. It's the nature of

the beast. And it is why, after more than a decade of covering the Olympics, I've come to greatly prefer the Winter Games.

It's a matter of personal taste: Winter sports such as alpine and cross-country skiing are things that I actually do, from my home in the northwestern corner of the United States. But it's also a matter of professional pragmatism: The Winter Games are much smaller than their summer counterpart. The entire schedule for the complete seventeen days fits on one sheet of paper—albeit one with type that grows harder and harder to read every time the torch is relit.

With fewer choices, the odds are that you'll be there when, say, Kjetil André Aamodt of Norway closes out his spectacular career by becoming both the youngest and oldest man ever to win an alpine skiing gold medal. It's simply more manageable.

This has been true of the Winter Games throughout history, until the recent shift to host cities that are major metropolitan areas. Most of the Winter Games up through Lillehammer in 1994 had a small-town, folksy feel. They were truly intimate events, the kind of scene where any of the 4,000 permanent residents of a small burg like Lake Placid, New York, could actually rub elbows with winter-sport legends such as Ingemar Stenmark or Eric Heiden at a local café. For that reason alone, the Winter Games, at least until recent years, have always brought their own unique, alpine-village charm.

Of course, such remote, high-altitude locales present their own challenges, some of which, through history, have threatened to bring the Games to a halt. Since their very beginning high in the Alps at Chamonix, the Winter Games seem to have carried a weather curse. Mountain towns that haven't had a warm spell since Columbus sailed can be relied on to have one just in time for the Olympics, sending host nations into a frenzied panic and the schedule into complete disarray. It happens. You adjust. Once it all begins, and that runner touches off the cauldron in whatever inventive way the latest host city has devised to launch the Games, you're quickly sucked into the maw of scheduling, harried transit, and fatigue. And as a journalist, you always seem to be about a half-day behind.

Complicating things further is the fact that there are two often wildly differing versions of reality during an Olympic Games: the one athletes and spectators see, feel, touch, taste, and smell—and the glossy, usually tape-delayed version you see back at home, on TV. Ever since the 1960 Squaw Valley Games, the first Olympics to be broadcast more or less in their entirety on television, the TV version—which those of us on the ground really have no access to—has largely set the agenda. It's the one our editors—not to mention billions of global Olympic watchers—are plugged into. If a particular story—a figure skating judging scandal, say—dominates TV coverage, it quickly will dominate the lives of people at the Games themselves. At that point, our own version of what's most important at the Olympics that day is essentially rendered moot. TV, in addition to paying most of the Olympics' bills, also plots its story lines, simply because it is the prism through which most of the world experiences the Games.

In some cases, those story lines are obvious, and TV gets it right. It's difficult even for grumpy cynics to argue, for example, with the made-for-TV grandeur of an Olympics opening or closing ceremony. I'll make a confession here that I might not make on a crowded bus full of journalists: I'm a ceremony geek. To me, the pomp and pageantry of the opening and closing ceremonies, while admittedly usually over the top, provides many of the more memorable moments at any Olympics, because they emphasize the Games' great cultural melting pot. Some folks blow the ceremonies off; journalists watch the TV feedback at the press center and write about it as if they'd been right in its midst. It's a lot easier that way, frankly (again, transport and logistics). Not me. I want to be there, to live it and feel it, even if that means, as it did in Salt Lake City, fighting through crowds to get to the press center, where I sat, fingers completely frozen from being out in the 20-degree weather for three hours, and attempted to write a coherent story for page one of the next day's paper, in about 15 minutes.

Afterward, I remember feeling the way I do after every Olympics: exhausted, wrung out, used up—and buzzed.

Why? The Olympics is unlike anything else out there. It is a rare moment in time when all the people of the world come together as one to do something besides attempt to kill one another. The planet stops, at least for a second, and turns its focus on one place, one competition, for three medals. Gold, silver, bronze.

It is that complicated and that simple and, when it all works as well as it can, that beautiful.

From an inside perspective, inside the arenas, inside the locker rooms, inside the offices and ceremonies and what passes as media housing, the Olympics are a lot like they must seem from the outside. Just extremely amplified. The lows—the backstabbing between national federations, the politics, the sponsor money-grubbing, the insane caste system in which Olympic Family are treated like royalty while local residents of the host city are snubbed or even physically relocated—seem even lower from up close.

But the highs—Croatian skier Janica Kostelić persevering to become the greatest female alpine skier in Olympic history in spite of growing up in a nation, Croatia, that had no ski team and barely had a country—are that much higher when the stars are right there, within your reach, where you can see their tears and feel their exultation.

There's no way to truly describe how it feels to stand there as history unfolds. I will go to my grave remembering the clock ticking down to zero on the first-ever women's gold medal hockey game, where the United States edged out Canada for the gold medal in 1998. Athletes from both teams—they had and still have a rivalry that borders on hate—dropped gloves and sticks and hugged one another, reveling in the historic significance. For once, it wasn't about who won. It was about female hockey players who had dared to dream, all those years, on playgrounds and ice rinks around the world. They had arrived. Arrivals are great stories. We all stood there and watched, and there wasn't a dry eye in the place. That's what makes it all worthwhile. Deadlines be damned; this is history, and if you don't pause to soak it all up, you're either dead or a fool.

Covering the Olympics is a special privilege, and no matter how much we media people gripe about schedules and deadlines, deep down, each of us ringheads knows it and embraces it. The Olympics can be maddening. But when the magic happens and you're close enough to reach out and touch it, it's very real.

That, in fact, was a large part of the motivation for this book. As an Olympics observer, I am far from an expert on the Games, past or present. I'm just a guy who happened to be lucky enough to fall into a job that takes me on a worldwide tour in

U.S. figure skater Kristi Yamaguchi carries the Olympic flame through the streets of Nagano in 1998.

pursuit of the flame every two years. I was fortunate enough at one point, in fact, to carry the flame, on the torch relay for the 2002 Salt Lake Games. It moved me, and some part of me will always feel the heat from that flame held high above my head.

It sounds corny, but if you're there, you understand. My hope for this book is to take you there, for a few moments, a few hours, or a few days, and help you draw closer to the true meaning of that flame, to help you get a better sense of what the Games represent.

One way to do that is to mine the Olympics' rich past. Another is to flesh out the rules, skills, equipment, and field of play to help you better understand—and, I hope, more fully enjoy—the Games in the present. Yet another is to bring to life some of the Winter Games' greatest stars—larger-than-life legends of the ice and snow.

I've endeavored to do all of that in this book, mixing my own firsthand knowledge of the modern Winter Olympics with archival knowledge of Games past. I believe a full grounding in the often folksy, occasionally zany, always heartwarming roots of the Winter Games is particularly relevant now, as we stand on the cusp of the 2010 Games in Vancouver, Canada, the largest metropolitan area ever to host a Winter Olympics and clearly the most diverse, globally focused city ever to take on the task.

The world has high hopes for the Sea to Sky Games, as they're known in British Columbia. As do I. The Games are literally right up the road from my home in the Pacific Northwest. They are, likewise, a short hop away for most Americans. So my parting advice would be this: If you can, go. Find a way to fight through the maddening allocation process and get tickets. You're not likely to be disappointed. You might make for yourself a lifetime

Opposite: A journalist at work during the opening ceremonies for the 2006 Turin Winter Olympics.

memory. And if you can't go? Watch, read, listen, enjoy. Soak it up from home. The Olympics are a grand excuse for broadening ourselves, standing back and dropping the stock report and glimpsing, just for a moment, how we relate to, and fit in with, the rest of the world.

If you can find that moment and drink in that view, the Olympics will have been a success. And if this book helps push you closer to that viewpoint, I'll consider it a worthy endeavor as well.

A BRIEF GUIDE TO THE GUIDE

This book began with a simple goal: Assemble a compendium of knowledge about the Winter Olympics to help the average person better understand the Games. Whether you'll be watching in person or via broadcast, or just discussing the topic with friends, the information and stories compiled here will help you become conversant in any Winter Olympics sport. It's designed to give the casual fan of the Winter Games a broader context of the event throughout history, and fill in those knowledge gaps—how many jumps does a ski jumper take during the Nordic combined?—that we all have, particularly for sports most of us see only once every four years.

The material also is, I hope, interesting enough on its face—given all the lore, mystery, and fascinating backdrops of the Games—to be a worthwhile read, even for the decidedly non-Olympiphile.

Either way, this guide is organized in a way that makes it easy to skip around to something that piques your interest.

Sport by Sport

The book is organized by sporting event, grouped into ice sports and snow sports. Individual chapters describe individual pursuits—hockey, speedskating, cross-country skiing, and the like. Each chapter begins with an overview of the sport, often including an anecdote from my personal experience at the Olympics or compelling stories from Games past that illustrate the character of each given sport.

Spectator's Guide

The "Spectator's Guide" sections are a simple introduction to the sport: how it's competed, on what field of play, with what equipment, how one wins, and so on. Few people really know all the rules of the events they see so infrequently. And even those of us who witness them more often usually benefit from a refresher course.

History's Hits and Misses

Each Spectator's Guide is followed by a "History's Hits & Misses" section, a grab bag of great exploits, notable flops, unforgettable moments, and trivia from the annals of the sport in question. It's sort of

Tara Lipinski could not contain her exhilaration as she completed a jump combination in the short program at the Nagano Games in 1998.

the CliffsNotes on the subject, the basic boilerplate history any educated Olympic fan needs to know.

Record Book

Each chapter also features the "Record Book," a section describing prominent medalists in the sport. Note that I make no attempt here to include all medalists in a sport. Other published works, most notably David Wallechinsky's indispensable *The Complete Book of the Winter Olympics,* do that and more, listing the top finishers in each event for the entirety of the Games' history. Instead, I have attempted here to summarize, listing interesting trends (such as the Soviet Union's decades-long lock on the gold medal in pairs figure skating, or Canada's early dominance in ice hockey). I also have endeavored to single out prominent medalists, especially those with long Olympic careers and noteworthy medal hauls. Lastly, I've attempted to list all of the North American medalists for each sport. This is not intended as a slight on other deserving medalists; it's simply a reflection of the primary audience for this book: North Americans.

Next Stop

Each chapter concludes with the section "Next Stop," describing the venue where that sport will take place for the Vancouver 2010 Games. In some cases, these sections include detailed reviews of the actual field of play from athletes who have participated in test events at the venues (most of which are new). When appropriate, I've also included information on how to use the venue—for your own figure skating turns or weekend mogul attempts—when and if it's open and available for public use.

Legends of the Sport and Olympic Flashbacks

Interspersed throughout the book are two other features: "Legend of the Sport" pieces highlight an athlete whose Olympic Games performance truly qualifies him or her as legendary. The title is not bestowed lightly; you have to have done something remarkable to earn the label. Note that several of the newer sports don't include a "legend" because, frankly, I don't believe they've been around long enough for any athlete to have earned the title. "Olympic Flashbacks" are moment-in-time glimpses of my reporting of the Games. Each is a column filed from the Winter Olympics and published in the following day's *Seattle Times* as part of my general Olympic beat reporting. I reproduce them here because they say, in a manner more fresh and of-the-moment, more about an event than I could ever hope to say by re-creating it from memory. They are some of my favorite pieces filed from the Winter Olympics.

Dousing the flame: an exhausted journalist collapses into a noodle bowl at 3:00 AM on the last night of the 1998 Nagano Games.

ROOTS: A BRIEF HISTORY OF THE WINTER GAMES

❋ ❋ ❋ ❋ ❋

When you walk the streets of Chamonix, a jewel of a village in the French Alps, look up at the jutting peaks, breathe in the fresh air, and soak up what can only be described as mountain majesty, you might think it'd be a grand place for a Winter Olympics.

Well, it was. But you'd never know it from inspecting the place.

The town's Olympic past was, in fact, one of the reasons I traveled there, back in the early autumn of 2004, on a trek of Olympic discovery.

This was a Summer Olympics year, and on the way to Athens to cover the Summer Games, photojournalist Dean Rutz and I made a stop in Paris, where we strolled the Sorbonne, the sprawling university campus where the very notion of a modern Olympics was formulated and popularized by French aristocrat Pierre de Coubertin in the late 19th century. We soaked up a bit of that history, and after the Athens Games set out to find more, by returning to Paris and boarding a train for the Alps and, ultimately, Chamonix.

It's a magical little place, with charming old alpine-style buildings set on either side of the Arve River, which, in late summer, pushes milky glacial

flour through the town. As a student of both the Olympics and mountaineering, I'd always intended to visit here. This became a pilgrimage, of sorts, to the birthplace of the Winter Games.

I expected this to be a simple task: walk into town, look for the signs pointing to whatever was left of the Olympic infrastructure there, snap photos. But after two days of investigating the village, nary a sign of the famed five rings was found. I put the matter out of mind for a couple days, which was very easy to do, caught up as we were in the wealth of alpine hiking and sightseeing in the area. But I wanted to rub elbows with some piece of those famous first Games I'd read about long before. I wanted to stand on the site of the ice sheet, perhaps, where America's Charles Jewtraw won the first-ever Winter Olympic medal; where Gillis Grafström of Sweden, one of the sport's greatest innovators, performed; where a precocious Norwegian girl, Sonja Henie, first took

Opposite: Figure skater Midori Ito of Japan is granted her nation's highest Olympic honor: lighting the torch cauldron at the opening ceremonies.

to the ice as an 11-year-old phenom. I wanted to see some evidence of the ski trails and jump where a Norwegian with a classic Olympic name—Thorleif Haug—flew to three gold medals.

But none of this was in evidence. We took a daylong side trip to the excellent Olympic Museum, just to the north in Lausanne, Switzerland, where the archives displayed grand images of the first Games' quaint opening ceremonies, and some of its competitions. Back in Chamonix, we visited the Musée Alpin, mostly filled with tokens of the region's rich mountaineering history.

On one museum wall, however, was a display of black-and-white photographs of the Olympic ceremonies. One picture showed a national delegation, from Canada, I believe, marching into the parade grounds. In the background was the river, and behind it, a large, white-sided hotel.

My friend Elliott Almond, another Olympics buff and longtime "ringhead," pointed at it. "That hotel," he said, "is still there."

"Where?"

"Right up the street."

We walked over and went to the front desk, combining our embarrassingly inadequate French-language skills to get the clerk to summon the proprietor. Was this the hotel pictured in the first Winter Olympics photos?

Why yes, she said. The hotel had stood in place for a century. In 1924, it was owned by her grandfather, and had been passed down through the family. Behind the hotel, across the river, she pointed out the site of the Olympic parade grounds. We thanked her and walked across the bridge to the site.

There, at ground zero for the birth of the Winter Olympic movement, we found what can only accurately be described as the least attractive building in all of Chamonix—a trade school, with the typical, 1960s-style cement walls and complete lack of architectural imagination.

Around the far side, on the edge of a parking lot, we found it: Chamonix's only homage to the first Olympics. It was a modest stone-and-steel sign, denoting the dates and this place—home of the first-ever Winter Olympics, in 1924. It was a new height in understatement, but somehow, in the grand context of the Alps, appropriate. The people of Chamonix, we decided—and learned by asking some of them later—have neither the need nor the desire to exploit their role in Olympic history.

Easy for them, actually: They don't need it to draw tourists, who flocked here for the alpine grandeur long before the Games were invented, and will keep flocking here long after the first Games are forgotten—which, to most people, they already are. The city is known as the birthplace of modern alpinism, and today has become a thriving center for all practitioners of adventure sports, including parasailers who rain from the sky every summer afternoon, dropping from the tops of jutting peaks to the valley floor.

Chamonix, it seems, refrains from touting its Olympic past because it simply doesn't need to tout it. You've got your sign, and that's enough.

Thus ended, in something of an anticlimax, my personal quest to get a tactile feel for early Olympic history. And thus began a broader effort to get to know the Games even better by studying their history on paper, in books, pictures, memorabilia, and historical documents.

Along the way, I learned that the choice of host cities, as is evidenced by Chamonix, in the old days often was as much a product of chance as it was careful deliberation. The first Winter Games, in fact, weren't even officially designated as such until two years after their completion. Here's how it happened:

Ever since the first modern Games, held in 1894 in Greece, organizers had sought to bolster their athletic lineup—and, frankly, to broaden the

Games' appeal to northern European nations—by sprinkling in some winter sports. After fourteen years of deliberation—early Olympic officials didn't do anything without due consideration—ice skating finally debuted in 1908, in a seemingly odd place—at the London Summer Games.

The first Olympic skating contest featured now-familiar names, such as the men's champion, Sweden's Ulrich Salchow, father of the jump that now bears his name, and Madge Syers of Great Brit-

ain, crowned the ladies' champion. The event was a popular success, but it quickly became clear that an Olympics in the summer would never be a practical setting for any sports beyond ice skating or hockey, which even then could be staged indoors.

This realization led to a formal proposal, made in 1911 by an International Olympic Committee (IOC) member from Italy, Count Brunetta d'Ussaux, to encourage Stockholm, site of the 1912 Games, to either include winter sports or stage a separate winter event.

A tall stone-and-steel marker is all that remains of Winter Olympics I, in Chamonix, France, in 1924.

The notion was far from popular with the Scandinavian countries. Even though it was widely believed that they would dominate winter events, northern nations had been hosting their own Nordic Games for more than a decade, and they saw the Olympics as unfair, Johnny-come-lately competition.

They were outvoted by the IOC membership, which approved a separate Winter Games for 1916, with ice competitions in Berlin and Nordic skiing and jumping events at Feldberg Mountain in southern Germany. That plan was nixed by World War I, and when the next Olympics came around, in Antwerp, Belgium in 1920, they once again were Summer Games with a few winter elements—figure skating and hockey.

By then, de Coubertin, the IOC president and overall grand poobah, had soured on the idea of a separate Winter Olympics. Winter sports, then mostly associated with resorts for the well-heeled, were dismissed as "snobbish" activities for the rich (an irony, given de Coubertin's social status, not to mention that of the lion's share of other members of the IOC, then and to this day). But support for a Winter Games remained among many IOC members, who voted for an experimental adjunct to the 1924 Paris Summer Games. It was to be called the International Week of Winter Sports. The site: Chamonix.

The little town already had a ski jump, which was upgraded for the Games. Organizers quickly built a bobsled run, an ice stadium on the valley floor, and a shooting range and ski trails for the biathlon, which had been approved as a demonstration sport then known as "military patrol."

The Games began on January 25, 1924, with 258 athletes (13 of whom were women—all figure skaters) from 16 nations drawn to the Haute-Savoie region on the border between France and Italy. Athletes, as can be witnessed in grainy silent film in the IOC archives, marched into the opening ceremonies in full performance uniform, carrying their skis and hockey sticks and pulling their sleds.

The Games—which hosted 18- and 50-kilometer cross-country ski races; ski jumping and Nordic combined; speedskating races of 500, 1,500, 5,000, and 10,000 meters; four-man bobsled; hockey; and figure skating—were hailed as a complete success by most of the 10,000 spectators.

The majority of IOC members agreed. In 1926, the sports festival was redesignated the first Olympic Winter Games. A new tradition had begun.

The typical early Winter Games played out in a small mountain village, with fewer than two dozen nations and 300 to 700 athletes. The schedules and complexity increased during the 1950s, with more member nations added to the IOC and more events tagged on to existing sports.

Not until the 1964 Games in Innsbruck would the number of competitors leap to more than 1,000, a number that remained fairly level until the 1988 Games at Calgary, when the figure ballooned to 1,423 with the addition of new alpine ski events such as the super-giant slalom (super-G) and new team events for existing sports such as the Nordic combined and ski jumping.

In 1992 that growth spurt continued, with more than 1,800 athletes gathering for the Albertville Games, thanks to the introduction of two completely new sports—freestyle skiing and short-track speedskating. By the time snowboarding was introduced at the Nagano Games of 1998, the Winter Olympics had grown to 2,176 athletes from 72 nations, with 68 separate medal events. The last Winter Games, in Turin, saw 2,400 athletes compete in 78 medal events. Similar numbers are expected in the Vancouver Games of 2010.

The point: The explosion of the Winter Olympics into the major, multisport festival we know today is a fairly recent phenomenon, occurring mostly after the 1992 IOC vote to split the Winter Games into an alternating four-year cycle from the Summer Games. That decision was partially to accommodate broadcasters, who found their resources strained in covering a full Summer and Winter Games during the same year. But it also was intended to give the Winter Games their own cachet, on equal footing with the Summer Games, as one or the other now rolls around every two years.

Also worth noting is the progression of the size of the host cities, from small mountain towns to major urban centers such as Calgary, Nagano, Salt Lake City, and Turin, a city of 900,000 that became the largest host city ever in 2006—at least for a short while. Vancouver, with a metropolitan population of 2.3 million, will easily eclipse that mark when it raises the Olympic flag at B.C. Place in February 2010. The entire city of Chamonix would fit neatly into one corner of any of those cities' neighborhoods.

The 2014 host city—Sochi, Russia—will be a step back in the other direction. Only time will tell if that's the start of a retro trend or just an aberration in the march to bigger, more complex, and more expensive venues for the Games of the Winter Olympiad.

With all that in mind, let's take a look at what has come before:

1924: I Olympic Winter Games
Chamonix, France

More than 10,000 people attended the International Sports Week in 1924, in picturesque Chamonix, an event that drew athletes from 16 nations to the Alps to compete in hockey, bobsled, ski jumping, and skating. It wasn't until two years after the competition that Olympic officials officially branded them the first Olympic Winter Games. But all the athletes knew at the time that the festival, the first to bring competitors in so many disciplines together for a single winter sports event, was something special.

The inaugural Games will be remembered for the first-ever gold medal, awarded to speedskater Charles Jewtraw, from Lake Placid, New York, who won the 500 meters on an outdoor track that circled the parade grounds that had been used for the opening ceremony. The Games also crowned a repeat champion: Gillis Grafström of Sweden had won the figure skating competition at the 1920 Summer Games in Antwerp. Grafström, an early innovator credited with inventing the spiral and flying sit spin, took the gold easily in Chamonix.

The dominant figure at the Games was A. Clas Thunberg, a Finn who medaled in all five speedskating events. The first Games also marked the beginning of a long period of dominance for Canada's hockey team. They beat five opponents easily, rolling up a combined score of 110–3. The Chamonix Games also saw the debut of a gifted young figure skater, Sonja Henie, 11, of Norway. She finished eighth, but even at such a young age she displayed the talent that would carry her to history in the next three Olympics.

1928: II Olympic Winter Games
St. Moritz, Switzerland

The St. Moritz Games—the first to be held in a different country from the one hosting the Summer Olympics—were the first of many to be cursed by rain and unseasonably warm weather. The 10,000-meter speedskating race was never completed, as the ice literally began melting before it was finished. Rain shut the Games down for an entire day. Nearly a third of the competitors in the 50-kilometer cross-country ski race—difficult enough under optimal conditions—quit in frustration on a slushy course.

Sonja Henie of Norway, competing now as a veteran 15-year-old, soared to her first gold medal in women's figure skating. She would remain the youngest Olympic gold medalist for 74 years.

A highlight of the Games was the sliding events, held on the famous track that gave birth to the sports of bobsled, luge, and skeleton. The latter appeared as a new Olympic event, and Americans Jennison and John Heaton took advantage, winning the gold and silver medals, respectively.

Sonja Henie and competitors kick up their heels at the 1928 Winter Games in St. Moritz, Switzerland.

Gillis Grafström of Sweden was crowned men's figure skating champion for the third straight time, if you count his Summer Games appearance in 1920. Also repeating on the medal stand was A. Clas Thunberg, the Norwegian speedskating great, who added two more gold medals to his tally. Norwegian dominance at these Olympic Games was personified by skier Johan Grøttumsbråten, who won the 18-kilometer cross-country race and also the Nordic combined.

Canada continued its domination in hockey,

winning three games by a combined score of 38–0. And in pairs figure skating, the French duo of Andrée Joly and Pierre Brunet rocked the skating world when they both competed wearing black, shattering a tradition of women always wearing white. The pair later married and continued competing as Andrée and Pierre Brunet.

1932: III Olympic Winter Games
Lake Placid, New York, USA

The first Olympics outside Europe unfolded in an unlikely place—little Lake Placid, New York, an

Adirondack mountain village of 4,000 year-round residents that was bold enough to host a Games during the Great Depression. The expense of the long boat ride proved prohibitive for some European athletes: Only about half as many competed as in the St. Moritz Games four years earlier. Competitions were filled with relatively large numbers of North Americans, tainting the Games somewhat in the eyes of Europeans.

Americans enjoyed their home field advantage to win the overall medal tally. But it wasn't without controversy: Rules for sports such as speedskating were altered dramatically from preceding Olympics, with mass starts that benefited U.S. and Canadian skaters, who were the only ones familiar with them. The sport's greatest champion, A. Clas Thunberg of Finland, refused to even make the trip to compete. Americans took advantage, particularly skater Irving Jaffee, who won two gold medals.

Other competitive highlights: Having previously won a gold medal in boxing at the 1920 Summer Games, U.S. four-man bobsled crewman Eddie Eagan, riding in a sled piloted to victory by Billy Fiske, became the only person to win a gold medal in the Summer and Winter Games. He still holds that distinction today.

In skating, Gillis Grafström of Sweden, attempting to win his fourth straight title, skated an

Memorabilia from the 1932 Games is on display in the World Figure Skating Hall of Fame in Colorado.

incorrect compulsory figure, giving the gold medal to Karl Schafer of Austria. Sonja Henie defended her title, as did the Brunets in pairs.

Hoping the Games would provide a respite from chaotic, anxious times, the United States spent the then-extravagant sum of $750,000 on a new speedskating stadium, a ski jump, an ice rink, and a brand-new bobsled run. But it neglected some of the smaller details, such as attending to the cross-country course, where some skiers nearly got lost skiing through woods with ill-marked trails and no course attendants.

1936: IV Olympic Winter Games
Garmisch-Partenkirchen, Germany

The 1936 Games, in the twin Bavarian towns of Garmisch and Partenkirchen, were seen by Nazi leaders in Germany as a warm-up for the big 1936 Summer Games, which would become a premier propaganda event for Adolf Hitler. Most of the rest of the world—not to mention the IOC, which had awarded the Games to Germany in 1931, before Hitler's rise to power—resented this. Hitler himself reportedly had been unsure about the Olympics, which he claimed were "an invention of Jews and freemasons." But he came to appreciate their value as a propaganda tool, and he later embraced the Games—with his own rules. Only German photographers and videographers, for example, were allowed to record the competitions. An attempt by democratic nations to remove the Games from Germany after passage of the Nuremberg Laws, which stripped Jews of their civil rights, was denied by the IOC, whose only proviso was that Jews be allowed to participate. A worldwide boycott attempt fell flat, and the Games went on.

But not without other controversy. The Garmisch-Partenkirchen Games also saw the beginning of what would become a decades-long dispute over how to draw the line between amateur and professional athletes. With alpine skiing added for the first time, a dispute erupted between the IOC and the International Ski

Federation (FIS), the sport's governing body. The FIS believed instructors should be allowed to compete; the IOC barred them, saying they were professionals. The result: Skiers from Austria and Switzerland, including most of the top talents, boycotted the Games.

In figure skating, Sonja Henie won her third straight gold—an achievement yet to be matched. She retired from amateur competition after the Games—with ten straight world titles to match her three gold medals—and began what would be a long and prosperous career as an actress and professional skater. Austria's Karl Schafer repeated as men's champion. Norway's Ivar Ballangrud won three gold medals in speedskating, including the shortest race, the 500 meters, and the longest, the 10,000 meters. On the hockey rink, one of the Winter Games' greatest upsets occurred, with Great Britain beating Canada. A closer look at the rosters makes the win less spectacular: ten of the twelve players on Britain's team were living and playing in Canada.

1948: V Olympic Winter Games
St. Moritz, Switzerland

The 1948 Games brought the world back together in a familiar place—St. Moritz, which had escaped the ravages of war by being in a neutral country. The Games of 1940 had been awarded to Sapporo, Japan, which had been forced to withdraw in 1938 because of its ongoing war with China. St. Moritz and Garmisch-Partenkirchen offered themselves as backup sites, but the Games were canceled outright in late 1939 because of World War II.

When the world collected itself and regrouped for an Olympics in St. Moritz in 1948, emotions remained raw. Athletes from Germany and Japan were banned from competition, and Russia, under Stalin, didn't show. A host of other controversies marred the Games, including two hockey teams appearing to represent America, leading the IOC to refuse to ratify the results of the tournament, won by Canada.

But as usual, flashes of athletic grace outshone

the angst. America's Dick Button, performing the first double Axel in competition, won the men's figure skating title at the age of 18. Canada's Barbara Ann Scott won the women's gold. Ski jumping legend Birger Ruud of Norway attended the Games as a coach but decided to compete and, at age 36, won a silver medal. Similarly, on the bobsled track, America's John Heaton, age 39, returned to the site of his 1928 silver medal and won another, a full twenty years later.

1952: VI Olympic Winter Games
Oslo, Norway

By 1952, the Winter Games were long overdue to visit Norway, the birthplace of skiing and a dominant force in winter sports. In a break with tradition, the Olympic flame was ignited in the hearth of famed skier Sondre Nordheim (credited with inventing the modern ski binding) and carried on skis to Oslo by 94 skiers. The cauldron was lit by Olav Bjaaland, who had accompanied Roald Amundsen to the South Pole in 1911.

It was a grand Olympics for the home team, with speedskater Hjalmar ("Hjallis") Andersen winning three gold medals in speedskating, with record margins of victory in the 5,000 and 10,000 meters. On the slopes, America's Andrea Mead Lawrence won both the slalom and a new event, the giant slalom, at age 19. In men's competition, local hero Stein Eriksen won the giant slalom and took silver in the slalom, stealing the Olympic thunder at long last from skiers who had cut their teeth in the Alps.

Canada won the gold medal in hockey once more. Women's cross-country ski racing debuted at these Olympics, with Lydia Wideman of Finland claiming the first gold. In men's racing, Veikko Hakulinen of Finland won the grueling 50-kilometer race—the first of what would be seven Olympic medals. In figure skating, men's champion Dick Button repeated, once again unveiling a new move, the triple loop, in competition.

1956: VII Olympic Winter Games
Cortina d'Ampezzo, Italy

As debuts go, the Soviet Union's Olympic howdy in the Dolomites of Italy was an impressive one. Competing for the first time, the USSR captured the overall medal count, beating out Norway. Standout performances by the Soviets included gold medals in three of the four speedskating events and a shocking gold medal victory in ice hockey, ending Canada's long run atop the medal stand.

Weather again was a factor. First there was not enough snow, prompting an Army bucket brigade. Then there was too much, after a storm in which more than a foot fell. After that came a major thaw and then a hard freeze.

But competition went on, and the conditions did little to slow one skier. Anton "Toni" Sailer completed an historic sweep of all three races in alpine skiing, a feat that would not be equaled until Jean-Claude Killy pulled it off in the Grenoble Games of 1968. In ice skating, America's Tenley Albright overcame a nasty gash from a blade on one ankle to win America's first women's gold medal. Teammate Hayes Jenkins took the men's gold in what would be the last figure skating competition conducted outdoors.

One of the Cortina Games' most momentous events, however, had nothing to do with competition. They were the first Games to be partially televised, ushering in an era in which TV coverage played a greater and greater role in the scheduling of events. They also were the first Games to be heavily subsidized by sponsors who provided "official" products, such as Fiat cars.

1960: VIII Olympic Winter Games
Squaw Valley, California, USA

You could say that New York attorney/land developer Alexander Cushing had more than his fair share of chutzpah. When he bid on the 1960 Winter Games in 1955, Squaw Valley barely existed. The

Lake Tahoe ski resort consisted of a single chairlift, two rope tows, and a small lodge. And the "town" had a population of one—Cushing himself.

He dreamed big, however, and, reportedly by courting votes of IOC members in the Southern Hemisphere, convinced the IOC to pick an up-and-coming resort over previous hosts St. Moritz, Garmisch-Partenkirchen, and a new favorite, Innsbruck, Austria. In the next four years, the area went on a $15 million crash construction course, building first roads, bridges, and hotels and then an ice arena, speedskating track (the first Olympic track with refrigeration), more ski lifts, and a ski jumping hill.

What *wasn't* built created the most controversy— a bobsled track, which the organizing committee deemed too expensive. As a result, the Squaw Games were the only ones in Olympic history not to include the sport.

Still, these were the biggest Winter Games to date, drawing athletes from 30 nations. They also were among the more innovative, introducing an athletes' village and staging opening and closing ceremonies worthy of Hollywood, produced by none other than Walt Disney. The grand celebration included 1,300 musicians, 3,000 singers, 2,000 carrier pigeons, 20,000 balloons, ice sculptures, and fireworks.

These were the first Games to be fully televised, with the American contract granted to CBS, which bought the rights for $50,000. The Squaw Valley Games also were the first to use a computer, an early IBM model, to process results.

In competition, U.S. figure skater Carol Heiss won the gold medal. The men's competition was won by David Jenkins, the brother of 1956 gold medalist Hayes Jenkins.

Skiing, unfolding on some of the most difficult courses in Olympic history, saw its own history made as Jean Vuarnet of France won the downhill with some newfangled technology: metal-edged skis.

Penny Pitou of the United States took silver in the downhill and giant slalom. In cross-country, Finnish star Veikko Hakulinen won three more medals.

The speedskating star was Yevgeny Grishin of the Soviet Union, who repeated his victories in the 500 and 1,500 meters. Biathlon made its medal-sport debut here, with Klas Lestander of Sweden winning the first gold medal. Also new was women's speedskating, with Lydia Skoblikova of the USSR claiming gold in the 1,500 and 3,000 meters.

One of the Squaw Valley Games' greatest highlights, however, was a young U.S. hockey team's upset wins over Canada and the favored Soviets and then a come-from-behind gold medal victory over Czechoslovakia—a scenario that would repeat itself with uncanny similarities at the next Olympics to be held on U.S. soil, in 1980.

1964: IX Olympic Winter Games
Innsbruck, Austria

Innsbruck had waited a long time to get a Winter Olympics, and when the time came, winter fled. So little snow blanketed the mountains around Innsbruck that the Austrian army was enlisted for a Herculean task: They carved some 20,000 blocks of ice from the mountains and trucked them to the bobsled/luge run, and then hauled 40,000 cubic meters—about 52,000 cubic yards—of snow to the alpine ski courses. Torrential rainfall came next, further threatening the start of the Games.

But Innsbruck pulled it off. Of historical interest: Ski jumping gained a second individual event, the normal hill. And the sport of luge, after years of trying, finally debuted at the Olympics.

In competition, Soviet speedskating star Lydia Skoblikova continued her dominance, making history by sweeping all four speedskating events, giving her six gold medals, more than any other man or woman in the Winter Games at that time. A similar sweep came on the cross-country course, where Soviet skier Claudia Boyarskikh won all three events. In men's cross-country, Sixten Jernberg won the 50 kilometers to become the most decorated men's Winter Olympian to that point, with a total of nine medals.

In skiing, sisters Christine and Marielle Goitschel of France finished in first and second place in the slalom and, remarkably, also the giant slalom (Christine won the slalom, Marielle the giant slalom). In figure skating, the pair of Lyudmila Belousova and her husband, Oleg Protopopov, won the first of what would be successive pairs titles, launching a Soviet Union/Russian dominance of that event that continues to this day. In hockey, the USSR edged Canada for the gold medal.

Tragedy also struck the Games: A British luge racer, Kazimierz Kay-Skrzypecki, and an Australian downhill skier, Ross Milne, were killed during training runs. Weather conditions were cited as a factor.

1968: X Olympic Winter Games
Grenoble, France

The Grenoble Games were the most dispersed to date, largely because the industrial city of Grenoble wasn't close to snow. Only the ice skating competition was held there, with the rest of the Olympics farmed out to other villages, some as far as 40 miles (65 kilometers) away. Seven Olympic villages were used to house athletes and officials, giving the Games a feeling of many smaller world championship events in the same region, not one cohesive Olympics.

French skier Jean-Claude Killy dominated the headlines. Seeking to replicate Toni Sailer's earlier sweep of the alpine events on his home country's slopes, Killy pulled it off, but not without some good fortune. His chief rival in the third alpine event, Karl Schranz, beat Killy's time but was disqualified for missing gates after he said he saw a shadowy figure cross the slalom course. Until the pairs skating judging fiasco at the 2002 Salt Lake Games, it ranked as the greatest scandal in Winter Games history.

More controversy struck the luge course, where the defending women's gold medalist, East Germany's Ortrun Enderlein, and two teammates, apparently destined to sweep the medals, were disqualified for heating their sled runners. In figure skating, America's Peggy Fleming took gold, and Belousova and Protopopov repeated as pairs champions. In a rare double feat, Eugenio Monti of Italy, who had won a pair of silver and bronze medals piloting both the two- and four-man bobsleds at the two prior Olympic competitions, drove both to gold in Grenoble at age 40.

The Grenoble Games also were the first to include mandatory drug testing after events. No positive results were registered. For the first time, sex tests were administered to ensure that women really were women, after some controversy from previous Games. Again, no one failed. East Germans were allowed to compete under their own flag for the first time since the erection of the Berlin Wall.

1972: XI Olympic Winter Games
Sapporo, Japan

The 1972 Games were the first to be held outside Europe or America, and they began under a cloud. The Olympics' longtime bugaboo, the amateur/professional controversy, marred the Sapporo Games before they even began, when IOC president Avery Brundage, 84, banned Austrian ski superstar Karl Schranz because his acceptance of money from ski sponsors allegedly made him a professional. Brundage also threatened to ban as many as forty other skiers. The IOC's executive committee, foreseeing disaster and seeking a truce, compromised by letting Brundage make an example of Schranz, the World Cup overall champion. The Austrian skier returned home to a ticker-tape parade attended by 100,000 fans. Ten years later, the IOC, almost adding insult to injury, issued Schranz a declaration of participation for Sapporo.

As part of a greater protest over the IOC's

unwillingness to ban professional hockey players masquerading as amateurs for the Soviet Union and Czechoslovakia, Canada refused to send a hockey team to the Games. The result: The Soviets won their third straight gold medal in hockey.

Stars of the Games were Dutch speedskater Ard Schenk, who won three golds in speedskating, missing a full event sweep by a stumble in the 500 meters; and Soviet skier Galina Kulakova, who won all three women's cross-country events. In alpine skiing, two relative unknowns made headlines: Marie-Therese Nadig of Switzerland, 17, won both the downhill and the giant slalom. And Paquito Ochoa, who had never finished higher than sixth in World Cup competition, won gold in the men's slalom—the first Winter gold medal for Spain. In luge, Anna-Maria Müller of East Germany, disqualified in the runner-heating scandal four years earlier, gained some vindication, winning a gold medal. For the hometown fans, the big story of the Games was the Japanese sweep in ski jumping, led by new national hero Yukio Kasaya, who claimed Japan's first-ever Winter gold medal.

1976: XII Olympic Winter Games
Innsbruck, Austria

The 1976 Games were meant to be in America. The IOC originally awarded the bid to Denver, which planned to celebrate America's bicentennial by raising the Olympic flag. But someone forgot to ask the people of Colorado, who voted overwhelmingly not to spend state money on the effort. Former host Innsbruck stepped up to bail out the IOC and take on its second Games.

They seemed a bit cursed from the start, with unseasonably warm weather in the mountains and a full-blown flu epidemic in the Olympic Village. Sickness actually affected the Games' results: Eight-time medalist Galina Kulakova of the Soviet Union was disqualified from a race because she had used a nasal spray containing a banned substance to fight off a cold. But the Games continued, with memorable moments.

The big story was Austrian Franz Klammer's out-of-control run to glory to win the men's downhill on his home mountain. It overshadowed a stellar performance by Rosi Mittermaier, 25, of Germany, who won two gold medals and nearly became the first woman to sweep the three traditional alpine events. Kathy Kreiner, 18, of Canada nipped her by twelve-hundredths of a second in the giant slalom.

Ice dancing debuted here as a medal event. Dorothy Hamill won the women's gold medal in figure skating for America. Soviet pairs skater Irina Rodnina, newly paired with husband Aleksandr Zaytsev, won the second of what would be three straight gold medals, an Olympic record. She had won gold with partner Aleksey Ulanov in 1972. The Soviet hockey team, the clear class of the competition with its professional "amateurs," won its fourth straight gold medal.

1980: XIII Olympic Winter Games
Lake Placid, New York, USA

The tiny burg of Lake Placid had considerable difficulties in making its second Olympics work. A state of emergency had to be declared when bus service failed, leaving thousands of spectators stranded. Ticket distribution was disastrous, and logistics in general were a challenge, in spite of the fact that all Olympic venues were within sight of one another.

But three big stories, two on ice and one on snow, overshadowed all the problems. America's young, largely unknown hockey team, seeded seventh of eight teams, pulled off the most stunning upset in Winter Olympic history, beating its heavily favored Cold War rival, the Soviet Union, in a game now known as the "Miracle on Ice." The scrappy team,

Opposite: The spires supporting the Olympic flame cauldron from the 1980 Games still stand in a field outside Lake Placid, New York.

Brian Boitano was America's top male figure skater through the 1980s.

coached by Herb Brooks, then knocked off Finland to win the gold medal, sending the country into a frenzy and elevating the Winter Games into the American consciousness as they had never been before.

In skiing, Swedish great Ingemar Stenmark, the most prolific World Cup winner in history, broke through to win both the slalom and giant slalom. Hanni Wenzel equaled the feat on the women's side, making Liechtenstein the smallest country to win an

Olympic gold medal. Both did so in the first Olympics ever to employ artificial snow, as the weather gods once again conspired to play havoc with Olympic alpine ski scheduling.

On the Olympic Oval, American speedskater Eric Heiden did the unimaginable, winning gold medals in all five speedskating races, from 500 meters to 10,000. His last victory, in the 10,000, came after he overslept and almost missed the race—he'd been out celebrating the U.S. hockey team's victory over the Soviets the night before.

Soviet biathlete Aleksandr Tikhonov won his fourth straight gold medal. Another historical footnote: Taiwan became the first country to boycott the Winter Olympics. The delegation, under pressure by IOC officials seeking to court China, refused to change its name to Taiwan from its preferred Republic of China, feeling so strongly about the issue that they decided to stay home instead.

1984: XIV Olympic Winter Games
Sarajevo, Yugoslavia

The first Winter Games ever in a Socialist country seem charmingly innocent in the hindsight of history. Nobody knew at the time that the delightful host city in the Balkans and its welcoming people would be devastated by the Bosnian civil war in the coming decade.

The Games will be remembered for Yugoslavian skier Jure Franko's silver medal in the giant slalom—the first medal for his country. Cross-country skier Marja-Liisa Kirvesniemi of Finland won all three individual races. Speedskaters Gaétan Boucher of Canada and Karin Enke of East Germany won two gold medals each.

Americans had a rare Winter Games breakthrough in alpine skiing: Bill Johnson, surprising everyone but himself, won the downhill. Twin brothers Phil and Steve Mahre won gold and silver in the slalom; Debbie Armstrong and Christin Cooper were first and second in the women's giant slalom.

At the Zetra Figure Skating Center, Germany's Katarina Witt won the women's competition, and ice dancers Jayne Torvill and Christopher Dean of Britain won gold with a classic performance skated to Ravel's *Bolero,* earning a full set of perfect scores. Eight years later, the building was reduced to rubble in the country's civil war, and the bobsled run was used as a Serb guerilla artillery position, becoming pocked with landmines.

These Games also saw significant expansion, with 12 nations added to the party after IOC Chairman Juan Antonio Samaranch provided financing for athletes from warm-weather nations like Egypt and Senegal.

1988: XV Olympic Winter Games
Calgary, Alberta, Canada

The Calgary Games marked the expansion of sports events into the configuration we're more familiar with today. Alpine skiing events grew from three to five with the introduction of the super-G and the return of the alpine combined. Nordic combined and ski jumping both got their own team competitions. The result: more athletes, more events, more days. The Games grew for the first time to 16 days, stretching over three weekends.

Stars of the Games were Alberto Tomba of Italy, who won the slalom and giant slalom; Pirmin Zurbriggen of Switzerland, who won the downhill gold and giant slalom bronze; Vreni Schneider of Switzerland, who won the women's slalom and giant slalom; Matti Nykanen of Finland, who won three ski jumping medals; Dutch speedskater Yvonne van Gennip, who won three gold medals; Katarina Witt of Germany, who skated to her second straight figure skating gold medal; and Brian Boitano of America, who won the much-hyped "battle of the Brians" over Canadian hopeful Brian Orser.

In another notable event, Christa Rothenburger of East Germany won the 1,000 meters in speedskating. Later in the year she won a silver medal in cycling at the Seoul Games, becoming the first person to medal in a Summer and Winter Games in the same year. Also, America's Debi Thomas won bronze in figure skating, the first Winter Olympic medal won by a black athlete.

The sad story of the Games belonged to U.S. speedskater Dan Jansen, a favorite in the 500 and 1,000 meters, who learned during the Games that his sister had died of cancer. Jansen fell in both races and would go on to repeat his errors in the Albertville Games before finally earning a medal breakthrough in his swan-song race at Lillehammer.

1992: XVI Olympic Winter Games
Albertville, France

The Albertville Games of 1992 marked the end of the practice of staging Summer and Winter Games during the same year. They were also notable for long bus rides: Only 18 of 57 events were held in Albertville; the rest were scattered throughout resort towns in the Alps. The Games also continued to expand, with the addition of freestyle skiing, women's biathlon, and short-track speedskating as medal events.

It was a grand Olympics for Norway, which took every single cross-country ski race, led by skiing legends Björn Dæhlie and Vegard Ulvang, each of whom left with three golds and a silver. Women's cross-country star Raisa Smetanina of the Unified Team (formerly the USSR) made history by winning a gold medal in the 4x5-kilometer relay—her 10th medal over five Olympic Games. Her teammate, Lyubov Yegorova, won three golds.

The star of the speedskating track was America's Bonnie Blair, who defended her title in the 500 and also won the 1,000 meters, much to the delight of a boisterous contingent of backers from her hometown. East Germany's Gunda Neimann won golds in the 3,000 and 5,000 meters and a silver in the 1,500. The new sport of short track was dominated by South Korea; Kim Ki-Hoon won both individual men's events.

In skiing, Alberto Tomba won the giant slalom but was nudged by less than three tenths of a second in the slalom. He still became the first alpine skier to win the same event twice. Figure skater Kristi Yamaguchi won the gold for America. In the overall medals standings, a unified German team finished ahead of the Soviet Union.

1994: XVII Olympic Winter Games
Lillehammer, Norway

The return of the Winter Games to Norway was a marked success; most observers believe it to be the best-organized, most popular Winter Games ever. Crowds were huge, with more than 100,000 fans at cross-country skiing and 150,000 at ski jumping. These Olympics also came very quickly for spectators accustomed to seeing the Games every four years, as the gap was shortened to two years to put the Summer and Winter Games on opposite cycles, alternating every two years.

The Games began in typical Norwegian Nordic fashion, with the Olympic flame carried to the opening ceremonies stadium by cross-country skiers, then flown into the ceremony by a ski jumper holding it aloft.

The star of the Games, not surprisingly, was a Norwegian: speedskater Johann Olav Koss, who won three speedskating races, breaking the world record in each, and then announced that he was giving his prize money to charity. And the Games concluded in a fever pitch as Norway and Italy dueled in a classic cross-country ski relay ultimately won, by inches, by Italy, in front of a crowd of more than 100,000. The individual cross-country stars were Bjørn Dæhlie of Norway, who won two gold

America's Tommy Moe shocked the world by winning the men's downhill at the 1994 Lillehammer Games.

medals; teammate Thomas Alsgaard, with two; Manuela Di Centa of Italy, who won medals in all five events; and Lyubov Yegorova of Russia, who won three gold medals to bring her total to six. Yegorova's record—and in fact her entire career—was later tainted when she tested positive for a steroid substance at the 1997 Nordic World Championships.

In alpine skiing, Vreni Schneider of Switzerland won gold, silver, and bronze medals. America's Tommy Moe and Diann Roffe were surprise winners in the men's downhill and women's super-G. America's greatest star was again Bonnie Blair, who added two gold medals to her impressive resume. But its newest star was Dan Jansen, who overcame years of Olympic futility and family tragedy by winning gold in the 1,000 meters, his last Olympic race.

In the biathlon, Myriam Bédard of Canada won both individual races, making her a national hero in her homeland. Figure skaters Ekaterina Gordeeva and Sergei Grinkov of Russia repeated their gold medal in pairs.

In North America, the Lillehammer Games always will be remembered most, however, for the scandal involving figure skaters Tonya Harding and Nancy Kerrigan. Kerrigan, who had been kneecapped by an associate of a jealous Harding before the Olympics, skated to silver behind Oksana Baiul of Ukraine. Harding bawled about a broken lace and finished out of the running.

Europeans will remember the Lillehammer Games as the first in which former Soviet Republics such as Ukraine, Georgia, and Russia competed as independent nations, rather than under the banner of the Soviet Union or, as in the previous Olympics, the Unified Team.

1998: XVIII Olympic Winter Games
Nagano, Japan

Nagano saw the Winter Games expand once more, with the addition of snowboarding, curling, and women's hockey as medal sports, bringing the number of events to a record 68. Japan's first Winter Games in 26 years were hamstrung by weather: not a lack of snow but too much, causing frequent schedule juggling for the alpine ski events.

The Games also were notable for their first-ever inclusion of National Hockey League stars. Although the rules had been changed to allow them to compete much earlier, 1998 was the first time the NHL took a two-week break in the middle of its season to allow players to compete. The Czech Republic beat Russia 1–0 in the gold medal game.

In snowboarding, Canada's Ross Rebagliati made headlines by winning the event's first gold medal, then, after he tested positive for marijuana use, having it stripped and later returned.

In figure skating, 15-year-old Tara Lipinski upset favored Michelle Kwan to win the gold medal for America. Cross-country star Bjørn Dæhlie of Norway won three more gold medals and a silver, bringing his all-time Winter Games medal haul to 12, eight of them gold. Women's cross-country skier Larissa Lazutina of Russia won five medals, including four in individual events. Her results would be tainted by her disqualification for doping at the next Games in Salt Lake City.

In alpine skiing, America's Picabo Street was an upset gold medalist in the super-G. But the Games' greatest star was Austrian World Cup legend Hermann Maier, who suffered a spectacular fall in the downhill but recovered to win the super-G three days later. He later won the giant slalom. Katja Seizinger of Germany won her second straight downhill gold—an Olympic first.

The United States won the first gold medal in women's hockey, beating Canada 3–1 in the gold medal match. Luge legend Georg Hackl of Germany won his third consecutive gold medal. Japan's shining moment once again came at the ski jump, where the nation won the team jumping competition.

2002: XIX Olympic Winter Games
Salt Lake City, Utah, USA

Salt Lake City's Games were born in scandal, nearly collapsing on themselves after it was revealed that organizing committee members, apparently following then-standard protocol, had blatantly bribed IOC members to win the Games. The committee's house was cleaned, with businessman Mitt Romney assuming the reins and quickly putting the Games back on course. The Games, held only five months after the September 11, 2001, terror attacks in New York City and Washington, D.C., also began under extremely tight security, with heavily armed soldiers patrolling venues protected by razor-wire fencing.

Beyond that drama, the Salt Lake Winter Games saw the return of skeleton racing, last competed in 1948 at St. Moritz, and the debut of women's bobsled. Both padded the medal count of the home team. U.S. slider Jimmy Shea, a third-generation Olympian, won the men's skeleton contest, and Jill Bakken and Vonetta Flowers won the inaugural women's bobsled race, making Flowers the first black athlete to win a Winter gold medal in an individual event. Canadian Jarome Iginla later became the first black male gold medalist, in hockey. Canada also won the gold medal in women's hockey.

A highlight came in short-track speedskating, where Australia's Steven Bradbury became the "accidental medalist" by being the last man standing in a 1,000-meter final in which all other competitors crashed in the final turn. Freestyle skier Alisa Camplin, competing with two ankle fractures, won another surprise gold medal for Australia.

The alpine ski star was Janica Kostelić of Croatia, who won three gold medals and one silver in Park City. Georg Hackl of Germany didn't win, but with a silver medal became the first athlete in history to earn a medal in the same individual event five times in a row. Short-track speedskater Yang Yang (A) made history by winning China's first Winter Games medal.

In biathlon, Ole Einar Bjoerndalen of Norway won gold in all four events; Samppa Lajunen of Finland won all three Nordic combined contests.

In short track, America's Apolo Anton Ohno came back from a fall in the 1,000 meters to win the 1,500 after South Korea's Kim Dong-Sung was disqualified for impeding, which sent the Korean delegation—and, apparently, much of the nation—into a tizzy, resulting in death threats to Ohno and a threat, not fulfilled, that the Koreans would boycott the closing ceremony. In ski jumping, Switzerland's Simon Ammann won both individual events—the first man to do so in 14 years.

The story that simply wouldn't go away, however, came once again in figure skating, where Canadian pairs skaters Jamie Sale and David Pelletier appeared to have outperformed Russian pair Elena Berezhnaya and Anton Sikharulidze, but judges placed the Canadian pair second. After reports that a French judge had "traded" her first-place vote with another judge for a favored result in another event, the IOC decided to award a second set of golds to Sale and Pelletier.

The Salt Lake Games also were notable for doping scandals, particularly among the ranks of cross-country skiers. Multiple-medal winners Johann Mühlegg of Spain and Larissa Lazutina and Olga Danilova of Russia all were stripped of medals after testing positive for darbepoetin, a drug that boosts red blood cell levels.

2006: XX Olympic Winter Games
Turin, Italy

Italy's first Games in 50 years got off to a big bang with an opening ceremony solo by Luciano Pavarotti—his last public performance. Ice events took place in the often smog-shrouded city of

Opposite: A tall suspension bridge connected the athlete's village with other Olympic buildings during the 2006 Turin Games.

For opening ceremonies in Turin, Italy, acrobats formed the shape of a dove.

Turin, with snow events scattered at venues in the nearby Alps.

The Turin Games set another attendance record, for both athletes and participating nations. But they failed to do so at the box office; empty seats were in evidence at early-round hockey matches and other contests.

A couple of legends were solidified on the ski slopes. Austrian superstar Hermann Maier, who had owned World Cup competition in the late '90s perhaps more solidly than any skier since Ingemar Stenmark, survived a stupendous crash—he sailed some 60 feet through the air, landing on his head and shoulder—not only to get up and ski down the mountain, but to return within days to win the giant slalom. Norway's Kjetil André Aamodt, winning the super-G, became the oldest (34) skier to win an alpine gold medal (after having been the youngest to do so at age 20, at the Albertville Games), and the oldest athlete to earn four medals in the same event. It made him the most decorated Olympic alpine skier ever, with eight medals from five Olympics. Half an hour later, Croatian sensation Janica Kostelić won the alpine combined, one of three medals added to her historic alpine medal haul.

South Korea won 10 medals in speedskating, with Jin Sun-Yu winning three golds for the women's team and speedster Ahn Hyun-Soo winning three golds for the men. Evgeni Plushenko dominated the men's figure skating contest, while

Shizuka Arakawa of Japan was a surprise winner for the women, besting America's Sasha Cohen. In the pairs competition, Dan Zhang and Hao Zhang overcame Dan's horrendous crash on an attempted quadruple salchow in the final to win a silver medal after she received medical attention.

In speedskating, Canada's Cindy Klassen medaled in five of six events; America's Joey Cheek medaled twice. Another speedskater, Claudia Pechstein of Germany, won a gold and silver to become the first athlete to earn nine career medals over five Olympics in speedskating, cementing her place as one of the sport's all-time greats. Apolo Anton Ohno of the United States won a gold medal in the 500-meter short track—his fifth medal, tying him with Eric Heiden for the most Winter Games medals by a single U.S. athlete in any sport.

Michael Greis of Germany won three gold medals in biathlon. André Lange drove both the two-man and four-man bobsleds to gold medals for Germany. And snowboard cross, a gang race likened to motocross racing, debuted to excellent TV ratings.

VANCOUVER EDITION: THE SEA TO SKY GAMES

❄ ❄ ❄ ❄ ❄

It is a city known for going nuts from time to time. But usually not this early in the day. On the morning of July 2, 2003, GM Place, a stadium that is normally the home of screaming fans of the NHL's Vancouver Canucks, was filled with 10,000 screaming fans of a *potential* Olympic Games—at about 5:30 in the morning.

You have to get up early if you want to land an Olympics. The time warp was made necessary by the fact that the International Olympic Committee (IOC), gathered to select the host city for the 2010 Winter Games, was meeting at midday in Prague, Czech Republic. So the Vancouver organizers opened the doors at dawn, allowing members of the public to file in for the big announcement, shown on the stadium's scoreboard video screens.

It wasn't just the public sitting there, anxious, fidgeting, not wanting to think about what would happen if the decision went the other way. The heart of Canada's Olympic movement was there, too: athletes, coaches, sponsors, politicians, and business tycoons. Snowboarder Ross Rebagliati, he of the notorious one-toke-over-the-line performance-

impeding drug bust after winning the first-ever gold medal in snowboarding at Nagano, was sitting in a portable chair right about at what normally would be GM Place's hockey-rink blue line. He looked nervous. Everybody did. You could cut the tension with a plastic yogurt spoon from a Tim Horton's, and some people were.

By 7:30 AM, a buzz began sweeping through the building. You could literally see it start at the stage in the center of the rink and spread through the crowd of VIPs, then up into the stands. An announcement had been issued from Prague: Salzburg, one of three candidate cities for the 2010 Olympic Winter Games, had been eliminated in the first round of voting.

The collective sigh of relief nearly blew the doors open in the arena service tunnels. Salzburg had been considered the chief rival of Vancouver, which, along with alpine partner Whistler, was seeking to host the first Winter Games on the west coast of North America in 50 years. The reasoning behind this relief was obvious: The other host candidate was Pyeongchang, South Korea. And recent saber-rattling across the border in North Korea made any international event on the Korean peninsula seem unlikely.

Canada felt ready to party. But another hour dragged by, with no word from Prague, and the nervousness returned. And for good reason, it later turned out: Unbeknownst to Canadians, Pyeongchang had actually led the balloting in the first count but couldn't pull a solid enough majority to end the matter there. The final selection would depend on the split of those Salzburg voters seeking new suitors. In the end, most of them switched to Vancouver, which had serenaded delegates with a slick, heart-tugging music video of spectacular scenic backdrops, set to Vancouver rocker Bryan Adams' song "Here I Am."

Canada's thriving green, white, and blue city on the salt water had won the Games of the XXI Winter Olympiad by a mere three votes, 56–53.

When IOC President Jacques Rogge made the announcement via video, the crowd went berserk. Fireworks banged. Thousands of grown adults stood and hugged one another and cried. Music played, and people danced. You almost expected someone to produce the Stanley Cup, hold it high over their head, kiss it, and then pass it around.

It was exultation, yes, but mostly relief. Vancouver's flirtation with the Olympic Games was no new spur-of-the-moment idea. Various groups in the province of British Columbia, in fact, had been submitting bids for various Olympics since 1968. The village of Whistler itself had been founded as part of a developer's dream to draw the Winter Games to a tiny site and build around them, much as the organizers of the last western North American Games, at Squaw Valley, California, had done in 1960.

Over the years, a certain amount of momentum had built up, and before this vote, it had reached a near crescendo in B.C., where some 50,000 people had already come forward to act as the 25,000 needed Games volunteers.

Now, with the vote secured, Vancouverites and Whistler residents spent a full day partying. And then set to work to the task at hand, which, by any measure, was sobering.

A DAUNTING TASK

Vancouver, the largest, warmest, wettest metro area ever to host a Winter Games, would need a budget of $1.7 billion (Canadian) to build venues and other Olympic infrastructure and operate the Games. It would need $200 million—and likely much more—just for security. It would need even more money for other, off-budget yet critical work, such as a costly light-rail project. It would need to turn the precipitously cliff-hanging Sea to Sky Highway between Vancouver and Whistler into a safe, efficient, multilane freeway. In a Canadian province that is extremely sensitive to environmental degradation, it would need to build a giant bobsled/luge run on the face of Blackcomb Mountain, and carve out a large area in the nearby peaceful, forested Callaghan Valley to build ski jumps and cross-country trails.

The Vancouver Organizing Committee, or VANOC, would need to build an expanded hockey rink at the University of British Columbia, a new speedskating oval to the south, in Richmond, and a new curling rink in the central city. It would need to finance and launch the tripling in size of a cruise-ship terminal/convention center at water's edge into a sprawling media center; it would need to rebuild Pacific Place, an aging ice arena, into a modern facility for the world's best figure skaters. At the time it also believed that it would need to revamp the very building we all stood in that morning, GM Place, to accommodate the larger, Olympic-sized ice rink for the medal rounds of hockey.

There was more: Outside, just across the street, stood B.C. Place Stadium, another timeworn public building. This stadium, with an air-supported fabric roof, had seen better days. The home of the B.C. Lions football team would need to be spruced up to literally host the world in opening and closing ceremonies—the first in Olympic history to unfold indoors. And within a few years, a violent winter storm would make it clear that the building didn't just need detailing—it needed an entirely new roof.

The truth is, there was a lot more. But this was the public outline everyone knew by heart.

Hearts and minds needed to be swayed as well. While the Olympic organizing effort had received solid support from the general public, not everyone was sold. Vancouver is a progressive city with a strong bent toward using public resources directly for the public good, whether that be healthcare, community services, or, increasingly, housing programs to get the city's burgeoning homeless population—attracted to Vancouver from around Canada in part because of its mild winter weather—off the streets. Some politically active Vancouverites saw spending in excess of $2 billion on a 17-day festival for men and women in sausage-casing speed suits, all for the amusement of "Olympic Family" jet-setters, to be an abomination.

Five years later, a handful of them still do. An impressive countdown clock in downtown Vancouver has been vandalized with paint bombs by Olympic opponents. Demonstrations by environmentalist and First Nations aboriginal groups have delayed—but never stopped—the massive, $600 million Sea

Canadian Olympic fans unfurl a giant Canadian flag at GM Place on the day the 2010 Games are officially awarded to Vancouver.

THE SEA TO SKY GAMES AT A GLANCE

Olympic Winter Games dates: February 12 to 28, 2010
Paralympic Winter Games dates: March 12 to 21, 2010
Number of Olympic athletes and officials: 5,000
Number of Paralympic athletes and officials: 1,700
Countries participating in the Olympic Winter Games: 80+
Countries participating in the Paralympic Winter Games: 40+
2010 Games events tickets available: 1.6 million
Estimated number of media representatives: 10,000
Estimated number of Games volunteers: 25,000

to Sky Highway program. When IOC members visited the city in February 2008 for a progress report, protesters strained against riot police in an attempt to enter their hotel conference room and let their thoughts be known directly, face-to-face.

Olympic supporters, however, can point, justifiably and proudly, to what has been accomplished in those same five years since the bid.

"OWN THE PODIUM"

Canadians still smart over the paltry home-country medal count at the nation's two other Olympics—Montreal in 1976 and Calgary in 1988. The home team collected nary a gold medal in the Montreal Summer Games, which also turned into a financial disaster. And remarkably, it failed to garner gold again at the Calgary Games, where Canada's best results were silver medals won by figure skaters Brian Orser and Elizabeth Manley.

Canada has vowed to avoid a repeat of that embarrassment. This determination quickly morphed into an actual public/private partnership known as Own the Podium, whose goal is what the name, in no uncertain terms, indicates. Canada expects to do what America did with its Games at Salt Lake City in 2002—use the home snow and ice advantage to

post its most impressive winter results ever.

Money is a major portion of this effort: The federal government and private donors put up $110 million to cover enhanced training and other costs. But venue access is another crucial element of the program. The goal is to maximize Canadian athletes' prep time on the field of play. This is particularly important in the bobsled/luge/skeleton competitions and in alpine and Nordic skiing, where venues differ greatly from place to place and familiarity breeds athletic confidence. Certainly, test events will bring the world's greatest athletes to compete on Vancouver's 2010 ski runs and ice sheets, for World Cup play and other competition. But completion of the venues almost two years in advance of the Games should also give home athletes practice time that no competitors can come close to matching.

Just one example: The men's downhill run, at Whistler, will be run on a course that's been reconfigured since the last World Cup race on the run, a decade ago. No World Cup races will be run there before the Olympics. Only Canadian skiers will have access to the intricacies of its bumps, jumps, and curves. This isn't a novel Canadian concept. Other nations have done the same at other Olympics, with varying degrees of success.

THE VENUES

Of course, nothing is more key to the Own the Podium goal—or to the success of an Olympics itself—than the venues. Vancouver's, like those in many other modern host cities, will be spread out across a fairly large region. But unlike other recent Games, particularly those in the Alps of Europe, the 2010 venues are split almost equally between two places, depending on whether they involve ice or snow.

The opening and closing ceremonies and all the flat ice events—hockey, figure skating, speedskating, short track, and curling—will take place in Vancouver and environs, connected by an efficient public transit service consisting of buses, light rail, and ferries:

○ Hockey will be spread between a greatly expanded ice facility at the University of British Columbia, or UBC, on the city's west side, and Canada Hockey Place (as GM Place has been renamed for the duration of the Games), in the downtown central district. After receiving the bid, VANOC was faced with a tab of up to $10 million to reconfigure 18,630-seat GM Place to accommodate an Olympic-sized ice rink, which is about 4.5 meters (15 feet) wider than NHL ice. But the group successfully petitioned the International Hockey Federation to break with 84 years of tradition and allow Olympic hockey to be played on NHL-sized ice. From that moment on, the rink was ready to go. UBC Thunderbird Arena, which will seat 7,200, is expected to see its first play by the winter of 2009.

○ Figure skating will take place on Olympic-sized ice at the remodeled Pacific Coliseum, on the city's east side. The building, which will seat 14,239 for the Olympics, will also be the home of short-track speedskating, one of the Winter Games' most visually spectacular events.

○ Curling will commence on new ice sheets at a revamped facility near Nat Bailey Stadium, in Hillcrest Park.

○ Speedskating will unfold at the Richmond Oval, part of a major new waterfront development project in the city's south suburb, near the airport. It is the first Olympic Oval ever built at near sea level. An extension of the city's elevated light-rail system southward to Vancouver International Airport should ease access to this facility.

The snow events, for the most part, will be based in and around Whistler, the vacation-resort village home to about 10,000 full-time residents, swelling to 55,000 when its many hotels and condos are fully booked:

○ Alpine skiing will take place on the face of Whistler, where the men's downhill run, named after famed "Crazy Canuck" ski racer Dave Murray, is a former World Cup site. The newly configured women's

A NEW MEDAL EVENT—AND OTHERS STILL ON THE DRAWING BOARD

Approved for Vancouver 2010: Skier cross.
Rejected and still trying: Biathlon mixed relay, mixed doubles curling, team alpine skiing, team bobsled and skeleton, team luge, women's ski jumping

B.C. Place and Canada Hockey Place stadiums will be the center of attention during the 2010 Winter Games in Vancouver.

downhill run will be one of the steepest in the world.

- Cross-country skiing, ski jumping, Nordic combined, and biathlon will take place at Whistler Olympic Park, a completely new facility carved out of mostly untrammeled forest west of Whistler.
- Sliding sports will be held at the new Whistler Sliding Centre, tucked between Whistler and Blackcomb ski resorts.

Whistler will also have its own athletes' village, media housing and work facilities, and medals plaza for nightly awards ceremonies.

The exceptions to the city/mountain division are the sports of freestyle skiing and snowboarding, both of which will take place at Cypress Mountain, a popular alpine and cross-country day-skiing area in the hills of West Vancouver, 20 minutes out of downtown. Cypress will host the traditional freestyle moguls and aerials contest for skiers, as well as the halfpipe and parallel giant slalom races, plus the popular snowboard cross races, which debuted in Turin. All are spectator events with a powerful "wow" factor and likely will be well attended.

Many of the venues will double as venues for the Paralympic Games, which run right after the

2010 OLYMPIC SYMBOLISM

Official symbol: Ilaanaq the Inunnguaq

Ilaanaq is an *inukshuk*, a stumpy, stony creature made of rocks piled, as in Inuit tradition, like a cairn or trail marker. (The name *Ilaanaq* is a native word for "friend.") The design is based on an *inukshuk* actually built of stone for the Expo '86 World's Fair, later donated to the city. It now resides on English Bay Beach in Stanley Park.

Official mascots:

- Miga, a mythical sea bear, part orca and part bear
- Quatchi, a Sasquatch
- Sumi, the Paralympic Games mascot, is an animal guardian spirit with the wings of the mythical thunderbird, and the legs of the black bear
- Mukmuk, a Vancouver Island marmot who is not an official mascot, just a friend of the furry family

Olympics, from March 12 to March 21. The Paralympics, an international event for disabled athletes held annually since 1960 (for summer events) and 1976 (for the Winter Games), will feature 1,700 athletes from six different disability groups. They will compete in alpine and cross-country skiing, biathlon, sledge hockey, and wheelchair curling, using the same venues as the Olympic Games.

THE DEADLY WILD CARD—COASTAL WEATHER

All of these venues appear to be well constructed, well planned, carefully designed, and ready to roll. And about half of them could see all of that foresight go for naught if the weather fails to cooperate. What most people don't realize about Whistler Blackcomb, a global snow-play destination consistently rated tops in North America for skiing and snowboarding, is that it sits at a relatively low elevation, at close proximity to salt water.

The dual ski mountains of Whistler and Blackcomb offer truly spectacular terrain and a full mile of vertical drop—the largest in North America. But

to offer good skiing at all times somewhere on the mountains, they really *need* all that vertical. The base village at Whistler is just a touch over 600 meters (2,000 feet) in elevation. Snow is always ample here by mid-February, so that shouldn't be a concern. But at some point nearly every winter, the area is struck by "Pineapple Express" storms that batter B.C. and the northwestern United States with warm, wet weather straight from the South Pacific.

What that often means in Whistler Village is rain, which could create havoc with alpine ski events requiring a hard, fast course. And what it means on the mountains above, sometimes, is fog. Not just your ordinary, this-is-a-nuisance fog, but blinding, I-can't-find-my-way-off-the-mountain fog. If it were to set in and stay during scheduled high-speed, dangerous events such as the downhill or super-G, scheduling mayhem could occur.

Then again, the weather might cooperate. When the weather is fine, few ski mountains in the world are as pleasant a place to be as Whistler Blackcomb. In fact, a World Cup men's and women's alpine ski event took place at Whistler in mid-February 2008, and came off with nary a hitch, weather or otherwise, with the race surfaces earning high marks from the world's best skiers.

Another potential problem spot is Cypress Mountain. At 914 meters (3,000 feet), Cypress sits 305 meters (1,000 feet) higher than Whistler Village but is closer to salt water. It too is prone to wet weather and fog. A World Cup aerials and moguls contest there in the winter of 2008 was shut down partway through when fog, rain, and warm temperatures rolled in and refused to leave. It was so foggy at the venue, in fact, that spectators could barely see the bottom of the moguls course right in front of them, let alone the top. By the end of the first scheduled day of competition, an army of volunteers was running around with snow shovels, scooping water that had formed in giant, hot-chocolate-colored lakes at the base area.

It was a wakeup call to VANOC—as well as an embarrassment, said local media. A headline in the *Vancouver Province* said it all: "Worst fears realized as mild weather wreaks havoc at 2010 ski venue." Canadian officials did all they could do—they took it in stride.

"It's really a matter of us to have some really solid contingency plans for when this happens," said Cathy Priestner Allinger, vice president of sport for VANOC.

Ice sports in the city, conversely, should unfold on schedule, barring unforeseen events. But typical Vancouver weather in February— light rain and about 41 degrees F—does present an aesthetic challenge for the Games. A majority of Olympic spectators very well could visit the Games and attend many events without ever seeing a flake of snow.

Fortunately, all the major networks will have a stockpile of footage showing the city and its surrounding mountains at its sun-splashed, snowy best.

Impenetrable fog, an occasional fact of life at Olympic venues such as Cypress Mountain, is a constant worry to Olympic organizers.

B.C. AND VANCOUVER— NOTHING IN THE WORLD LIKE THEM

Let there be no mistake: Vancouver and its environs, when the weather cooperates, are stunning, and together they will form a unique and perhaps

TICKET FACTS

Olympic fans ready to book a train, plane, or car trip to Vancouver would be best served by chilling out for a second and considering the ugly truth: Tickets are at a premium for almost any Olympics, and they will be at a huge premium for the Sea to Sky Games.

In fact, by the time you read this, the vast majority of the 1.6 million tickets for Vancouver events very likely will have been sold. Ticket sales began for Canadian residents only in October 2008, through an online process at www.vancouver2010.com. A second round of ticket sales, again for Canadians only, was set to disperse the remaining tickets, if any, in early 2009.

Americans hoping to hop the border to see the Games likely will be dismayed to learn that they cannot get in on the general advance ticket sales offered to the Canadian public—at least not without recruiting some willing Canadian surrogate to go through the process for them. Instead, they'll go through the same routine as they would to obtain tickets to the Olympics in, say, Turin, dealing with one of two authorized brokers, who will sell tickets and travel packages based on a ticket allotment determined by the IOC. Those two agencies are Jet Set Sports (www.jetsetsports.com) for corporate groups, and CoSport (www.cosport.com) for individuals, the two ticket agencies licensed by the U.S. Olympic Committee. Such agencies typically have some allotment of tickets available to late-in-the-Games purchasers—unfortunately, often at premium prices.

Foreign visitors in the city of Vancouver or town of Whistler might be able to buy tickets to nightly medals ceremonies in B.C. Place Stadium and Whistler Village, respectively. Those are also ticketed events, with entertainment and other hoopla before the awarding of medals won that day at nearby venues. At press time, a ticket plan for these victory celebrations was still being formulated. Check the official website for more information.

Paralympic tickets will be distributed separately, and later on the calendar. Some tickets likely will be available for Paralympics events through 2009. See www.vancouver2010.com for details.

As usual, up to 30 percent of all Olympic tickets will be made available to Olympic Family members—big-time sponsoring corporations and IOC members themselves. Vancouver organizers say they will make a special effort to ensure that any tickets bought by Olympic Family members but not used by their holders are made available once more to the general public. But that's a tough thing to do unless those Family members make their intentions known well beforehand. Unused Olympic Family tickets were blamed for many of the vacant seats at venues during the Turin Games—a black eye on the event that was not lost on Vancouver's organizers.

unforgettable Winter Olympic backdrop. No Winter Olympics have ever been attempted at a place like it: a large, diverse, metropolitan, sophisticated urban area with a backdrop of blue salt water and stunning snow-capped mountains.

The city, 38 kilometers (24 miles) north of the U.S. border, is as majestic as any in North America. It is bordered to the north by Burrard Inlet, an inland finger of salt water stretching to the Strait of Georgia and then the Pacific Ocean, and to the south by the massive Fraser River, whose sprawling delta cradles the city and 20 other local municipalities in a 3,000-square-kilometer (1,158-square-mile) triangle. Nearly every way you turn in the city, a waterfront is not far away.

Vancouver is consistently rated one of the top vacation spots in the world by major travel magazines. It is home to 180 municipal parks, including its forested crown jewel, Stanley Park, which occupies a large peninsula in Burrard Inlet, near the city center. It has distinct, vibrant neighborhoods, including the largest Chinatown in North America. Indeed, it's a city that has nearly everything, from mind-blowing sushi to great coffee to mile after mile of waterfront bike paths and hundreds of acres of in-city forestland. Vancouver has a large, modern, international airport, with ample direct service to both Europe and Asia, which lie in nearly equal distances in opposite directions. To put it simply, there's a reason it's one of the fastest-growing cities in all of North America.

Likewise, Whistler is tough to beat as a mountain-resort destination, offering the comforts of fine hotels and the rugged allure of real wilderness—with real bears, real mountain lions, real lakes and trees, and really big rocks—right outside of town.

All of this will look spectacular in the opening TV montages. Count on it.

Of course, Vancouver also has its uglier side, including a large homeless population and an active drug culture—acknowledged, in a practice that would be shocking to neighbors to the south, by government health officials who sometimes distribute drugs to addicts, to keep them on an even keel.

TICKET PRICES (IN CANADIAN DOLLARS)

Alpine skiing: $120 to $150

Cross-country skiing/biathlon: $25 to $75

Bobsled/luge/skeleton: $30 to $85

Curling: $65 to $125

Figure skating: $50 (ice dance compulsories) to $525 (gala exhibition)

Freestyle skiing: $50 to $125

Hockey: $25 (women's preliminaries) to $775 (men's gold medal game)

Short-track speedskating: $50 to $150

Ski jumping: $80 to $210

Snowboarding: $50 to $150

Speedskating: $95 to $185

Opening ceremony: $175 to $1,100

Closing ceremony: $175 to $775

But the city, its surrounding province, and its surrounding nation are likely to put on a show that makes those problem areas a minor footnote.

Marketing studies point to a population eager not simply to host the Games, but to attend them as well. Selling the estimated 1.6 million tickets for these Games should not be a problem. Interest among Canadian winter-sports fanatics is expected to be high, and these Games will be smack in the center of a population center of 2.3 million people (actually, more than 5 million if you factor in the population of metropolitan Seattle, just 193 kilometers [120 miles] to the south).

Games organizers, sensitive to criticism about the prices and availability of tickets at previous Olympics, vowed to make more tickets and more affordable options available for hometown spectators (as opposed to, say, higher-paying foreign groups, which buy tickets in blocks). They promised to sell more than 100,000 Games tickets (about 6 percent

The sprawling cruise ship terminal/convention center will serve as the Main Press Centre for the Vancouver 2010 Games.

TRANSPORTATION

Getting to and from venues in Vancouver should be easier than in some previous host cities, thanks to a diversified light-rail/bus/ferry network criss-crossing the city. Details on how to get from point A to point B to witness event C were still being worked out when this book went to press. But you can count on one thing: Expect to use public transportation. This definitely will be true for getting to any venue in Vancouver proper. And it's likely to also be true for those hoping to commute the 120 kilometers (75 miles) to Whistler to see alpine events. The Sea to Sky Highway is likely to be limited, at least between Squamish and Whistler, to official transport only during the Games. And once there, access to the three venues around Whistler Village will be by bus as well.

of the total) for $25 Canadian, and said that half of all Games tickets will be sold for $100 or less. Tickets for premium events, however, such as the opening and closing ceremonies, the men's and women's figure skating finals, and most hockey, especially the medal rounds, are likely to seem prohibitively expensive to many fans.

THE GAMES' LASTING LEGACY

With that degree of public interest, the 2010 Games, barring some unforeseen hang-ups, have all the elements needed to make Maple Leaf Nation proud. Canada's last Winter Games, in Calgary, were considered a success by the IOC because of their organization and expansion of winter events. Unlike many other Olympics, they also were completed without any legacy of debt to rankle otherwise supportive politicians in Alberta or Ottawa.

And that might be the ultimate factor in judging the success of Vancouver's Games. To land a modern Olympics, the host city and provincial government must literally put their credit on the line, stipulating that local taxpayers, not the IOC, are responsible for any cost overruns beyond the Games' roughly $2 billion budget. That's a lot to ask and has scared away many other potential Olympic cities.

Vancouverites, however, seem to have embraced the challenge, so profound is their wish to put their own unique, natural, coastal Canadian brand on a worldwide tradition such as the Olympics. VANOC officials believe that the Games, if they operate as planned, will leave a profit solid enough to operate most of the Games facilities into perpetuity as "legacy venues."

The UBC ice rink will be used for university and community sports and training. The Richmond Oval will be a community athletic center and continue to host major speedskating competitions and other sports events. B.C. Place will continue as a government-owned pro sports arena. The curling center will maintain some of its ice sheets, with the rest of its space converted to a community facility with an Olympic-sized swimming pool. Pacific Place Coliseum will continue to be a multipurpose arena for minor league hockey and many other events. Canada Hockey Place will go back to being GM Place and the home of the Vancouver Canucks, a venue for concerts and the like. Cypress Mountain will revert to its pre-Games use as a popular recreational ski and snowboard venue.

In Whistler, the scenic, naturally beautiful Whistler Olympic Park, in a mountainous, forested

The Richmond Oval, (shown under construction here) on the banks of the Fraser River, will host speedskating, then convert to a massive multi function sports facility after the 2010 Games.

valley with spectacular views of surrounding Coast Range peaks, will be a recreational and competition center for cross-country skiing, biathlon, and ski jumping (most of it already is open to recreational use well in advance of the Olympics). Whistler Sliding Centre will remain an international training and competition facility for bobsled, luge, and skeleton athletes, complementing the single existing sled track at Calgary. It might, as have other tracks after their Games use, also offer public rides on bobsleds or modified luge sleds.

The noncompetition venues will find noncompetition uses: The media centers will revert to their convention center role, and the athletes' villages will be converted to housing—providing, in Whistler, some much-needed affordable residences for workers in the town's thriving tourist industry and others.

The key to all this, of course, is money. The Games must generate enough cash to pay the bills and leave an endowment for the future, to prevent the Olympic facilities from becoming white elephants, as they have in some other Olympic host cities. Some IOC critics, in the wake of massive cost overruns and public subsidies of the Games in Athens in 2002 and, to a much lesser extent, in Turin in 2006 (loss estimates vary between $80 million and more than $200 million), have begun to argue that re-creating the massive, costly Olympic infrastructure in a new locale every two years is folly; they say the Olympics should rotate between two or more "permanent" homes, where competitions can be repeated with little public investment.

The IOC has resisted this notion, for obvious reasons. Olympic advocates are borderline evangelical about the value of the Olympic experience. For every bad taste left in the mouth of a host city, they point to other examples of the Olympic Games becoming a unique source of national pride—a coming together of the people of the host nation that proves almost magical. And they're right: The Summer Games of Sydney in 2000 and the Winter Games of Lillehammer in 1994 are strong examples of that very phenomenon. The IOC still believes that its mission is to bring that same experience, and offer that same opportunity, to people around the world who've never touched it before. As long as people are still willing to foot the bills, the IOC will be willing to bring the Games to them.

PUTTING ON A GOOD SHOW

Like Americans, Canadians appreciate a good show and a good party. And the Sea to Sky Games should provide exactly that. Canada, more than perhaps any Olympic nation except Norway, knows and loves

VANCOUVER AT A GLANCE

Population: City limits: About 600,000. Metro area: 2.3 million (2008)

Language: Primarily English; federal government officials speak English and French. Vancouver is a highly multicultural city. After English and Chinese, the most common languages are Punjabi, German, Italian, French, Tagalog (Filipino), and Spanish. More than half of Vancouver's school-age children have been raised speaking a language other than English.

Climate: Pacific maritime, with generally mild year-round temperatures averaging in the high 70s Fahrenheit in summer and the low 40s in winter. The average daily temperature in February, the time of the Olympics, is 44 degrees.

Currency: In addition to Canadian currency, most Vancouver establishments accept U.S. dollars and Japanese yen. The Canadian dollar is a large golden coin, named the Loonie for the bird figure on its face. A smaller, gold-and-silver-colored coin is worth $2 and is nicknamed the "toonie."

Taxes: Visitors to Canada pay a 10 percent tax on lodging and liquor, as well as a 7 percent provincial sales tax and 5 percent federal goods and services tax for most other things.

Time zone: Vancouver is in the Pacific Time Zone. Daylight savings time is observed.

Visitor information: Tourism Vancouver's visitor information center is downtown at the Plaza Level, Waterfront Centre, 200 Burrard St. Phone: 604-683-2000. It also operates information centers at the Vancouver International Airport, the Peace Arch border crossing, and a seasonal desk at the cruise ship terminal at Canada Hockey Place. See www.tourismvancouver.com.

winter sports. From jam-packed, screaming throngs at hockey games to exuberant, multinational crowds for alpine skiing in Whistler—already a notable party town well before the Olympic bid was awarded—look for these to be an Olympics to remember. Even curling—yes, curling—is likely to draw large throngs in Canada, which is home, by various estimates, to 80 to 90 percent of the world's curlers. Major curling tournaments, or bonspiels, draw large TV ratings in Canada. Bottom line: Don't expect the empty-seats phenomenon that plagued the Olympics in Athens and Turin to strike Vancouver.

That sense of public ownership is key to any Olympics that go down in history as wildly successful. Although some opposition to the Vancouver Games remains, opinion polls show broad public support for the effort. Vancouverites, above all else, are immensely proud of the city they've built for themselves, and they see the Games as a way to show it off to the world. That's the same sentiment one sensed in Sydney before their Games, and it translated into a special experience because of it.

On a larger scale, Olympic officials yearn for that magic to reappear in British Columbia for their

Springtime visitors enjoy the views along the Sea to Sky Highway, which received $600 million in improvements to ease the journey between Vancouver and Whistler.

Vancouver Mayor Sam Sullivan accepts the Olympic flag from Turin officials during the closing ceremony for the 2006 Winter Games.

own, more selfish reasons. Games that become a special event in their host nations tend to play better around the world on television, and TV inarguably is the economic engine driving the modern Games. And the fact is that recent trends in viewership of the Olympics, particularly the Winter Games, have not been good. IOC officials reported record global viewership for the Turin Games. But ratings in the lucrative American market were down. Journalists

toiling away in Turin during the most hectic portion of those Games were dismayed to hear from home that the Games were drawing less of a national television share than a popular reality show, *Dancing with the Stars.*

For the Games to continue to re-create themselves every four years, that trend must not continue. Major television networks like NBC Universal, which owns a multibillion-dollar contract for the

Olympics through 2012, are hoping the allure of Vancouver—and its proximity to the United States, placing major events in prime time for American markets—can help stem the tide of declining ratings. The Vancouver Games have the potential to do just that. New, TV-friendly sports like snowboard cross, which was launched to rave reviews in Turin, and now skier cross, to be competed for the first time at Cypress Mountain, have the potential to draw younger viewers more oriented to the X Games than the Olympic Games. And Americans have a natural affinity with, and ongoing curiosity about, their neighbors to the north, right across the longest undefended border on the planet.

"The world's eyes are going to be on B.C.," provincial premier Gordon Campbell said in a speech in early 2008. "And it will be your chance to show off the great diversity of B.C., the richness of our province and the vastness and diversity of our country."

He then went a step further, bringing the focus back to where it really belongs.

"We're going to be the best Olympics ever for athletes."

Those are the dual standards by which great Olympics are judged. And when Sam Sullivan, then the popular quadriplegic mayor of Vancouver, rolled his wheelchair up a ramp to accept the Olympic flag from hosts in Turin, the eyes of the Olympic world shifted to B.C.

Opposite: The Lake Placid Oval, site of Eric Heiden's monumental five-gold-medal performance in 1980

PART ONE

ICE SPORTS

BOBSLED, LUGE, SKELETON

❄ ❄ ❄ ❄ ❄

More than 40 years after the fact, a handful of Lake Placid old-timers still recall all the details. It was a typical February day at Lake Placid—bitter cold. Overcast. Foreboding.

Ice on the Olympic bobsled run at Mount Van Hoevenberg was hard, even brittle, witnesses recall. And the bobsledders gathered to compete in the annual four-man bobsled race for the 1966 Diamond Trophy knew what that meant: difficulty controlling sleds, especially on tracks with curves as tight as those on Mount Van Ho, which had seen its share of spectacular crashes over the years.

But none was as spectacular, and ultimately horrific, as the one awaiting an Italian sled driver on Zig-Zag, one of the old Lake Placid course's most notorious curves.

In fact, a crash on Zig-Zag, which slams riders into a sharp curve to the left and then back to the right (hence the Zig and the Zag), had already created a course delay on this fateful day—a U.S. sled rode too high up the turn and slammed into a permanent wooden lip at the top of the course, causing head injuries to two sliders. That lip had

its own ominous history: It was installed after the 1932 Olympics, at which two German sleds rocketed right off the course. Still, many drivers feared it, and another U.S. driver had withdrawn from the race after the first crash this day at Zig-Zag, according to a detailed account in the book *Lake Placid: The Olympic Years, 1932–1980,* by George and Steven Ortloff.

The sled in question, driven by two-time Olympic medalist and 1965 world champion Sergio Zardini, who had relocated to Canada, was next in line after the crash on Zig-Zag. As the Italian and his crewmen began barreling down the run, the crowd began drifting toward Zig-Zag.

Zardini, with the fastest time in the first heat of the day, was charging hard, with speeds approaching 90 mph (144 kilometers per hour) in the straightaway above Zig-Zag. The sled rocketed through the Zig portion of the double curve correctly, but its runners lost hold in the transition area between turns, and the sled tipped violently and slid, scraping along on its left side and completely out of control, into the sheer wall of Zag. There, it careened to the top of

World Cup bobsledders enter the sweeping Shady Curve on the Lake Placid bobsled track at Mount Van Hoevenberg, near Lake Placid, New York.

the curve and scraped, with ferocious impact, along the wooden overhang, all the way through the turn.

Unfortunately, the highest point on the sled—and the first thing to hit that wooden roof at 60 mph—was Zardini's head. His leather helmet flew off, leaving his face and skull to be literally planed by the rough-hewn wood. Teammate Mike Young, seated behind him, also contacted the lip but managed to duck and cover his head. The impact yanked both men from the sled, which continued to slide downhill with the two other crewmen. The two ejected riders' bodies slid slowly and lifelessly down the course, eventually coming to a stop, a trail of blood behind Zardini. And the public-address announcer called out the coded words alerting emergency crews to a potential fatality: "Eighty-two at Zag!"

Emergency crews attended to Young, who was unconscious, but suffered relatively minor injuries, and put the driver on a stretcher and into a waiting ambulance. And there, a young Jim Rogers, broadcasting the race for WNBZ Radio, poked his head into the back to check on the driver's fate.

Rogers, retelling the tale 41 years later, after one of the tours he gives as a volunteer at the Lake Placid Olympic Center, said he has tried, unsuccessfully, to forget it ever since.

"All of his head was gone," Rogers recalled. "He was just wearing a soft leather helmet, and it was torn off. I very nearly lost my lunch."

As a local priest moved in to administer last rites, Rogers was still on the air. He did some fast thinking: "Ladies and gentlemen," he said, "we're going to have to take a commercial break."

The race was canceled, much to the relief of photographer Kay Jones, who captured live images of the horrific crash, and the one preceding it, for the New York *Daily News.* Her brother, Fred Fortune, was the next racer in line.

The fatal crash was the second in international bobsled competition that year, and the third fatal wreck in the sport's history at Mount Van Hoevenberg. We recount the story here not to revive the horrible pathos of the moment, or simply to tell a lurid tale, but to offer perspective on a little-appreciated aspect of winter competition.

Bobsled, luge, and skeleton, the Winter Games' three sliding sports, are all events in which a person, given a bad twist of fate, can die.

It is not common, especially with modern safety improvements. The track at Mount Van Hoevenberg, for example, has been rebuilt twice since that fateful day—once for the 1980 Winter Games, and again in 2000, when it was re-routed to make it safer. But fatal or near-fatal accidents remain a part of the sport, and not just bobsled. A luge racer was killed during a training run for the 1964 Innsbruck Games.

The point: It is one thing to throw around terms like "courageous" or "heroic" in discussions about sports in which an athlete chasing a round ball faces, at worst, a sprained ankle, broken bone, or concussion. The words take on new meaning when you engage in a sport subject to natural and manmade hazards, one so precise that one false muscle twitch could take your life. To drive a bobsled, luge, or skeleton is to live, literally, on the edge between glory (such as it is, in this case) and disaster.

All of this adds an extra dimension of drama to a sport that, frankly, needs no such boost to make it alluring for spectators. The sliding sports stand out, perhaps above all other Winter Games pursuits, for their sheer, spine-tingling extremes.

It's fun to watch any of the three sports on TV. But it is a complete rush to witness them in person. Because of the compressed angles from long-throw telephoto lenses, television tends to rob many speed sports of their true impact. The effect is even more profound in sliding sports; only spectators at the scene can fully appreciate their speed and ferocity.

People watching at the track don't just watch sleds go down the course at 128 to 144 kilometers per hour (80 to 90 mph). They feel them. The passing of a bobsled is heralded 15 to 20 seconds before it even comes into view. The ground rumbles. A low, throaty roar, like a jet plane on takeoff or a runaway locomotive, begins to wash down the hill. And seconds later, before you are even prepared to turn your head and look, SHA-WHOOSH!, the sled is here in a glimpse and then gone in a blur, the bright colors of its cowling and the occupants' helmets smearing into a visual and aural blur, like an impressionist painting set to rock music.

It's an overpowering experience—one that any Winter Games visitor should make the time and effort to feel for him or herself.

Anyone lucky enough to catch a competition at Lake Placid, Calgary, Salt Lake–Park City, and now Whistler Blackcomb will go away knowing, in a visceral way, what's really at stake in the sliding sports: It takes an awful lot of preparation, skill, raw strength, and luck to win a medal in bobsled, luge, or skeleton. And given the tragic ramifications of error, some fairly uncommon valor.

SPECTATOR'S GUIDE

The sliding sports are a sort of blue-collar special at the Olympics. Because fans are allowed to spread out along the entire course, thousands of tickets are usually available, and bobsled, skeleton, and luge are not usually among the Games' biggest draws. That makes them rather affordable, in Olympic-ticket terms. And once you're there, the thrill is inescapable.

Fans can stand right along most parts of the track—even on bridges over the top of it, in some places. Few Olympic sports allow you to get close enough to actually feel the jet wash of passing competitors. It's truly spectacular, and a thrill even for spectators with only a casual interest in who wins.

Field of Play

Bobsled, luge, and skeleton athletes all compete on the same field of play: frozen, U-shaped tracks of steep-banked ice that twist their way down mountainsides. The only difference for the three sports in terms of the track is that they start at different points on the mountain—bobsledders and singles lugers typically start higher than skeleton riders and doubles lugers. Women also start lower on the course than men.

Most modern ice tracks are built of concrete, which is covered by a thin layer of refrigerated ice and meticulously manicured, although a handful of old-style "natural" courses made from pouring freezing water on snow still exist in Europe—one of which is still used for World Cup competitions, the highest level of the sport.

Curves on the courses are very steeply banked—near vertical, in the case of horseshoe turns. The curves make each track unique. Although each sliding track shares common traits (on average, they are between 1,000 and 1,500 meters [3,280 and 4,921 feet] long and about 1.5 meters [5 feet] wide, with slope grades ranging from 8 to 15 percent), there is no standard sliding track. Each course must have a hairpin turn, a left turn, a right turn, and a labyrinth, but, like the downhill course in skiing, each has its own unique layout and characteristics, often reflective of the terrain onto which it's built. This is part of the tradition and allure of the sport, and it keeps things interesting for competitors and spectators alike.

North America's four existing ice tracks serve as good examples of how different courses can be: The current Lake Placid track, one of the most "technical," or curvy on the World Cup circuit, has 20 curves for men and 17 for women; Calgary's track offers only 14 curves for men and 10 for women; the track at Park City, Utah, has 14 curves for men and 12 for women. These courses range from 1,455 meters (4,773 feet) in length for men's competition at Lake Placid to only 1,086 meters (3,563 feet) for women at Calgary.

The fourth track, completed in 2008 on the slopes of Blackcomb Mountain for the 2010 Vancouver Games, looks to be one of the fastest courses in the world, with 16 curves over a 1,450-meter men's course that, even in its infancy, has proven steep enough to produce some truly spine-tingling moments. For more on the Whistler track, see page 77.

Generally, the higher and colder the location of the track, the faster the ice will be. Warmer ice allows the razor-sharp runners to sink in farther, creating greater friction. And in a sport so dependent on aerodynamics, thinner air at higher elevations creates less drag on sleds.

Format, Rules, and Strategy

Each bobsled run begins with racers standing outside the sled, pushing hard and digging in with spiked cleats for up to 50 meters as the sled runners slide in

grooves on a level ice surface before all team members pile in and tuck down for the downhill run.

At the Olympics, bobsledders take four runs. Starts are crucial: A fraction of a second edge at the top of the course can turn into several seconds by the time the team reaches the bottom. To gain maximum advantage, many modern bobsled drivers have begun recruiting sled "pushers" from the ranks of elite track-and-field athletes. Race times are recorded in hundredths of seconds, and the difference between first and second—or, at the Olympics, between a medal and no medal—is often minuscule.

In luge, as in bobsled, the start is key. Luge sliders don't run and jump into their sleds. They start seated atop it, hands on two bars sticking out of a start gate at hip level. They then rock back and forth and use their arms to launch themselves down the track, pushing with their spiked gloves for additional speed.

All that's left from that point on is steering—and chilling out. The key to sliding extremely fast, ironically, is to relax, most luge drivers say. That's tough to do when you're hurtling at 144 kilometers per hour (90 mph) down a ribbon of ice.

Lugers can undergo forces five times that of gravity and, because of the way their heads are situated, can't see directly where they're going. Sound like fun? It's even more complicated when done with a partner. Doubles luge teams sit tightly bunched, with the heavier slider or "rear driver" on the top, or rear, of the sled and the lighter, front "driver" nestled between his legs.

Singles lugers get four runs over two days; doubles lugers get two runs on one day. It's a dangerous sport: The sleds are so sensitive that even slight head movements can make a sled and rider, who is

Opposite: U.S. skeleton slider Eric Bernotas leaves the finish area of the track after winning a World Cup race at Mount Van Hoevenberg.

attached only by gravity and a firm hand grip, veer off the course. Luge times are kept in milliseconds (thousandths of a second).

In skeleton, starts are made with the slider standing, crouched forward, hands on the sides of the low-slung sled as he or she sprints about 50 meters in spiked cleats before leaping onto the sled face first. In the descent position, sliders keep their hands along their sides, their chins barely off the ice. They steer by shifting their body weight.

Skeleton riders take two runs on the same day, and their times are tracked in hundredths of a second.

In all three sliding sports, the lowest cumulative time wins. The fastest sleds are those that negotiate curves in the closest semblance to a straight line. Sleds bumping and banging into the icy sidewalls lose tremendous amounts of speed. Drivers who run "clean" through the course, avoiding bumps and entering and exiting turns gracefully and efficiently, will post the fastest times.

Training and Equipment

The sliding sports, perhaps more than any other, meld the dual talents of athleticism and technological prowess. Because heavier sleds naturally slide faster, bobsled, skeleton, and luge, the old joke went, were the only sports one could train for by heavy lifting—of multiple beers. No longer. Weight restrictions placed on sleds and riders ended all that, making taut bodies the new norm for athletes engaged in the sport.

Sliding athletes are generally incredibly fit: wiry and strong from top to bottom, with lightning-quick reflexes and the steely nerve it takes to fling your body down a ribbon of ice at more than 80 mph. They're heavily into weight training, sprints, hopping over hurdles, and other strength and agility exercises. Lugers need to have particularly strong necks, upper bodies, and lower legs, as those parts are used to control the course of the sled.

Although the sliding vehicles vary greatly, the other gear has some similarities. All sliding athletes wear form-fitting synthetic speed suits to cut down on wind drag. All wear low-top shoes with spikes on the bottom to gain purchase in the starting area. And all wear impact helmets with face shields to prevent injury. Gloves vary between the pursuits. A luger's gloves stand out because of the spikes along the fingertips, used to continue pushing off the ice after leaving the start gate.

Sleds have evolved from crude toys, really, to precision instruments, with closely protected secrets contained in their runners, floorboards, seats, and cowlings. Yet even the fastest sled in the world will finish last if it's not pushed and driven by athletes every bit as sculpted and honed as the equipment.

Inside the Bobsled

Bobsleds—sleek, aerodynamic, rocket-shaped sleds made of metal and fiberglass that reach speeds in excess of 128 kilometers per hour (80 mph)—have rope-operated steering mechanisms and are the most easily steered of the three sleds. Attaining top speed is dependent on weight, aerodynamics, ice temperature, and the sharpness and composition of the steel runners, in addition to the skill of the driver, who has the task of negotiating fully vertical banked turns in a precise way to avoid crashes. After the start, nondriving crew members are essentially ballast, keeping their heads down and all limbs out of the way.

Combined athlete/sled weight limits have been imposed since 1952. Today, the maximum is 630 kilograms or 1,389 pounds for a four-man sled, 390 kilograms or 859 pounds for a two-man sled, and 340 kilograms or 750 pounds for a two-woman sled. This injects a bit of math wizardry into the sport, as drivers must carefully consider the strength-to-weight ratio of each team member to reach optimum performance, particularly in the crucial race starts.

Bobsleds have brakes, which can be applied only in the finishing straight, where traveling uphill causes the sled to slow somewhat on its own.

Doubles luge sliders attack the course at the 1998 Nagano Games.

Luge's Inner Workings

Luge drivers, who slide feet first on their backs, on narrow sleds, achieve even higher speeds than their bobsledding counterparts—exceeding 137 kilometers per hour (85 mph), and their equipment couldn't be more different. Luge sleds are small and flexible, with runners angled inwards. Drivers lie on their backs and steer by applying pressure to the runners with their calves and to the sled surface with their shoulders, not with a steering wheel.

Because weight is a key to speed, weight limits are strict. A singles sled must weigh between 21 and 25 kilograms, or 46 and 55 pounds; a doubles sled must be between 25 and 30 kilograms, or 55 and 66 pounds. There is no weight limit per se for the athletes, but the total weight of the sled and its driver(s) is tightly controlled; lighter athletes often add supplemental weights to their bodies—under a complicated, prescribed formula—to hit the maximum allowances. Doubles lugers, for example, are allowed up to 180 kilograms, or 396 pounds, of weight between them. And yes, officials do check: Sleds and sliders are weighed in after each run.

Luge sleds have no brakes; they're stopped by pulling up on the front of the sled, digging in the rear runners, and simultaneously braking with the feet in the finish area, where the sled slides uphill in a deceleration lane.

Skeleton Facts of Life

Skeleton sleds are heavier, rectangular sleds, 79 to 119 centimeters (31 to 47 inches) long and 46 centimeters (18 inches) wide, with a fiberglass top sheet over steel runners placed 33 to 38 centimeters (13 to 15 inches) apart. The combined weight of the sled and sledder is capped at 115 kilograms (253 pounds) for men (42 kilograms for the sled alone) and 92 kilograms (203 pounds) for women (35 kilograms for the sled alone).

Skeleton sleds also have no brakes; racers slow

A skeleton sled, with rounded runners, is a far less precise instrument than a bobsled or luge sled.

them by sitting up and putting their feet down on the ground over the course of the finish area, which runs back uphill toward the starting position to allow slowing by gravity.

HISTORY'S HITS AND MISSES

Bobsled, or "bobsleigh" to some, is so named because early sliders, in flat portions of the tracks, would bob their heads in an attempt to generate momentum and pick up speed. *Luge* is the French word for "sled," while skeleton got its name because the stripped-down early versions of the head-first sled looked like a metal skeleton.

OLYMPIC FLASHBACK
SALT LAKE CITY GAMES

Feb. 20, 2002

Reported by Ron C. Judd for The Seattle Times

PARK CITY, Utah—In the end, it was all much adieu about nothing.

Remember the anguished goodbyes, the tumultuous driver/pusher split-ups that threatened to overshadow the grand introduction of women's bobsled into the Winter Olympics?

Historical footnotes.

Because yesterday, as skies darkened over Park City and snow began to settle, it all came down to two women's tenacity—an unquenchable thirst for being first down the mountain.

It was only fitting—and almost too perfect—that one would turn out to be Jill Bakken, 25, a Portland, Oregon native, a 1995 Lake Washington High School grad, a women's bobsled pioneer, and, as of last night, an Olympic gold medalist. And that the other would be 28-year-old Vonetta Flowers, who became, as far as anyone could determine, the first black athlete from any nation to win a Winter Games gold.

You could see it coming. For weeks, headlines and the swirl of scandal surrounding Bakken's more famous, just-a-tad faster teammate, driver Jean Racine, whose unceremonious ditching of best friend and longtime sliding partner Jen Davidson set off a national sports-world debate: What's more important? Best friends or first place?

It's all about winning, Racine maintained. She swapped a friendship for a few hundredths of a second.

In the wrong direction, it turned out. Last night, when it really mattered, the woman Racine chose to replace Davidson struggled with a hamstring injury. Racine posted the second-worst start times of the entire field.

Do you believe in karma?

Pretty good time to start.

What goes around came around—hard—yesterday for Racine, America's top-ranked driver, who finished fifth with limping partner Gea Johnson.

"I'm not going to think about any regrets right now," Racine said after the race. "I have four years to think about it."

Here's hoping she uses them.

Meanwhile, it is with great pleasure that we say goodbye, Mean Jean.

And hello, Jill Thrill.

Because last night in Park City, Bakken and partner Flowers, riding relatively pressure-free air, blew away the world, winning America's first ever women's bobsled gold medal with a combined time of 1:37.76—three tenths of a second faster than Sandra Prokoff and Ulrike Holzner of Germany and a half-second faster than Germany's Susi-Lisa Erdmann and Nicole Herschmann.

It was a fitting end. Flowers, who had no idea of her place in history until informed later, said through tears after the race she's more interested in raising a family than continuing a career of careening down frozen streambeds at 80 mph.

And Bakken, who couldn't stop smiling or crying either, seems poised to give U.S. women's bobsled what it needs most: a fresh face.

Here's what's behind it.

A high-school homecoming queen, Bakken was a multisport athlete at Lake Washington—and basic speed freak wherever she went. She eventually dropped her high-speed ski runs in Washington's Cascades—but only because she suspected she could go way, way faster in a bobsled.

At the time, there was no formal U.S. women's

program. Bakken entered it, anyway, traveling to Lake Placid to run sleds with anyone and everyone crazy enough to get in with her. She was the first woman in the program, and last night became the first American to win a bobsled gold.

She's also a part-time soldier with the Army National Guard. Bakken, pressed for money during the nonfunded years of bobsled, joined the Army's World Class Athlete program with her longtime pusher, Shauna Rohbock. As such, they're unable to accept commercial endorsements until their contract with Uncle Sam runs out—or they get out of it, whichever comes first.

For the past six years, she's stuck with bobsled driving in spite of a spate of painful injuries—a blown-out knee, a ripped Achilles tendon, chronic back injuries, a half-dozen other ailments. All of it endured for one shot at two fast, clean runs in front of hometown fans at the Olympics.

Teammates and coaches call her the most-liked person in the program—the one woman they'd all like to see win the gold.

They had no idea how sweet it would be when it happened.

Bakken, although she still seems stunned, sounded fully comfortable with her new role as leading lady for U.S. bobsledding. She didn't see any reason last night's race can't do for women's bobsled what the U.S. women's hockey gold medal in Nagano did for that sport.

"Having women compete in this Olympics . . . will give people the opportunity to see what it's all about," she said.

She and Flowers both said their victory seemed especially sweet given that, for months, they've been the overlooked duo in U.S. women's bobsledding.

"Jill and I tried to stay out of the soap opera," Flowers said. "We tried to stay focused. A lot of people saw us as the 'other team.' We had to come out and prove a lot of people wrong."

The manner in which they became the "other team" is instructive. Bakken made her own last-minute partner switch before these Olympics, but managed to stay below the seat-swapping controversy all winter, for all the right reasons.

When she replaced longtime pusher—and friend—Rohbock with Flowers, Bakken discussed it at length with Rohbock, then offered them a chance to come to the track and duel it out, head to head—an opportunity Racine never provided Davidson. Rohbock also was injured at the time, and didn't contest the decision.

There also was the none-too-small matter of publicity: Racine and Davidson had literally sold their sisterhood image—for a half-million or more—to all available corporate buyers well before the Olympics, creating an instant air of hypocrisy when Davidson was dumped (a distinction Racine still seems unable to grasp).

Bakken never fostered that pretension—a fact that's obvious in her continued strong friendship with Rohbock. Her former partner was among the first to embrace Bakken and Flowers—a new friend—last night at the finish.

"Shauna," Bakken would say later, "was there with me tonight, just as much as Vonetta was."

A lesson there, perhaps. Racine had it all wrong. It's not always a choice between friends and medals. It's a simple choice between right and wrong.

How do you know the difference? The same way Jill Bakken did last night.

If you've got the medal in one hand and your friend in the other, take it to the bank: You've done it right.

Sliding for Fun and, Later, Glory

Bobsled is older than the Winter Games themselves. It began in St. Moritz, Switzerland, where local vacationers, largely Brits bored with the pokey pursuits of cross-country skiing and snowshoeing, began racing toboggans and sleds, which they bolted together to hold more occupants. Alas, much of this racing was done in village streets, prompting a local hotel owner to brainstorm a dedicated track on the mountainside. It was operational sometime around 1870. Drivers soon tricked out their sleds for even greater speed. A local racing club put on its first competition in January 1898.

Local aficionados soon began working on an improved track for formal competition, and the famed Olympia Bobrun St. Moritz–Celerina was born in 1903, built entirely of natural ice. It remains the only natural ice (nonrefrigerated) track in major competition today, with work crews rebuilding it over a three-week period every winter.

The *Fédération Internationale de Bobsleigh et de Tobogganing* (FIBT) was founded in 1923 and continues to govern the sport, as well as skeleton, today.

Bobsled was a charter event at the 1924 Chamonix Games and continued an Olympic run uninterrupted until the Squaw Valley Games of 1960, when the local organizing committee decided to save money by not building a sledding track. Two-man bobsledding debuted at the 1932 Games, and two-woman's bobsledding debuted at Salt Lake City in 2002.

Luge was a latecomer to the sliding ranks. The first world championships took place in Oslo in 1955, with many anticipating that luge would replace skeleton in the Winter Olympics. In 1957, the *Fédération Internationale de Luge de Course* (FIL) was founded, and it still governs the sport today. The first Olympic competition, for both singles and doubles, was in Innsbruck in 1964.

Skeleton was developed in St. Moritz, first by sliders racing from St. Moritz to the nearby town of Celerina and then on the local Cresta Run, where a national competition took place in 1887. That track also was the site of the sport's first Olympic competitions, in 1928 and 1948. Skeleton then disappeared from the Games until its reinstatement at the Salt Lake City Olympics of 2002.

Billy Fiske, Sliding into History

The second and third Winter Games, in 1928 at St. Moritz and 1932 at Lake Placid, turned into playgrounds for America's Billy Fiske, who would become a legend on and, later, off the Olympic ice.

By some accounts, Fiske, a daredevil by nature, got to be an Olympic bobsled driver at age 16 the old-fashioned way: by asking. Fiske, Olympic historian Bud Greenspan recounts in his book *Frozen in Time: The Greatest Moments at the Winter Olympics,* was a 16-year-old on vacation at St. Moritz over the 1927 holidays when he was introduced to Jay O'Brien, chair of the U.S. Olympic Bobsled Committee.

Fiske said he wanted to drive for O'Brien's team. O'Brien, learning Fiske's age, told him to come back in four years. But a few days later, a second sled, USA II, was entered in the contest, with Fiske on the roster. And a month after that, Billy Fiske drove it to first place at St. Moritz, beating his own compatriots (a sled that included O'Brien as a crewman) by a half-second.

In doing so, Fiske and his team proved, emphatically, that one need be neither long in the tooth nor experienced to win a gold medal, at least not back then. Not only was Fiske a bobsled rookie, but three of his teammates jumped into the sled stone cold after answering a want ad in a Paris newspaper. None had ever seen a bobsled, let alone ridden in one. As reported by Olympic historian David

Wallechinsky, sled pusher Geoffrey Mason showed up for practice a couple of weeks before the Olympics, won a gold medal, then never rode in an international bobsled race again.

At the 1932 Games, defending champion Fiske was back, with new teammates (including O'Brien as a pusher). Temperatures were so warm in Lake Placid that the bobsled runs were postponed, resuming after the Games were completed. When they did, Fiske won by two seconds over the USA II sled, the Saranac Lake Red Devils, driven by Henry Homburger. O'Brien, 48 at the time, became the oldest Winter Olympic medalist ever.

When World War II commenced, Fiske became the first American to sign up for the British Royal Air Force. After shooting down several enemy planes, Fiske was critically wounded in the 1940 Battle of Britain. He managed to land the plane but died the next day at the age of 29. He was the first American pilot to die in combat in World War II.

Another famed member of that '32 squad was, Edward "Eddie" Patrick Francis Eagan, a Denver native who rose from poverty to become a Rhodes Scholar and attorney. Eagan, competing with virtually no sledding experience in the Lake Placid Games, made history by becoming the first (and still only) person to win a gold medal in both the Winter and Summer Olympics. Eagan had previously won a gold medal in boxing (light-heavyweight) in the 1920 Antwerp Games.

American Ingenuity

Fiske and company weren't the only athletic entrepreneurs at the '32 Games. Local residents J. Hubert and Curtis Stevens won the gold medal in two-man bobsled, employing a bit of American ingenuity via a now-illegal trick: heating their bobsled runners with a blowtorch. Some people, allegedly, still try it, though most of them get caught.

An Italian Sled Legend

Eugenio Monti must have had winter sports in his blood. A talented alpine skier, he was an Italian national champion before a knee injury ended his career in 1951. Rather than quit, he simply switched sliding implements, swapping his skis for a bobsled. In 1956, in his hometown of Cortina d'Ampezzo, Monti won silver medals in both the two-man and four-man events—a disappointment, as he considered the course to be in his backyard.

With the absence of a sledding track at Squaw Valley in 1960, Monti had to wait until 1964 at Innsbruck to resume his gold medal quest. There he again faltered slightly, sliding to bronze medals in both events. But he'll forever be remembered for an act of sportsmanship—lending a replacement bolt to a British team, which went on to win the two-man gold medal.

Monti, believing his medal days were over, retired. But two years later, a sled mate devised a speedier sled, and Monti was lured back. At age 40, he drove again in the 1968 Grenoble Games, and in the two-man race, something of a miracle occurred: Monti's sled and a German sled tied for first place, with identical times after four runs. Under the rules in place at the time, the sled with the single fastest run time won. Monti's course record on his fourth run earned him, at long last, the gold medal. Before the Games ended, he added a second, in the four-man. He retired as one of the most successful bobsled drivers ever.

Canada's Famous "Playboy Bobsledders"

At the time, it was almost as ludicrous as the notion of a bobsled team from Jamaica. Even though Canada had a long reputation as a winter-sports haven, the nation hadn't fielded a single bobsled team in Olympic competition.

It was no surprise, then, that people were

grinning when Peter Kirby, Douglas Anakin, and brothers John and Vic Emery showed up in Innsbruck to do battle in 1964. The Montreal quartet was widely viewed as a bunch of spoiled playboys—rich ski bums out to party and, in their spare time, make a few token bobsled runs.

It was hardly the case. Vic Emery was a Harvard MBA, John Emery was a plastic surgeon, Kirby

U.S. bobsledder Erin Pac brings her doubles sled to a finish at a World Cup race.

was a geologist, and Anakin was a teacher. They put all that brain power to work. With no track to train on in Canada, the team trained in a gym and used the Lake Placid course for its limited on-ice time. They paid their own way to the Olympics, where photographs showed three of the four racers decked out in football helmets.

But they shocked the world by setting a course record on their first run, and they went on to win the gold medal over the favored Austrian squad by nearly a full second. What's more, Vic Emery and Kirby narrowly missed adding a second medal in the two-man competition, where they finished fourth.

Proving they were no fluke, Vic Emery and Kirby, with new teammates Michael Young and Gerald Presley, won the world championships the next year in St. Moritz. All four of the Canadian gold medalists—the only gold medalists for Canada at the Innsbruck Games—were subsequently enshrined in the Canadian Olympic Hall of Fame.

Bow Down to Bo-Dyn

If those bobsleds with American flags on the front have something of a race car look to them, it's no coincidence. In 1992, NASCAR driver Geoff Bodine, the winner of the 1986 Daytona 500, donated nearly $200,000 to launch the nonprofit Bo-Dyn Bobsled Project. Bodine's money, and the expertise of automotive engineer Bob Cuneo of Connecticut, led to U.S. bobsleds with lower-profile, more aerodynamic bodies and more responsive steering than past sleds.

They were the first made-in-America sleds used by U.S. racers since 1956, and they have proven highly successful, with four Olympic medals and a pair of overall World Cup championships. An annual fundraiser for the project, the Chevy Geoff Bodine Bobsled Challenge, pits NASCAR drivers against National Hot Rod Association drag racers every winter on the track at Lake Placid.

Cool Runnings, for Real Mon

To this day, a lot of people probably think it was all just a movie stunt. They're half right.

The fielding of a team of Jamaicans in Olympic bobsled competition truly was a stunt—one organized by Americans George Fitch and William Maloney, who had business ties in Jamaica and recruited military members to slide for the island nation.

The sledders themselves, later immortalized in the movie *Cool Runnings,* trained hard—and, predictably, flopped in Calgary. But they wound up sticking with the sport, moving up in the ranks in subsequent international competitions. By the 1994 Olympics in Lillehammer, they were a respectable team, finishing in 14th place—ahead of the fastest sleds from the United States, Italy, France, and Russia.

Somewhere in Nagano, There's a Spare Silver Medal

After four runs at the 1998 Nagano Games, the two-man bobsled teams of Pierre Lueders and David MacEachern of Canada and Gunther Huber and Antonio Tartaglia of Italy finished dead even in cumulative time: 3:37.24 to 3:37.24. As it turns out, it wasn't the first-ever tie in bobsled. Recall that the previous deadlock, in 1968, had led to an "awarded victory" to the team with the fastest single run.

The rules had changed by Nagano, however, where the two teams were declared co-gold medalists. Lueders and MacEachern were the first Canadians since the famous '64 squad to win the four-man bob.

Sitting Back in Steerage

If you think modern luge sleds look tricky to control, imagine the original ones. A major turning point in the sport we know today came in the 1930s, when Austrian slider Marti Tietze, a four-time European champion, pioneered the flexible sled, which allowed sliders to steer by moving their feet along the front of the runners. Before that? People steered largely by dragging their hands on the track—not something you want to do for a long time, if you value the use of your hands.

America Gets on the Luge Scoreboard

One sunny day in 1998, near Nagano, Japan, America's Chris Thorpe, Gordy Sheer, Mark Grimmette, and Brian Martin shattered a massive barrier, becoming not only the first Americans, but also the first North Americans, to medal in luge. Their win was the result of an effort begun more than four decades before.

When luge was added to the Olympics for the 1964 Games, America had no formal luge training program. Team members were mainly U.S. soldiers who were stationed in Europe and had ready access to sled tracks. Home-front sliders were limited to those willing to risk life and limb sliding on the old track at Lake Placid, which was designed for bobsledders.

All that changed in 1979, when the old Lake Placid track was replaced by America's first refrigerated multisport track for the 1980 Winter Olympics. At around the same time, the sport's parent organization, USA Luge, was formed, establishing a national team and training program. Today, that group has one of the most aggressive recruiting programs in all of Olympic sports. Elite-level luge athletes and coaches tour the country in the summer offseason, holding luge tryout camps for aspiring young athletes.

The most promising prospects—picked for their natural ability to run a course on a luge sled fitted with wheels—are invited to USA Luge training camps. Many of these kids have graduated to the U.S. national team and even the Winter Olympics. In recent years, the U.S. men's and women's singles sliders have begun to catch up with the men's doubles

Mark Grimmette and Brian Martin broke the ice for U.S. luge medalists at the 1998 Nagano Games.

teams. American slider Courtney Zablocki finished fourth at the 2006 Turin Games—the highest finish ever for an American woman. And singles luger Tony Benshoof also finished fourth in Turin, the highest finish ever for an American male singles luger.

Meet the Sheas—Times Three

When Lake Placid's Jim Shea took to the icy skeleton course at Utah Olympic Park near Park City in February, 2002, he believed he had some company on his sled. Shea was the son of Jim Shea Sr., who had competed in the Nordic combined and cross-country skiing at the 1964 Innsbruck Games. Jim Sr.'s father, in turn, was Jack Shea, the first American to win two gold Winter Games medals, in the 500- and 1,500-meter speedskating events at the Lake Placid Games of 1932. Shea became the toast of New York at the completion of the Lake Placid Games, and he and his son, and later his grandson, were local celebrities for generations.

Jim Shea the latter, or "Jimmy," as he is known to most, was the most unlikely medalist of the trio. He was a bobsled driver who switched to skeleton in 1995, at least partially because of the dramatically lower equipment costs. Jimmy Shea, who overcame a difficult childhood marked by the learning disability dyslexia (he says he still finds it difficult to read), became the first American to win a World Cup skeleton championship in 1999. His charge to the medal stand in 2002 was made even more dramatic by sudden tragedy: Grandfather Jack Shea was killed by a drunk driver in Lake Placid in a traffic accident two weeks before the Salt Lake Games. Jimmy Shea honored his legacy by following in his grandfather's footsteps to take the Athlete's Oath at the Salt Lake opening ceremony.

In competition on February 20, 2002, America's first third-generation Olympian carried a photo of his grandfather in his race helmet at Park City, crediting the spirit of Jack Shea for pushing him to victory over Austria's Martin Rettl, the gold medal favorite, by five hundredths of a second.

Hot Oil—Optional

Legendary Olympic luger Georg Hackl owns another world title of which he is equally proud: four-time World Wok Racing Champion.

Yes, that's wok, as in the circular Chinese cooking pan. Wok racing was born as a result of a bet on a German comedian's TV show and grew into its own "reality" sport, perfectly made for TV, complete with its own opening ceremony. Contestants—some athletes, but many B-movie stars and other subcelebrities—slide down German luge/bobsled runs seated on large woks, with ladles strapped to their feet to steer and prevent friction. Hackl won the race in 2004, 2005, 2007, and 2008, in the process establishing a one-man wok speed record of 91.70 kilometers per hour (about 57 mph, or about 30 mph slower than a top luge sled).

RECORD BOOK: BOBSLED

Not surprisingly, Germany and Switzerland, where the sport was invented, have garnered the most medals in men's two- and four-man and women's two-man bobsled since the sport's inception at the 1924 Games. The Germans have hauled in 37 medals (15 gold) compared to Switzerland's 30 (nine gold). Following on their heels is the United States, with 18 total medals. Italy has 12 total medals (thanks in no small part to Eugenio Monti's six); no other nation has more than four.

Most of the American medals stretch far back into history: gold in the five-man in 1928 at St. Moritz; gold and silver in the four-man and gold and bronze in the two-man at Lake Placid in 1932; gold and bronze in the two-man at Garmisch-Partenkirchen, 1936; gold and bronze in the four-man and bronze in the two-man at St. Moritz in

1948; silver in the four-man at Oslo, 1952; bronze in the four-man at Cortina d'Ampezzo, 1956; and then a long drought until a silver (**Todd Hays, Randy Jones, Bill Schuffenhauer,** and **Garrett Hines**) and a bronze (**Brian Shimer, Mike Kohn, Doug Sharp,** and **Dan Steele**) in the four-man at Salt Lake City in 2002. The American women's team of **Jill Bakken** and **Vonetta Flowers** grabbed gold in the inaugural women's Olympic competition at Salt Lake City in 2002.

Canada, which first won gold in the four-man at Innsbruck in 1964, has been surging in recent years. The Canadian pair of **Pierre Lueders** and **David MacEachern** won gold at Nagano in 1998; the team of Lueders and **Lascell Brown** won silver again at Turin in 2006.

RECORD BOOK: MEN'S LUGE

Italy, Germany, Austria, and the USSR/Russia have owned the luge medal stand for decades, winning 97 of 102 medals awarded in the sport since its inception in 1964. After total domination throughout the 1970s by the East and West Germans, the singles sport has been ruled in more recent years by three nations: the unified Germany, in the form of one **Georg Hackl;** Italy, via **Armin Zoeggeler;** and Austria, specifically **Markus Prock.** Hackl won his first medal, a silver, at the Calgary Games in 1988, when he still slid for West Germany, finishing behind East German **Jens Mueller.** He then captured gold in 1992 at Albertville, in 1994 at Lillehammer, and in 1998 at Nagano, before finishing second behind the surging Zoeggeler at Salt Lake City in 2002, capping one of the most amazingly long Olympic medal runs of any Winter Games athlete. Zoeggeler, in addition to his Salt Lake gold and a repeat performance at Turin, in 2006, owns a silver medal from Nagano and a bronze from Lillehammer. Prock won bronze in Salt Lake City and silver medals in Lillehammer and Albertville.

LEGEND OF THE SPORT
GEORG HACKL, GERMANY, SINGLES LUGE

Born: 9 September 1966, Berchtesgaden, Germany
Olympics: Calgary, Albertville, Lillehammer, Nagano, Salt Lake City, Turin
Medals: 3 gold, 2 silver

Few Olympic athletes have owned a sport like Georg (pronounced: "GAY-org") Hackl, the Speeding Weisswurst ("white sausage") from Berchtesgaden, Germany.

Hackl, who grew up not far from the famed Bavarian sled track at Königssee, hopped on a luge at 11 and fell in love with the sport. He was 22 when he qualified for his first Olympics, in Calgary in 1988, as the recently crowned European champion. But he was beaten out of the starting gate—literally—by fellow countryman Jens Mueller, leaving him with the silver medal and a somewhat bitter taste.

Georg Hackl of Germany stands as an all-time legend in the sport of luge.

Hackl returned home and had a special practice start range built for him at the Königssee course, then returned to win the gold medal at the Albertville Games of 1992, edging out Marcus Prock of Austria in a close competition. In a rematch at the '94 Lillehammer Games, Hackl narrowly beat the Austrian again, this time with a four-run combined time of 3:21.571 to Prock's 3:21.584. The IOC illustrates the closest finish in luge history thusly: If they had been racing all those runs in a straight line, Hackl would have won by less than 35 centimeters (about 14 inches) after 5.6 kilometers (3.5 miles) of sliding.

In 1998, Hackl entered the Nagano Games as an underdog for once: He had performed uncharacteristically poorly on the World Cup circuit that year—on purpose, some critics argued, to disguise the effectiveness of a newfangled, self-designed sled and new aerodynamic luge booties (yellow). Other sliders filed an official protest over the booties, but it was rejected. And so were they. On the course, Hackl was his usual Olympic self, completing all four runs faster than his competitors (a first for a male luger at the Olympics) and winning easily over Armin Zoeggeler of Italy and Mueller of Germany.

He finally was pushed from the top rung of the medal stand—albeit not completely off it—in the 2002 Games in Salt Lake City. Hackl, seeking an unprecedented fourth straight gold medal in the same event, was edged by Zoeggeler. He settled for the silver, but it was historic: He became the first Olympian to ever win five consecutive medals in the same event.

In the weeks before the 2006 Turin Games, Hackl, recovering from neck surgery, barely qualified for the German team. But the aging veteran, dubbed the "Godfather of Luge" by competitors, returned to the ice one last time for his sixth Games, sliding to a seventh-place finish at age 40.

"If you have a big task, it makes your life interesting, it gives it a bigger sense," Hackl told *USA Today*. "I always told myself that I can relax when I am in the graveyard."

Hackl's battles with Prock and Zoeggeler, coupled with his unprecedented Olympic medals run—not to mention 22 world championship medals—make him a true Olympic legend, on the ice and off. He also will long be remembered for his skills on the drawing board—he designed and built many of his own sleds—and his ability to psych out opponents, particularly during the Olympics.

The Speeding Weisswurst, so named because of the way he looked in that skintight speed suit stretched over a 5-foot-7, 175-pound frame, recently declared that he's finally ready to retire—to coaching.

Italian luge slider Armin Zoeggeler accepts his gold medal before a raucous crowd in downtown Turin, Italy during the 2006 Winter Games.

Doubles luge also has been dominated by Germany, Austria, and Italy (one of the three nations has won every gold medal since the sport's Olympic inception in 1964), with the occasional Soviet/Russian silver or bronze medal thrown in. At the 1988 Calgary Games, the Germans outdid themselves, sweeping the first four places in the event. That winning streak was finally cracked in 1998 at the Nagano Games, when America's **Chris Thorpe** and **Gordy Sheer** took the silver behind **Stefan Krausse** and **Jan Behrendt** of Germany, and the U.S. team of **Mark Grimmette** and **Brian Martin**

took the bronze. Grimmette and Martin returned to capture silver at the 2002 Salt Lake Olympics, where teammates Thorpe and **Clay Ives** took the bronze. Canada awaits its first luge medal. Might the Blackcomb track provide the magical spark?

RECORD BOOK: WOMEN'S LUGE

Germany has owned women's luge even more thoroughly than it has the men's events. Of the 36 medals awarded since the inception of women's luge at Innsbruck in 1976, Germans have captured 25.

In recent Olympics, three women have dominated the podium: Germany's **Silke Kraushaar** (gold in Nagano, bronze in Salt Lake, silver in Turin) and **Sylke Otto** (gold in Salt Lake and Turin); and Austria's **Barbara Niedernhuber** (silver in Nagano and Salt Lake City).

RECORD BOOK: MEN'S SKELETON

In men's skeleton, America was on top from the get-go, with a gold medal for **Jennison Heaton** and silver for his younger brother, **John,** in the first Olympic skeleton tourney in 1928 on the famed Cresta course at St. Moritz. Jennison Heaton also was the driver of the U.S. sled claiming silver in the men's five-man bobsled (the only time the event was held in a five-man configuration) at the same 1928 Olympics.

Skeleton reappeared when the Games returned to St. Moritz after the war period in 1948, with the gold claimed by **Nino Bibbia** of Italy, who made Connecticut's **John Heaton,** now 39, settle once again for silver after making a remarkable return performance 20 years after his first Olympic medal in the same event.

When the sport returned to the Olympics in 2002, after a long pause, an American man once again ascended to the top of the medal stand—again with a compelling family connection. Gold medalist **Jim Shea** of Lake Placid, New York, was a third-generation Olympian. At Turin in 2006, however, Canadians suddenly and spectacularly dominated the event, with **Gibson Duff** taking the gold and teammate **Jeff Pain** earning the silver.

RECORD BOOK: WOMEN'S SKELETON

In 2002, when skeleton returned to the Olympics at the Salt Lake City Games, Americans **Tristan Gale** and **Lea Ann Parsley** captured gold and silver, respectively, in the women's event.

In Turin four years later, **Maya Pedersen** of Switzerland took gold, with **Shelley Rudman** of Switzerland sliding to second place and Canada's **Mellisa Hollingsworth-Richards** taking the bronze.

NEXT STOP: WHISTLER SLIDING CENTRE

Location: Blackcomb Mountain, Whistler, B.C.
Spectator capacity: 12,000
Elevation: 785 meters (2,575 feet) at the base; 935 meters (3,067 feet) at the top
Other events: Alpine ski venues at Whistler Creekside are nearby
Medal ceremonies: Whistler Village Celebration Plaza

Bobsled, luge, and skeleton will be staged at the all-new Whistler Sliding Centre, near the base of Blackcomb Mountain in the resort town of Whistler. The track, with a capacity of 12,000 fans, is walking distance from Whistler's main resort village.

Construction of the 1,450-meter track, with 16 turns, was largely complete in the spring of 2008, when a group of international bobsled and luge officials and athletes from Austria, Canada, Germany, Britain, Italy, Russia, and the United States arrived for training runs to certify the course. They took runs in bobsleds, luge, and skeleton sleds from six different starting positions on the track, working from top to bottom.

It proved, by most accounts, extremely fast—and nearly ready to race, a rarity with a new track.

"This is a great track that will challenge all the skills of the modern sliding athletes," said Bob Storey, president of FIBT, the international bobsled federation. "It is fast, technical, demanding, and interesting."

A luge colleague echoed his sentiments: "There

are lots of technical tracks around the world, but this one is so unique because of the speed—that is what makes it so challenging," said Walter Plaikner, a technical delegate for FIL, the international luge federation.

How fast? U.S. luger Tony Benshoof, who holds the official world luge sled speed record at 86.6 mph, says it's only a matter of time before many racers blow right by that mark on the Whistler track.

"We were going 145 [kilometers per hour, or about 90 mph] in training gear and training steels," said Benshoof, a two-time Olympian. "I'm guessing, on good ice . . . it's going to be 95 miles per hour for sure."

Until now, the 2002 Olympic course in Park City, Utah, has been widely considered the world's fastest track, although Benshoof notched two runs at 139 kilometers per hour (86.5 mph) each on the Olympic course for the 2006 Turin Games.

Benshoof confirmed the opinion of Canadian skeleton slider Jon Montgomery, who looked at the track layout during construction and predicted that it "will be a real pumpkin-squasher," referring to high speeds and their accompanying g-force. Although tracks at lower altitudes generally are believed to be slower, due to warmer ice conditions, the Whistler track, with a bottom elevation of only 785 meters (2,575 feet), apparently makes up for that with its steep pitch.

"It's amazing how the track drops from curve one to the exit of curve two," Benshoof says. "I kind of dubbed it 'Waterfall' for a couple of reasons. First of all, there is a waterfall that travels underneath it, but man, you also feel like you're going off a waterfall when you come down it because you go from zero to 120 [kilometers per hour] in the course of about 10 seconds."

The bottom half of the course is even faster.

"On the bottom half, you go into warp speed . . . you really do," Benshoof says. "It wasn't until the last day [of four] that those curves started slowing down in my head. Before that, it was just a big blur."

Bobsled, Luge, Skeleton 2010 Schedule

February 13–14: Men's luge

February 15–16: Women's luge

February 17: Doubles luge

February 18–19: Men's and women's skeleton

February 20–21: Two-man bobsled

February 23–24: Women's bobsled

February 26–27: Four-man bobsled

CURLING

❄ ❄ ❄ ❄ ❄

"Although some people may snicker at curling's inclusion in the Olympics, it does further the International Olympic Committee's movement towards democracy by allowing non-athletes to take part in the Winter Olympics."

> —Olympic historian David Wallechinsky,
> introducing the curling chapter in
> *The Complete Book of the Winter Olympics*

Ouch.

Although rabid fans of sliding granite stones along a sheet of ice—that means you, Canada—might bristle at the insinuation, Wallechinsky makes a valid point. When it comes to sweat, grit, daring, and toil—the very ingredients of many of the Winter Games' most alluring events—curling, a board game played on foot, clearly doesn't measure up.

In fact, it makes ice dancing look like an Ironman triathlon.

Which is not to say it doesn't belong, if one is of the opinion that games of strategy and skill deserve an equal footing in the medal-sports world.

That's exactly what curling is. We part with critics who say it's not a sport; it clearly is. But it undoubtedly is a sport of a different color. Reference books on all things sport don't classify it as either an ice or a snow sport, but as a sport (or the more condescending "game") of "precision and accuracy." As such, curling is lumped in with other closest-to-the-pin pursuits such as shooting, archery, billiards, lawn bowling, pétanque, lane bowling, and golf.

Some of those, the astute Olympiphile will notice, also are Olympic medal sports. So don't be getting all huffy about curling's inclusion in the modern Games, curling aficionados say.

It took a long time getting here. Curling was a demonstration sport at Chamonix in 1924 and again five more times throughout the history of the modern Games, until the IOC finally put it on the medal stand in Nagano in 1998. At the time, many people believed, with good reason, that it would prove a boon to Canada, where curling, which has its deepest roots in Scotland, has been embraced like nowhere else on the planet.

The game is played by upward of a million

Canadians. Somewhere between 80 and 95 percent of the world's curlers live in Canada, according to various estimates (we'd love to know who makes such estimations, and to get a good look at their methodology). The game enjoys crazy-high TV ratings north of the border. Tens of thousands of curling clubs exist from Vancouver to Regina to St. John, welcoming curlers for league play much as bowling alleys do—or at least did—in the United States.

Throughout the year, those clubs descend on regional cities for big-time curling tournaments, or bonspiels—crunch time for any self-respecting Canadian curler since the sport was introduced by Scottish immigrants around 1760.

Alas, Canada's sheer numbers haven't translated to sheer dominance in the Olympics. The nation may own some 30 world titles, but it has snared only a couple of medals—notably, the Sandra Schmirler team's inaugural gold at the Nagano Games. And the rest of the world isn't waiting for the Canadians to get their Olympic groove on.

The sport, thanks largely to increased global exposure through Olympic TV broadcasts, has become increasingly popular in Scandinavia. Even Americans have begun picking up brooms and stones in areas outside curling's traditional hotspots, such as Minnesota, home of the U.S. Curling Association, an umbrella organization with 16,000 members in 135 curling clubs. Those numbers have grown by about 20 percent after each of the last two Winter Games, officials say.

The sport also is catching on in other nations looking for easy ways to increase their medal-count production, notably China.

But let's be honest: Curling is not, and likely never will be, a mainstream, highlights-on-*SportsCenter* kind of activity. Its world championships for 2008 were held in Fargo, North Dakota. It's not big time, big city, or high profile.

But for many people, that's the charm. "I think at its core the reason why I really, really enjoy watching curling is I think it's the only chance I have at ever winning an Olympic medal in my life," Ethan A. Brosowsky, a Los Angeles actor and producer, told the *New York Times* in 2006. "You look at downhill skiing or bobsledding and say, 'I can never do that, not in a million years.' But with curling it's different." In that way, it's the one everyman's sport in the increasingly specialized modern Games.

As such, it has its own idiosyncrasies, ranging from cute to bizarre. Above all else, curlers consider themselves sportsmen. Every match begins with handshakes all around and a good-luck admonition: "Good curling!" The winning team, by tradition, buys the losers a round of drinks—and that's not Gatorade in those glasses.

In spite of the protests of some who liken it to contract bridge, curling's Olympic future looks sound, especially in the short term. The sport has managed to attract a fair amount of attention—and new fans—in places where it had never been played before, notably Nagano and Turin.

Imagine the great swell of national pride when Canada, home to 94 percent—or pick your high number—of the people with curling brooms in their closets, welcomes the world to its own home rink, the friendliest curling ice the Olympics is ever likely to see.

It might be enough to make the nation's top contenders tear up. Or maybe, for the first time, actually work up a sweat.

SPECTATOR'S GUIDE

Much of the derision surrounding curling as an Olympic sport can be attributed to a widespread lack of knowledge about how the game actually works. Taking a few moments to familiarize oneself with the rules and setup can turn it into an enjoyable, albeit low-key, spectator sport. If you choose not to understand its inner workings, curling will look, well, just silly.

Field of Play

Curling is a game of skill and strategy played on a rectangular sheet of ice measuring 138 feet (42 meters) long and a little over 14 feet (4.2 meters) wide. At each end of the rink is a "house," a series of concentric rings that looks like a large target painted under the ice. The center circle, or the bull's-eye of the target, is called the button. A line running through the center of the button, from side to side as players face it, is called the tee line. Surrounding the button are three more concentric target rings measuring 4 feet, 8 feet, and 12 feet (1.2, 2.4, and 3.7 meters) wide, respectively.

At each end of the ice, behind the house, is a "hack"—two rubber blocks that serve as a push-off point for curlers, team members who deliver 42-pound curling "stones" toward the house on the other end by sliding them carefully along the ice for some distance and then releasing them.

The U.S. Curling Team at the 2006 Games in Turin

Another prominent feature of the rink is the "hog line," a red line about a fourth of the way down the rink on each end that delineates the final point at which a curler can release a stone.

Curling ice is groomed to keep it perfectly level, then, unlike other competition ice, treated with a light spray of water before each game. The water freezes in place to form a granular surface more conducive to stone sliding.

Format, Rules, and Strategy

In some ways, curling is quite similar to lawn bowling or shuffleboard: The object is to place stones as near to the button, or center of the target, as possible while preventing the other team's stones from doing the same. You're awarded 1 point for every stone you have closer to the button than your opposition's closest stone. (Thus, only one team scores during each "end" of play.)

Teams consist of four curlers per side—a "skip," or team captain who stands at the opposing house and directs shots from teammates; a "vice skip" or "third" at the other end of the ice, helping with strategy; and a "lead" and "second," whose job it is to throw the first and second stones and then influence their path down the ice by "sweeping" the ice in front of the stone with specially made brooms. The vice skip and skip also deliver stones, curling third and fourth, respectively. When the skip curls, the vice skip takes his or her place in the opposite house.

Using a broom for balance, curlers push off the hack at the end of the rink and slide ahead on one forward foot and one knee, holding the stone by the handle and releasing it with a spin—this is the "curl"—to give it the proper trajectory. A properly curled stone is often likened to a very slow-breaking curveball; the degree of spin gives it lateral movement.

The skip will direct two teammates to sweep the ice in front of an approaching stone, either to change its curl or to make it travel farther by reducing the friction on the ice in front of it.

The two teams alternate stone throws until all curlers have thrown two stones, for a total of 16. This constitutes one "end" of a game. (An end is like an inning in baseball.) Every game has 10 ends. The points are tallied up after each end, and the scoring team goes first in the next end, in which the stones are thrown in the opposite direction.

The team with the most points at the end of 10 ends wins. If it's a tie, an extra end is played.

Strategy revolves around placement. Curlers can aim to deliver a "draw" stone, or one that stops somewhere within the playing surface, or a "takeout"—a shot designed specifically to bounce the other team's stone out of the field of play. Strategically placed draw stones that come to rest in front of another stone, thereby preventing the opposition from taking that stone out, are called "guard stones."

Watch it for a while and, although you might not pick up all the confusing terminology (for example, in curling the term "rink" is synonymous with "team," as in "the Pete Fenson rink"), the game will begin to make sense.

Because each team curls eight stones per end, the maximum score for an end is 8 points, but teams usually wind up scoring 1 to 3 points. A game of 10 ends typically lasts about 2.5 hours, or about 15 minutes per end.

Training and Equipment

Although advocates point out that sweepers must be nimble on their feet and wind up walking the equivalent of up to 2 miles per match, this is hardly a sport you're likely to see featured in a Gatorade commercial. It is, however, undoubtedly a precision pursuit. So the best training for curling is curling. Lots of practice makes perfect.

Curling is the one door left slightly ajar in the Olympics for "normal" folks—people without stupendous athletic ability. Most curlers have full-time careers outside their sport: Pete Fenson, captain or "skip" of the U.S. men's bronze medal team at the Turin Games, operates a two-restaurant pizza chain, Dave's Pizza, in Bemedji and Brainerd, Minnesota. Other Olympic curlers have been housewives, bankers, salesmen, science teachers, students, and consultants. Most of them are introduced to the sport through family or friends who belong to local curling leagues. The best of them advance to regional, then national competitions.

Dress is ice casual; curlers wear what appear to be track suits, with stretchy pants for all that bending and jackets that can be taken off should a curler manage to get warm.

Curling stones are made of granite, almost all of which is quarried in Scotland and delivered around the world in extremely low-riding container ships. They're round spheres, slightly concave on the top and bottom, carefully balanced, with a plastic handle affixed to the top. Stones weigh 42 pounds (19 kilograms), with a diameter of 1 foot (30 centimeters) and a height of about 4.5 inches (11.5 centimeters). They never lift off the ice during competition—or at least one would hope not.

Shoes are low-cut, bowling style, allowing for ankle flexing while delivering the stone. The sole of the shoe on the foot used to slide out front during delivery (the left shoe for a right-hander) is slippery. The other shoe has a nonslip rubber sole.

Brooms have plastic handles and look an awful lot like a kitchen sponge mop, with a universal joint at the head allowing it to flex in all directions.

HISTORY'S HITS AND MISSES

Curling originated on the frozen ponds of Scotland, where it is believed to have been introduced by Flemish immigrants in the 16th or 17th century. The rules were standardized in 1716, but the first governing body, the Grand Caledonian Curling Club, was not founded until 1838. The first major tournament took place in Edinburgh in 1847.

Curling was most likely a demonstration sport (some debate lingers about this) at the inaugural 1924 Chamonix Games, and it would be a demo sport five more times (1932, 1936, 1964, 1988, and 1992) before earning medal status at the Nagano Games of 1998. World championships began in 1959 for men (then known as the Scotch Cup) and in 1979 for women. They now take place every year.

The USA's First Curling Medal

It took three Olympic Games for America to earn its first curling medal—a bronze captured by the Pete Fenson rink in Turin in 2006. Fenson himself secured the victory by placing a carefully targeted stone inside of a British draw, giving the U.S. squad an 8–6 victory.

"Our job's done here," he said afterward.

It was a big job. The medal was not only the first Olympic curling medal for the United States but the first U.S. curling medal in a major men's competition in two decades. Coupled with Canada's gold medal in the same event, it was a long-awaited North American moment of glory for fans of curling.

You Heard It Right—Curling's Sex Symbols

Cassandra "Cassie" Johnson and her sister, Jamie, were a good story for plenty of reasons going into the 2006 Turin Games. Growing up in the curling hotbed of Bemidji, Minnesota—also the hometown of bronze-medal-winning skip Pete Fenson—the sisters were fourth-generation practitioners of the sport, and some media outlets, including *Sports Illustrated,* picked them to win America's first curling medal in the Games in Italy.

LEGEND OF THE SPORT
SANDRA SCHMIRLER, CANADA, CURLING

Born: 11 June 1963, Biggar, Saskatchewan, Canada
Olympics: Nagano
Medal: 1 team gold

Canada is perhaps the only nation in the world where a curler can achieve household-name status. And none achieved it in quite as lasting a way as Sandra Schmirler, aka Schmirler the Curler.

Schmirler, a Saskatchewan native born with a club foot, wanted to play hockey. But her high school in Biggar didn't have a team, so she took up curling instead, practicing at first on natural ice in local fields. Serving as skip of a local squad, she won a provincial championship in 1991 and the Canadian championship in 1993. She was a three-time world champion when the sport finally earned medal status for the 1998 Nagano Games. Less than two months after having her first child, she led her rink, composed of herself and

fellow Saskatchewan natives Jan Betker, Joan McCusker, and Marcia Gudereit, to Nagano. After surviving a white-knuckle finish against a strong British squad in the Olympic semifinals, they won the gold medal match 7–5 over Denmark.

Schmirler became a celebrity in Canada and was known for bringing her gold medal out for all to see, and try on, at community events in Biggar and Regina. Tragically, only four months after her father died of cancer, and only two months after the birth of her second child, Schmirler was diagnosed with cancer. She died in 2000 at age 36. Fifteen hundred mourners attended her funeral, which was broadcast on national television. But her legacy lives on, through the Sandra Schmirler Foundation, a charity focusing on neonatal care in Canada. Its motto: "Champions start small."

Sandra Schmirler releases a stone during a curling match.

But their looks propelled them further into the spotlight. The sisters, to their shock and some degree of dismay, wound up on plenty of Olympic "hot athlete" websites during the Games. Cassie's bio page on NBC's website became one of the most visited during the Games, and she reportedly received dozens of marriage proposals from all over the globe at the U.S. team's official blog, which got so overloaded that it crashed.

Alas, their performance on the ice in Pinerolo didn't match the hype. The Johnson sisters' rink finished 2–7 in round-robin play, a disappointing eighth overall in the Olympics. Both say they're aiming to make the 2010 Games. But sorry, guys, they're both taken. Cassie Johnson became engaged right after the Turin Games and is now Cassie Potter. Her older sister now goes by Jamie Haskell.

Great Moments in Curling-Smack-Talk History

Canada was a predominant favorite to win the men's gold medal in the inaugural medal tournament in Nagano in 1998. One team member, George Karrys, was so cocky going into the gold medal match against Switzerland, which Canada already had beaten 8–3 in pool play, that he summed up the global curling hierarchy thusly:

"Probably the 50th or 60th ranked club team in Canada could beat the best team in Europe," Karrys crowed.

He was quickly corrected by team skip Mike Harris, who chimed in: "Actually, it's more like the top 40."

Final score of the gold medal match: Switzerland 9, Canada 3.

RECORD BOOK: CURLING

In men's curling, medals were awarded for the 1924 Chamonix Games, with Great Britain, Sweden, and France finishing first, second, and third. Some debate still exists as to whether it was an "official" medal event; the medals are, however, listed in the International Olympic Committee's official database. The sport then disappeared as a medal event until Nagano in 1998.

In the Nagano Olympics, Switzerland claimed gold, Canada silver, and Norway bronze. Norway moved up to gold at the Salt Lake Games, with Canada again earning silver and bronze going to Switzerland. At the 2006 Turin Games, Canada took gold, Finland silver, and the United States, earning its first-ever curling medal, claimed the bronze.

In women's competition, Canada, led by skip Sandra Schmirler, took gold, Denmark silver, and Sweden bronze at the Nagano Games. Great Britain took the gold in Salt Lake City, with Switzerland and Canada taking silver and bronze, respectively. At the 2006 Turin Games, Sweden took gold, Switzerland silver, and Canada bronze.

NEXT STOP: VANCOUVER OLYMPIC CENTRE

Location: Queen Elizabeth Park, Vancouver, B.C.

Spectator capacity: 6,000

Elevation: 74 meters (242 feet)

Other events: Wheelchair curling (Paralympics)

Medal ceremonies: B.C. Place Stadium

The 2010 Games' gift to the Vancouver Parks Department, Vancouver Olympic Centre will host the world's greatest curlers near the grounds of Queen Elizabeth Park, in the Riley Park/Little Mountain neighborhood.

A new arena with temporary seating for the Olympics, the complex will be converted to a multipurpose community recreation center with

Curlers in the 2010 Winter Games will compete in an all-new venue near Vancouver's Queen Elizabeth Park.

an ice hockey rink, gymnasium, library, and eight curling sheets after the Games. A new city Aquatic Centre with a 50-meter pool will be built next door.

The facility is adjacent to Nat Bailey Stadium, a minor-league baseball park that is home to the Class A Northwest League Vancouver Canadians (part of the Oakland A's organization) and the University of British Columbia Thunderbirds baseball team. Historical footnote: The stadium is named after the late Nat Bailey, a tireless Vancouver baseball advocate and former part owner of the Vancouver Mounties franchise. Bailey, whose White Spot restaurant

chain continues in operation, is credited with building Canada's first drive-in and developing the first car-hop tray.

Curling 2010 Schedule

February 16–23: Men's and women's curling, three draws daily

February 24: Men's and women's tiebreakers

February 25: Men's and women's semifinals

February 26: Women's medal round

February 27: Men's medal round

FIGURE SKATING

❄ ❄ ❄ ❄ ❄

Olympic figure skating is not, thank goodness, what it often appears to be on the surface.

At first, second, or even tenth glance, the casual observer is probably caught up in, and distracted by, the sheer sequin-and-mousse frivolity of it all.

Seriously: What other sport in the world has a designated "kiss-and-cry" area for competitors? For what other competition do hard-as-nails athletes spend hours donning makeup and linked-doily gowns designed by the likes of Vera Wang? What other sport makes and breaks careers—and in some cases, even lives—with competitions decided not by measurable results, but by the fly-by-night opinions of anonymous judges, some of whom may or may not have been paid to look the other way?

And—let's cut right to the chase here—what other sport puts on what it calls a "ladies" competition and still invites Tonya Harding?

The point: It's easy to look at figure skating's sequined fringe and consider the entire affair a joke. And some parts of it are. But when you see it enough times live, up close, and witness the grimaces and feel the pain and bask in the joy of the athletes on and off the ice, the TV channel in your brain changes from Looney Tunes to *True Grit*.

Then you spend a lot of time watching it, and you learn. You talk to people who know and love the sport, and you learn more. You sit down for coffee with someone like Dick Button, a master skater before becoming king of the commentators, and you soak up even more.

Figure skating, you eventually decide, for all its foibles, is the showcase event of any Winter Olympics for good reason. At its highest level, artistic skating is perhaps the greatest melding of power and grace in all of competitive sport. Top skaters have ballet liquidity and distance-runner stamina. They can make a quadruple-triple-triple combination look as effortless as a wink, then literally turn around and strike a spiral pose so profound it appears to have been sketched by Picasso. And then fall flat on their butts.

No other sport provides that eye-popping symmetry, that impossible contradiction, that she's-this-close-to-the-gold-medal-and-OH!-that's-a-shame fragility. And no other stage for this play is as dramatic and fitting as the ice arena at a Winter Olympic Games.

This is a high-wire act with no nets. You're out there by yourself, with an entire world watching, banking your future on a four-minute free skate program in which a jump launched a fraction of a second too soon or too late will send you crashing to the ice—and prompt some guy at a bar in Iowa to wince at the TV screen and wisecrack, "*That's gonna leave a mark!*"

It is not for the meek. Watching America's Michelle Kwan skate a near-perfect short program in Nagano, my first up-close experience with the sport, I was struck between the eyes by the cool precision and gritty eloquence of what could only be called high art on ice.

Later, at subsequent national championships and Winter Games, I found myself drawn, more and more, to the ice arenas for what we in the press box refer to as "the figs." Each trip provided a highlight that marked my reluctant education as a figure skating watcher and—I've finally been forced to admit—figure skating fan:

Like the drama of watching America's Tara

The Russian dance team of Roman Kostomarov and Tatiana Navka won the gold medal in ice dance at the Turin Games.

Lipinski—at age 15, one of the youngest Winter Games competitors ever—leap over the field to steal a gold medal from the favored Kwan in Nagano. Something about her bugged me. Still does. But you couldn't help appreciating the grit.

Or watching the dramatic ladies' final redux in Salt Lake City in 2002, when unheralded 16-year-old Sara Hughes claimed gold over the stunned also-rans: Irina Slutskaya, who took silver, and the apparently Olympic-cursed Kwan, the five-time world champion, who settled for bronze.

Like watching Kwan, in 2005, capture her eighth-straight U.S. championship, her ninth overall, tying the legendary Maribel Vinson Owen for the most titles, with a flawless performance in Portland, Oregon. Watching her soar with that timeless spiral, you couldn't help wondering about—and lamenting—the fact that the greatest female ever to strap on skates never put it all together when it counted most, with all the world watching.

Or sitting in the press box as graceful, powerful American skater Sasha Cohen brought an Olympic crowd to its feet at the Palavela in the 2006 Turin Winter Games, only to stumble in the free skate and be surpassed, once more, for the gold medal—this time by Japan's graceful Shizuka Arakawa.

Like witnessing firsthand the power and agility of the endless squadrons of great Russian skaters, from pairs Tatiana Totmianina and Maxim Marinin to the incomparable Evgeni Plushenko, who nearly stole the Turin Games with his all-but-perfect gold medal performances.

Or watching the next generation of junior skaters—they look like grade-schoolers—some of whom will be medal contenders or even medalists at the Pacific Coliseum in Vancouver—rise through the ranks, completing multiple-jump combinations that would have been unthinkable at this level even a decade ago.

Each of those moments stands as a bookmark in my personal skating trial by fire. Sometimes you have to get up close and personal to appreciate a sport already appreciated by millions from afar—especially by women, who consistently rank figure skating at the top of sports preference polls.

If you're one of the doubters, a little boning up here might be all that's required to have you hooting with appreciation for a properly executed triple salchow. You might wind up confronting, as I did, an inescapable truth:

Beneath all that glitter and mascara and corny music—sometimes *way* beneath them—true athletic beauty resides. Learning to recognize it, and fully appreciating it when it appears, is learning to relish the greatest show on ice.

SPECTATOR'S GUIDE
It looks like a sport where you just strap on skates, get going fast, and do something crazy. But every second and every motion of a skater's routine is carefully choreographed, and practiced ad nauseam. Because the sport is now ruled by a new and extremely complicated scoring system, a bit of background on the ins and outs can help spectators better appreciate what's going right—or, often, horribly wrong—on the ice.

Field of Play
Olympic ice rinks for figure skating are 30 meters (99 feet) wide and 60 meters (198 feet) long—a few feet short of an Olympic-sized hockey rink. Some international competitions, and often major events such as the U.S. Olympic trials, are conducted on smaller, professional hockey-rink-sized ice. In either case, skaters wind up using every inch of it. Modern skaters have the advantage of skating on ice that's reconditioned after every half-dozen performances. In the old days, this wasn't the case. In earlier Olympics, figure skating took place on outdoor rinks, where wind, weather and ice conditions were major factors.

Format, Rules, and Strategy

The term "figure skating" has become something of a misnomer. Compulsory figures, that slow, tedious, meticulous tracing of set patterns on the ice by competitors, were axed from international competition in 1990. The move came largely as a result of greater TV coverage of skating, which focused on the athletic aspects of the sport at the expense of the compulsory figures, which, for TV purposes, are like watching paint dry.

Today's singles and pairs skaters simply skate two programs: a short program, about two and a half minutes long, and a free skate, about four minutes long for women, closer to four and a half for men.

Beginning with the 2006 Turin Olympics, skaters have been forced to adapt to a new international scoring system installed in the wake of the 2002 Salt Lake judging scandal. It throws out the old 6.0 mark of perfection and replaces it with a complicated, much more detailed, computer-driven system that, frankly, is clearly understood by only a handful of badly-in-need-of-a-life figure skating wonks.

"Do you understand the new scoring system?" skating legend and ABC commentator Dick Button asked during an interview at the 2007 U.S. Nationals. "Because I don't."

Here's an oversimplified way to explain it: Under the old system, you essentially started with perfect 6.0 marks for required elements and had points chipped away for things you either flubbed or failed to attempt. The new system is zero-based, awarding you points—in great detail—for things you attempt and even more points for moves you successfully complete. Skaters know what point values are assigned to certain moves before they begin. That's how they now shape their programs to be competitive.

You still get two scores—one for technical elements, one for program components (the latter subdivided into five other categories)—and the highest score (thank God) still wins.

Further complicating matters, the International Skating Union, which brainstormed the system, has added an entirely new layer of "management," if you will: a panel of three "technical specialists," all equipped with TV replay monitors, who initially determine what kind of move was executed—whether a jump was a double or triple Axel, for example.

The judges then decide how well the move was performed, using a scale ranging from –3 to +3, which is then added to a predetermined point value for the jump (example: a triple Axel has a base value of 7.5; it can earn 10.5 if perfectly executed but drops to 4.5 if it's shaky).

So has the new system changed the way actual competitions play out? Absolutely. The old judging system, in addition to its simplistic 6.0 scale, also placed a higher value on skater's *placement* than on his or her actual scores. In other words, if one judge ranked a skater in first place with a score of 5.5 and another judge ranked a different skater in first place with a 5.9, those two marks were, for the purposes of the scoring system, the same.

Not anymore. The upshot is that under the old system, skaters who were anywhere below third or fourth place after the short program had, because of the placement, or ordinal, system, little to no hope of winning a competition, even with a sterling free skate. Today, skaters can leap ahead from much further back in the pack because their scores, theoretically, are based purely on what they do, not on how they did compared to someone else.

Make sense?

Well, sort of.

Many skaters say they like the new system, largely because it provides them with clear-cut feedback about what they've done wrong, thus giving them a roadmap to improvement the next time around. Some skating purists, however, complain that today's skaters are sacrificing overall artistry and flow in a mad dash to pile up points by completing or, in some cases simply attempting, difficult or ugly moves that have high point values.

Beyond that, as the public is forced through what's likely to be a long learning curve, there's no clear recognition of what a score means. Everybody used to know what it meant when Michelle Kwan drew a row of 6.0s. They don't really know what to think when she posts a short program score of 68. They ask, Out of what? A thousand? It's a fair question.

This has had a downer effect on the sport's fan base, some skating insiders insist.

"We've thrown away our icons," two-time gold medalist and longtime skating commentator Button said of the new system and its ditching of the old 6.0 perfect score. "How would you feel if you went to a baseball game and you couldn't yell at the umpires anymore?"

Nevertheless, the new system appears to be here to stay—whether anyone outside the inner skating world understands it or not.

Curiously, the new system may do little to prevent the very sort of corruption, exposed at the Salt Lake City Games, that spawned it in the first place. The new system has twelve judges, compared to nine under the old system. But unlike the previous system, where each judge's score was posted publicly, the new system's scoring scheme is kept anonymous.

Skating officials note, however, that scores are not anonymous to International Skating Union principals, who know who voted for which skater. And the technical scores are derived by choosing nine of the twelve judges' marks at random and then discarding the highest and lowest of those remaining.

Translation: It's still possible to bribe a judge, but it's not as easy to bribe the *right* judge—one who can provide a guaranteed result. These days, you might have to bribe more of them to cover your bets.

America's Sasha Cohen competes in the Palavela during the 2006 Winter Games.

LEGEND OF THE SPORT
RICHARD T. "DICK" BUTTON, USA, FIGURE SKATING

Born: 18 July 1929, Englewood, New Jersey
Olympics: St. Moritz (1948); Oslo
Medals: 2 gold

In the ornate lobby of the stately Davenport Hotel in Spokane, Washington, America's greatest Olympic skating legend puts his hands together, leans forward, and says something that might make your head spin like a skater in a death spiral.

"I didn't know what skating was about until after I had won two Olympics."

This from the man who performed the first double Axel and triple loop in competition—during the Olympics, no less—and generally is considered one of the sport's great innovators.

The comment, during the 2007 U.S. Figure Skating Championships, came in response to a simple question: "If you're Dick Button, 18 years old, with the program you

America's Dick Button won back-to-back gold medals at the 1948 and 1952 Winter Games.

skated at your first Olympics (in 1948), how would you fare under the scoring system we have today?"

"Crappily," says Button, the man who invented the flying camel spin.

Not because Button, a student of music credited with injecting a new athleticism mixed with lyrical grace into his sport in the post–World War II years, lacked the technical or athletic chops. Just because he never understood, he says, the true rhythm and melody of skating at its best until he added dance to the repertoire.

Button, who didn't begin skating until age 12, by 18 had won America's first gold medal in figure skating at the 1948 St. Moritz Games. He repeated the feat in 1952 in Oslo. But in his mind, the pair of gold medal performances were just warm-up stretches for his true quest: elevating figure skating to a plane it had never achieved by melding skating's athletic jumping with the lyrical grace, flow, and beautiful physical lines of dance.

The quest in the 1950s led Button to every dance class in New York City—classical, jazz, anything.

"I'd always stay in the back of the class. And I'd see these people who I knew were not as good of an athlete as I was."

He could do some of the same moves, he said. But not the same way, or with the same flow.

"I looked like a clumsy ice skater," he says. "They looked like dancers. So I was livid."

One day, he lost it. Button approached an instructor, demanding to know why his moves lacked the pizzazz of less-athletic students.

"She said, 'Well, what do they look like?'"

Button showed her, exaggerating, at least in his mind, the dancer's movements by performing a pirouette that nearly made him fall on his face.

"I said, 'That's what they look like!' And she said: '*Now* you look like a dancer!'"

"And I'm sitting there with my mouth dropping, thinking: You idiot. You absolute idiot, for not understanding this. At that moment, my camels went from this to this . . . and I became a better ice skater. It was then that I understood what dance and skating was all about."

Two halves, as he would say later about pairs skaters Ekaterina Gordeeva and Sergei Grinkov, that together formed a magical whole.

He has seen the same understanding, the same flow, timing, and grace, in a few other skaters, he says. Pressed for names, he mentions Tenley Albright, Carol Heiss, Barbara Ann Scott, Peggy Fleming, Dorothy Hamill. Reminded that his list contains no current stars, Button laughs.

"Don't pick on me!"

But he is making a serious point. Button fears that the sport's modern scoring system, which emphasizes jumps over fluidity, transitional skating, and other poetic elements of the sport, will make the skater who successfully mixes the grace of dance and the power of gymnastics an even rarer creature in the future.

The new, detail-oriented numeric scoring system, he believes, is an "overreaction" to concerns that the old one left too much power of general impression to individual judges.

"It's like automobiles," Button says. "Do you remember when they began to develop the fins? And then finally, it was, 'My God, what the hell are we doing?' The pendulum swings. I'm hoping that the pendulum will swing. It just needs to be rethought again to regain all the elements that make up skating."

If not, the world may be producing a new generation of skaters who can perform quadruple jumps one after another but not know how to skate well. And Button means that literally.

Some time ago, he gave away a free skating lesson to a charitable cause. The winning bidder bought it for her granddaughter.

"The child came out beautifully dressed and did a program that was really exquisite, and could probably do a double Axel and almost do a double Lutz," he recalls. "But she couldn't *skate* getting around the corner of the rink."

Competitive skaters have the same tendency, he says, choosing to ignore elements of skating that don't earn points, such as graceful back crossover steps and body positioning between jumps.

"They don't move well," he says. "Yes, they can do another triple jump. And yes, they can do another triple combination. But it looks like crap. Sorry I said that."

Button, by the way, has been uttering that "sorry" for nearly 50 years. To most Americans, he is far better known for his role as the expert, quick-witted, occasionally snarky television skating commentator than for his own skating career. Some of his blunt assessments of underperforming skaters have earned legendary status.

He famously told viewers as Angela Nikodinov took the ice at a major competition that now might be a good time for a "refrigerator break." And his impromptu transitions from praise to criticism are cuttingly funny. For instance, watching American skater Jenny Kirk fall in a long program: "Well, enough said about what she's good at."

While he's just doing his job, he regrets some of these comments later, particularly when they're pulled out of context of the overall performance. He says he's learned the hard way to watch what he says, particularly about current skaters. He does, after all, know all too well the struggle they face.

Even all these decades later, Button, who won five consecutive world championships between 1948 and 1952 and seven straight U.S. titles from 1946 to 1952, remembers both of his Olympic appearances clearly.

"I remember the mistakes," he says. "In the first Olympics, which was not very good skating, I did the best I could that day. The other Olympics, I did not do the best I could. I was overtrained. I made mistakes."

Even while making mistakes, he was a level above his peers. Button didn't just compete in the Olympics. He broke new ground in them. At the 1948 St. Moritz Games, Button, then a Harvard freshman, perfected a double Axel jump only days before the skating final. He brought it out in the pressure of the Olympics and nailed it, becoming the first skater to land one in competition.

By Oslo in 1952, he had developed a triple loop. He didn't need it to win but performed it anyway—again, the first landed in competition. But as a perfectionist, he still remembers most the program elements he could have improved.

He also recalls the overall Olympic experiences as special memories of an earlier, simpler Olympic era.

"Number one, both were skated outdoors," he says. "The first Olympics in 1948, the teams walking in were minuscule, the officials were few. (Skating) was outdoors in St. Moritz, and the people were all spread out on a bank. I've been back to that pond and I've said, 'My God, is this it?'"

Button laughs. But he made himself fit into that element, wearing a short black jacket to set off his jumping moves against the white surrounding peaks in a daytime competition. The scene was a bit less quaint at his next Olympics.

"The Olympic arena in 1952 in Oslo was outdoors on a huge football field, and the skating rink was lined by a little edge of snow all the way around. The judges sat on the ice with their big straw boots and their great overcoats while they judged this thing. It was quite a different scene.

"For me, it was just eye-opening and gloriously, wonderfully exciting."

Retiring from the sport at a relatively young age, Button earned degrees from Harvard and Harvard Law School. He then began one of the longest broadcast careers in U.S. history. He first narrated Olympic skating in Squaw Valley, California, in 1960 for CBS, then switched to ABC, where he worked major competitions for 40 years, winning an Emmy in the process. That included Olympic coverage through 1988, when ABC lost the broadcast rights.

Button's commentary became so synonymous with figure skating that fans attending major events said it seemed odd to watch skaters without it.

He leads a slower life these days, having suffered a serious skull fracture and brain injury in a fall while ice skating on New Year's Eve, 2000. Mostly recovered except for a loss of hearing in one ear, he serves as a national spokesman for the Brain Injury Association of America.

He splits his time between New York City and an upstate farm. He will be 80 when the Vancouver 2010 Games commence.

He remains the youngest man ever to win an Olympic skating competition. And likely will soon become the oldest to ever comment on one.

If you remember nothing else, keep this in mind: The one with the highest point total wins. You get more points for trying more difficult jumps, even more if you're successful. And you still get mandatory deductions when you fall. So, there's that.

And here's where the points will be applied:

Russia's Evgeni Plushenko, a master craftsman at work in Turin, Italy

A typical ladies' free-skate, or long, program today will have six to eight triple jumps, many in combinations; several combination spins; and a tricky straight-line step sequence. A typical men's free-skate program will have as many or more triple jumps and now, for top-level skaters, at least one or two quadruple jumps thrown in for good measure.

The Jumps

Jumps provide the most scoring bang for the buck in figure skating. With a little—okay, a lot—of practice, you can learn to identify them. Here's a list of the most common. Note that most of these jumps can be—and most often are—done with two to four revolutions before landing.

Jumps with a toe takeoff:

Lutzes: Launched by the right toe pick, with takeoff from the back outside edge of the left foot.

Flips: Launched by the right toe pick, with takeoff from the back inside edge of the left foot.

Toe loops: Launched by the left toe pick, with takeoff from the back outside edge of the right foot.

Jumps with an edge takeoff:

Axels: Because the jump is launched from a forward edge (the left outside edge), it has an extra half revolution, and thus it's considered the most difficult jump. It's landed on the back outside edge of the free foot.

Loops: Launched from a right back outside edge, landed on the same edge.

Salchows: Launched from a left back inside edge. Watch for the swinging opposite leg launching this one.

Pairs and Ice Dancing Scoring

Symmetry of movement is key for pairs, but the scoring is otherwise similar to that for singles. The main difference is that pairs obviously work from a different list of essential elements for their short program.

Ice dancing is all about flow. The sport emphasizes the grace of skating pairs, who essentially ballroom-dance their way around the ice rink.

Thus, scoring centers on how well the pairs move to music, how they execute their footwork, and how well they work together (*not,* as you might suspect, how little they are wearing out on the ice).

The primary difference in ice dancing comes in the competition format, which includes three rounds. The compulsory round, in which skaters complete a set of required maneuvers, is worth 20 percent of the final score. Next is an "original dance" round, in which all skaters get the same rhythm but can create their own routine to it. This round is worth 30 percent. The final round, worth half, is the free dance, with routines customized by each pair.

Judges apply the same scoring standards, with a technical score and program component score, as are applied to singles and pairs.

If you fail to understand a word of this, don't worry: You're not alone. Just wait for Button and Scott Hamilton to figure it out and explain it.

Training and Equipment

Figure skaters, not surprisingly, spend the vast majority of their time on the ice, practicing jumps, body positioning, spins, transitions, and footwork, often to the point of exhaustion. But this is a total-body sport, and the same types of training techniques—running, resistance and weight training, and reflex drills—used by other athletes have made their way into the modern figure skater's training quiver. Some top skaters also devote many hours to formal dance training and other pursuits bordering more on art than athleticism; it's necessary, they say, to become a complete skater, balancing fluidity with power.

Equipment has changed only modestly over the decades. Figure skates are boots with high ankles for support. Their blades are made of steel, which is not flat on the bottom, but concave, providing skaters with a sharp inside and outside edge from which to launch or carve turns. (The blades are so sharp that they're actually melting the ice for an instant, allowing forward motion on a thin layer of water.) Figure skates also have a blunt, serrated tip, called a toe pick, used to launch jumps and stop abruptly.

Skating uniforms aren't really uniforms at all, but costumes that become part of the show. They're all made of stretchy, breathable fabric—in every conceivable color and style combination, particularly in ice dancing, known for its avant-garde ensembles.

HISTORY'S HITS AND MISSES

Figure skating rates as the oldest Winter Games competition because, as a medal sport, it actually predates the Winter Olympics themselves. The sport was included in the Summer Games of 1908 and 1920 before settling into its wintry confines at Chamonix, France, in 1924.

In the early years, skating, like all other ice sports, was done outside. That made weather conditions—soft spots caused by sun exposure, a sheen of snow on the ice, and ever-present wind conditions—a major player in competitions. Early U.S. medalists Dick Button and Tenley Albright tell of the constant fear of having a meticulously trained-for program dashed by Mother Nature at the last second. It added an entire element to competition that modern skaters don't have to worry about. On the other hand, Olympic figure skating will never again have that charming feel you can only get skating outside in the fresh air in the shadow of snow-capped mountains in some quaint Bavarian village. Now it's all mega-arena, all the time.

OLYMPIC FLASHBACK
TURIN GAMES

Feb. 19, 2006
Reported by Ron C. Judd for The Seattle Times
Author's note: Sometimes, the ice dance can become a parody of itself. Years later,
I still can't help chuckling when I see the images from this event.

TURIN, Italy—Ice dance, its practitioners will tell you, is an art form that mirrors every facet of the miracle of a man and a woman coming together to become one.

The courtship. The union. The poetic symmetry.

The complete and unmitigated contempt when your partner drops you like a sack of dog chow in front of half a billion people at the Olympics.

Just ask Barbara Fusar-Poli of Italy, the designated dumpee Sunday night at the Palavela. She and partner Maurizio Margaglio, medal contenders skating before 6,095 flag-waving, hometown fans, were nearing the end of a stellar routine in the original dance when sequins became tangled and—bonk—down she went.

A frame-by-frame view is quite revealing: When Fusar Poli starts to fall, she loops her arm around her partner's neck, pulling him downward, perhaps to break her fall—or perhaps with clear malice and forethought, as if to say: If I'm going down, dude, you're coming with me.

Seconds later, the Italians, bronze medalists in Salt Lake City, scrambled to their feet, finished their routine and stood at center ice, preparing to paste on those cheesecake smiles and bow to the crowd.

Except Barbara wasn't quite ready to make happy yet. She was glowering at Maurizio with that special look reserved for guys who forget anniversaries, back the car over mothers-in-law, or misplace the kids at the airport.

For what seemed like an eternity, she stood there at center ice, glowering first at the ground, then at him, her eyes boring holes into his skull and out the other side.

Moments later, the traditional kiss-and-cry area was morphed to a spit-and-snit zone as he looked to the scoreboard to see their score sink from first place to seventh. She refused to look at him, staring in the opposite direction at the floor.

The crowd, watching all this on a megascreen, did a collective pucker and waited for the first blows.

Yikes. Ever hear of the Olympic truce, kids?

The only good news for these two was that they were far from alone in flubbing Sunday's original dance program, in which America's Tanith Belbin and Ben Agosto, who neither fell down nor wound up in the couples-counseling penalty box, vaulted from sixth to second—mostly over the bodies of fallen competitors.

Like those of Federica Faiella and Massimo Scali, the other top Italian pair. They, too, had cha-cha-sambaed their way to a near-perfect routine when the rhinestones came unriveted.

We go to the replay: In this instance, Faiella, perhaps slipping on a spot of Vaseline dropped by one of the dozens of men with bare chests and John Tesh haircuts on the ice before her, falls—and proceeds to tackle her partner from behind, dragging him to the ground like an offensive lineman beat on a pass rush.

Or consider Canada's Marie-France Dubreuil and Patrice Lauzon, who were doing one of those holy-cow moves where he holds her by the knee and she clings to his arm as he swings her wildly around his body like a discus when, inexplicably, they both broke the clasp. She fell to the ice with a splat audible in the cheap seats, landing on a hip and proving barely able to stand.

Her partner carried her out of the building.

It was carnage at a level not seen in the Palavela at any other time in the Olympics—which is saying something, given that they race short track on the same ice.

You're not supposed to fall in ice dance. It's supposed to be less about athleticism than its evil cousin, figure skating—a fact that has given rise to the sport's enduring bad rap: Ice dancers are skaters who can't land a jump.

That's never been completely true and certainly isn't now, as evidenced by Belbin and Agosto, who are supposed to make skeptical Americans suddenly care about this Vegas floor show masquerading as sport.

Most people likely have heard by now that Belbin, thanks to a literal emergency act of Congress (motto: New Orleans can wait), was able to legally emigrate from Canada to the U.S. just in time to compete in the Olympics.

But she apparently left in such a hurry that she had no time to bring much clothing along.

Like most of the female ice dancers, Belbin, who has the looks of a runway model, skates the saucy "Latin combination" approximately 57 percent naked. Ice dancing—and we're not going thumbs-up or thumbs-down on this, just passing it along—involves a lot of bare skin. And make no mistake: It's not that faux-flesh-colored sheer fabric that the figure skaters wear. It's the real thing, goose bumps and all.

Much already has been made about the eccentric attire of ice dancers, so we're not going there, except to point out that the new costume hue of choice—particularly among the American cha-cha artistes—is traffic-cone orange.

Ice-dancing insiders say this is to attract the attention of judges. Which is understandable, because clearly, without those flaming, Coast-Guard-orange bodices, most of these toned, half-naked, gyrating female skaters probably would be completely overlooked by male judges fascinated by the symmetry of the Olympic rings painted on the wall across the way.

We'll find out for sure tonight, when the event final, the free dance, will tie together all the loose ends:

Will the leaders, Tatiana Navka and Roman Kostomarov of Russia, avoid that killer Vaseline spot?

Will Belbin and Agosto bare enough of their souls—or perhaps their tushies—to grab a medal for the U.S.?

Will the International Olympic Committee need to page Dr. Phil to the kiss-and-cry to talk down the Italians?

Get ready to rumba.

Skaters Patrice Lauzon and Marie-France Dubreuil take a bad fall during an error-prone night in ice dancing at the 2006 Turin Games.

Skating's First Superstar

Sonja Henie's Olympic debut—as a precocious 11-year-old at Chamonix in 1924—was only the first stride in an Olympic skating career that has yet to be equaled. Norway's Henie (1912–1969) went on to become the only woman to win the ladies' title three consecutive times: St. Moritz in 1928, Lake Placid in 1932, and Garmisch-Partenkirchen in 1936.

Along the way, figure skating's first international starlet also won an unequaled ten straight world titles and later became a Hollywood star in the United States, memorably appearing in *Thin Ice* (1937) and *Sun Valley Serenade* (1941) while starring in wildly popular ice shows.

To date, no other woman has claimed three medals in ladies' singles, let alone three golds. You

Even at age 11, figure skater Sonja Henie showed star power at the first Winter Games in Chamonix, France, 1924.

can see one of her skating costumes—and marvel at the sheer dinkiness of it—at the World Figure Skating Hall of Fame in Colorado Springs, Colorado.

Notable First Leaps

The Axel jump separates the men from the boys, the women from the girls. It's tough to master and difficult to land in competition. The first Axel jump was performed by—surprise—a man named Axel Paulsen, who first completed it, oddly enough, wearing long-bladed *speed skates,* not figure skates.

Dick Button is credited with the first double Axel in competition, at the 1948 Winter Games in St. Moritz. Five years later, U.S. teammate Carol Heiss became the first woman to land a double Axel in competition. The triple Axel came 30 years down the road: Canada's Vern Taylor landed the first in competition at the 1978 world championships.

The women's triple Axel has remained highly elusive. Japan's Midori Ito landed the first, in 1988, and repeated the feat at the 1992 Winter Games in Albertville. America's Tonya Harding landed one at the U.S. championships in 1991 and remained the only U.S. woman to do so until young Kimmie Meissner completed the feat at the 2005 U.S. championships in Portland, Oregon. The same year, one of Meissner's expected chief competitors in Vancouver, Japan's Mao Asada, landed two in a single program at the Japanese championships.

In pairs skating, America's Rena Inoue and John Baldwin landed a throw triple Axel at the 2006 U.S. championships. They repeated the feat at the Turin Winter Games, becoming the first pair to land one in Olympic competition.

Tonya, Triple Axels, and Tire Irons

Nobody did less for the image, but more for the notoriety, of figure skating than Tonya Harding, the unlikely Olympian from suburban Portland,

Tonya Harding and Nancy Kerrigan were engaged in one of the Olympics' all-time soap operas before and during the 1994 Games in Lillehammer, Norway.

Oregon, who became the first U.S. woman to land a triple Axel in competition.

In her heyday, Harding was locked in a heated rivalry with fellow skater Nancy Kerrigan—who had to withdraw from the 1994 U.S. championships after she was whacked across the knee with a metal rod wielded by an assailant. Harding went on to win the Nationals—just as planned, as it turned out, when the plot unraveled and Harding was accused of conspiring with her husband, Jeff Gillooly, to arrange the hit on Kerrigan.

Harding was allowed to compete at the Winter Games in Lillehammer but self-destructed on the ice. Kerrigan, who was granted the second U.S. spot, memorably rose to the occasion for a silver medal. Both were outskated by Oksana Baiul of Ukraine.

Harding had waiting for her at home a ban for life from U.S. figure skating and went on to a career as a professional boxer and hubcap flinger. Ironically, the long-running scandal did for U.S. figure skating what no amount of athletic prowess had ever been able to do: made it dinner-table conversation, causing TV ratings to soar for years. Only recently has the soap-opera quality injected into the sport's image by Tonya begun to fade. Doesn't she have a younger sister?

A 6.0 for Deceit From the French Judge

The sport's second-biggest international scandal (let's face it: you've got to get up pretty early in the morning to make bigger figure skating headlines than Tonya Harding's kneecapping campaign) unfolded at the 2002 Salt Lake City Olympics, creating ripples that continue to come ashore today.

Skating watchers had long suspected that certain competitions were essentially rigged, creating the classic something's-fishy retort, "He still got a 6.0 from the Ukrainian judge," after a particularly dreadful performance. But not until Canada's Jamie Sale and David Pelletier crashed head-on with skating destiny at Salt Lake's Delta Center did anyone come up with the goods to prove it.

Sale and Pelletier skated a memorable, near-perfect free skate that had most of the world believing they had won the gold medal—which was awarded to Russia's comparatively shaky Elena Berezhnaya and Anton Sikharulidze instead.

After much booing, second-guessing, and, later, finger-pointing, French judge Marie-Reine Le

Gougne finally cracked under pressure, admitting she'd traded the first-place votes to the Russians for first-place votes for a French ice dancer, and a bottle of Stolichnaya. Okay, we made up the last part. The resulting scandal led to the rare awarding of *two* sets of gold medals—and a complete overhaul of skating's traditional 6.0 scoring system.

The Battle of the Brians

Canada's Brian Orser became famous in his early career for notable second-place finishes, including one at the Sarajevo Games, where he outscored American Scott Hamilton in both the short and long program but was edged out by Hamilton's superior scores in compulsory figures.

Orser's most-famous "second," however, came

Russian pairs team Elena Berezhnaya and Anton Sikharulidze shared gold medals with Canadians Jamie Sale and David Pelletier after a judging scandal at the 2002 Salt Lake Winter Games.

in the 1988 Calgary Games, where he battled with America's Brian Boitano in a memorable "Battle of the Brians."

Orser, before ever taking the ice as home-nation favorite, had added even more second-place finishes—at the 1984, 1985, and 1986 world championships. But he finally won that event in 1987, swapping his familiar second rung on the podium with Boitano, who had won in 1986.

Entering the Calgary Games, each was at his competitive peak—Orser was undefeated in major competitions that year—and the much-awaited clash was considered a toss-up. Boitano led after compulsory figures; Orser won the short program by a nose. In the long program, Boitano, in a costume with epaulets and skating to "Napoleon," went first and delivered a near-perfect routine that will long be remembered as the climax of his distinguished career.

Orser remained within striking distance, but the pressure—he had been chosen his nation's flag bearer in the opening ceremonies—got to him. He two-footed the landing on an early triple jump and subbed a double Axel for a triple near the end of the skate.

The outcome, however, still wasn't clear. Two judges rated the contest a tie, with four giving the nod to Orser and three to Boitano. Under the rules of the day, judges used the technical merit score to break the deadlock; both gave the edge there to Boitano. Orser, once again, stood second, this time on the medal platform in his home country in a contest that will be remembered as one of the greatest in figure skating history.

The two Brians, revisiting the Calgary Saddledome in 2008 for a documentary on the 20th anniversary of the event, said they'll always share a bond from the experience.

"There's this brotherhood or camaraderie we have until this day because no one, except each other, can understand what we went through that night," Boitano told Slam Sports. "I consider Brian a friend."

Orser agreed. "We played it out perfectly for the fans of the sport," he said. "Not just figure skating, but Olympic sport. We lived up to the billing."

Orser remains a force in the competitive skating world. He's a Toronto-based coach whose most recent star pupil is South Korean Kim Yu-Na, who holds the record for short- and free-skate points under the ISU's new scoring system and could be a medal threat at the 2010 Vancouver Games.

Tenley Albright—America's Gold Medal Icebreaker

Days before she was to take the ice at the Cortina d'Ampezzo Olympics of 1956, Tenley Albright was practicing outdoors when one of her skates hit a rut in the ice. She stumbled, with one skate striking the other—and slashing clean through, slicing her ankle to the bone.

Her father, a surgeon, rushed to Italy to sew her up. But she feared she wouldn't be able to compete. Somehow, when the time arrived, she decided the foot was stable enough to skate. And she performed flawlessly, holding a small lead over teammate Carol Heiss entering the final skate.

When she took the ice that day, a magical thing happened: As she skated to "The Barcarolle," a waltz from the opera *The Tales of Hoffmann,* the large crowd began singing the words to the orchestral theme—an international sing-along, right there in a little mountain village. "It was wonderful," she said of the massive chorus at the outdoor ice rink in the shadow of the Dolomites. "It made me forget about my injury."

When the scores were tallied, she had won the gold medal handily—the first by an American female skater.

Fifty years later, Albright, who went on to become a distinguished surgeon and cancer researcher in Boston, said that gold medal skate still seemed like only yesterday.

"This enormous feeling just sort of welled up

In 1956 Tenley Albright won the first gold medal for an American female figure skater.

in me," she said. "There was the most wonderful feeling of camaraderie. It made me feel like the sport was an international language."

It was the end of an era. The next Winter Games, at Squaw Valley in 1960, were the last to stage figure skating outdoors—and the first to be televised. Everything changed after that, with skaters facing increased pressure from fans and the media.

Not that first-time gold medalists ever got a pass on press scrutiny.

"We thought there was plenty at that time," Albright said. "We did have Movietone News, you know!"

Michelle Kwan—America's Greatest, but Snakebit Under the Rings

It isn't fair, but it's indisputable: Michelle Kwan, the greatest female skater of her generation and one of the greatest of all time, will be remembered by Olympic historians less for what she did accomplish than for the one thing she did not: win a gold medal.

Kwan, the five-time world and nine-time U.S. champion, grew from a precocious eight-year-old rookie with limitless talent to a mature woman skating with unprecedented poise, grace, and style before the eyes of an adoring American public. She became the living embodiment of figure skating persistence, passion, and perfection, and an idol to her fans.

Kwan spent half her life on medal stands in a career that saw her earn 53 scores of 6.0. Her five world titles tie her with Carol Heiss for the most ever for an American woman. Her nine national titles equaled the mark set by the legendary Maribel Vinson Owen from 1928 to 1937.

But she repeatedly crumpled—or was snakebit, depending on one's degree of affection for the woman—under the pressure of those five Olympic rings.

Kwan was a fresh face and a medal favorite entering the Nagano Games in 1998. Her main competition, 15-year-old Texan Tara Lipinski, was considered a major talent but too young to handle Olympic pressure.

Much was made of the two skaters' preparation: Lipinski got to Nagano early and lived the life of an Olympian, participating in the opening ceremonies and other events. Kwan came in late and stayed in a hotel. The serious approach appeared to be paying off for Kwan, who skated a sterling short program to take the lead into the free skate, where she skated

Opposite: Nine-time U.S. champion Michelle Kwan won every honor in her sport, except the Olympic Gold Medal.

first—and shone. Her routine included a couple of small mistakes, but most people in the building believed she had won the gold medal.

Then came Lipinski, the sprightly leaper who matched Kwan, triple jump for triple jump (seven in all), but made two of them into triple-triple combinations. That was the edge for an exuberant Lipinski, who became the youngest Olympic gold medal winner in an individual event.

By 2002 in Salt Lake, Lipinski had retired, and Kwan, who had switched coaches from Frank Carroll to Rafael Arutunian, was still chasing the one major prize missing from her trophy case. Her major competition was expected to be Irina Slutskaya of Russia. But another young American, Sara Hughes, 16, came along to spoil Kwan's coronation, capturing the gold medal and relegating Kwan to bronze, behind Slutskaya.

In the weeks before the 2006 Turin Games, Kwan, struggling under the new international scoring system, suffered a hip injury and failed to compete at the U.S. Figure Skating Championships, which also serve as the sport's Olympic trials. But she petitioned to be placed on the Olympic team anyway, and officials voted to comply. Once in Turin, however, Kwan took to the ice for an initial practice and clearly wasn't ready to perform.

She said a tearful goodbye to Turin—and, likely, her Olympic career—at a table in a news conference, rather than the medal stand.

Afterward, Kwan returned home, had her hip surgically repaired, and left competitive skating. She has said she will decide by 2009 whether to compete with the goal of making the U.S. Olympic team for Vancouver in 2010. At 29, she would be nearly twice as old as most of the medal favorites.

RECORD BOOK: MEN'S FIGURE SKATING

The most prolific medalist in men's figure skating is far from a household name outside his native Sweden. **Gillis Grafström** was an early skating innovator who pioneered the spiral, the change sit spin, and the flying sit spin. And judges were impressed: Grafström, the sport's only four-time medalist, won gold at Antwerp in 1920, Chamonix in 1924, and St. Moritz in 1928. He finally was dethroned four years later at Lake Placid, where, at age 38, he finished second behind Austria's **Karl Schäfer.**

North Americans have left a solid mark in men's figures. Young **Dick Button's** consecutive golds at St. Moritz in 1948 and Oslo in 1952 started a run for America: **Hayes Jenkins** led an American sweep at Cortina d'Ampezzo in 1956, with spinner extraordinaire **Ronnie Robertson** claiming silver and Jenkins' brother, David, taking bronze. **David Jenkins** went on to win the gold at Squaw Valley in 1960. **Scott Hamilton's** gold at Sarajevo in 1984 was followed by **Brian Boitano's** podium-topping performance four years later in Calgary.

And from there, the Russians took over, with five straight (and counting) gold medalists: **Viktor Petrenko** (1992, Albertville); **Alexey Urmanov** (1994, Lillehammer); **Ilia Kulik** (1998, Nagano); **Alexei Yagudin** (2002, Salt Lake City); and **Evgeni Plushenko** (2006, Turin).

Other U.S. men's silver medalists are **Timothy Wood** (1968, Grenoble) and **Paul Wylie** (1992, Albertville). Also winning bronze were **James Grogan** (1952, Oslo), **Scott Allen** (1964, Innsbruck), **Charles Tickner** (1980, Lake Placid), and **Timothy Goebel** (2002, Salt Lake City).

Canada's men's record book is highlighted by the consecutive silver medals of **Brian Orser** (1984 and 1988) and **Elvis Stojko** (1994 and 1998). **Toller Cranston** grabbed a bronze at Innsbruck in 1976; **Jeffrey Buttle** won bronze at Turin in 2006.

RECORD BOOK: WOMEN'S FIGURE SKATING

Sonja Henie is the only woman to win three consecutive gold medals: St. Moritz in 1928, Lake

Placid in 1932, and Garmisch-Partenkirchen in 1936. The closest competitor: **Katarina Witt** of Germany, who at Sarajevo in 1984 edged out a world champion, America's **Rosalynn Sumners,** and then successfully defended her gold medal at Calgary in 1988, narrowly besting hometown favorite **Elizabeth Manley** of Canada.

North Americans, however, have a long, distinguished history atop the ladies' podium: America's **Tenley Albright** was the first to win gold—in 1956 at Cortina d'Ampezzo, followed by **Carol Heiss** at Squaw Valley in 1960. **Peggy Fleming** won gold at Grenoble in 1968; **Dorothy Hamill** at Innsbruck in 1976; **Kristi Yamaguchi** at Albertville in 1992; 15-year-old **Tara Lipinski**, then the Winter Games' youngest individual-event gold medalist, won at Nagano in 1998; and **Sarah Hughes** at Salt Lake City in 2002. Silver medalists for the United States include **Michelle Kwan** at Nagano, 1998; **Nancy Kerrigan** at Lillehammer, 1994; Sumners in 1984; **Linda Fratianne** at Lake Placid in 1980; Heiss in 1956; Albright in 1952; and **Beatrix Loughran** in 1924 and 1928. Bronze medals were claimed by Loughran in 1928 at St. Moritz, **Maribel Vinson** at Lake Placid in 1932, **Barbara Roles** at Squaw Valley in 1960, **Janet Lynn** in 1972 at Sapporo, **Debi Thomas** in 1988 at Calgary, Nancy Kerrigan in 1992 at Albertville, and Kwan in 2002 at Salt Lake City.

Canada's **Barbara Ann Scott** took gold at St. Moritz in 1948 and remains the country's only ladies' gold medalist. **Karen Magnussen** (1972, Sapporo) and **Elizabeth Manley** (1988, Calgary) each won silver for Maple Leaf Nation.

RECORD BOOK: PAIRS FIGURE SKATING

In pairs skating, couples from the former Soviet Union or Russia claim one of the great gold medal strangleholds in Olympic history: 12 straight Olym-

pics have seen Russian pairs on the top of the podium—a dominance that will have lasted at least 46 years by the time competition begins in Vancouver. With the exception of the scandal-marred competition in 2002, you have to go all the way back to Squaw Valley in 1960 to find the last non-Russian gold medalists: **Barbara Wagner** and **Robert Paul** of Canada.

Not surprisingly, Russia also has produced the only repeat pairs gold medalists in Olympic history. **Irina Rodnina** and **Aleksandr Zaytsev**

Gillis Grafström's 1920 gold medal, the first awarded in figure skating, is on display at the World Figure Skating Hall of Fame in Colorado Springs, Colorado.

Great Britain's Jayne Torvill and Christopher Dean won the hearts of ice dance fans with their gold-medal-winning performance in Sarajevo.

won consecutive golds at Innsbruck in 1976 and Lake Placid in 1980. Rodnina, with a third gold at the 1972 Sapporo Games with a previous partner, **Aleksey Ulanov,** and compatriot **Artur Dmitriyev** (gold in 1992, silver in 1994, and gold in 1998) rank

as the most prolific pairs medalists of all time.

North Americans have claimed their share of pairs medals, although not many in recent years. America's **Sherwin Badger** and **Beatrix Loughran** won silver at Lake Placid in 1932; **Karol** and **Michael Kennedy** captured silver in Oslo in 1952; **Nancy** and **Ronald Luddington** won bronze at Squaw Valley in 1960; **Kitty** and **Peter Carruthers** took silver at Sarajevo in 1984; and **Jill Watson** and **Peter Oppegard** took bronze at Calgary in 1988. Canada's medal haul, in addition to Wagner and Paul's 1960 gold: **Suzanne Morrow** and **Wallace Diestelmeyer** won bronze at St. Moritz in 1948; **Frances Dafoe** and **Norris Bowden** took the silver at Cortina d'Ampezzo in 1956; **Debbi Wilkes** and **Guy Revell** won bronze at Innsbruck in 1976; **Isabelle Brasseur** and **Lloyd Eisler** took bronze at Albertville in 1992; and **Jamie Sale** and **David Pelletier** shared the gold with Russians **Anton Sikharulidze** and **Elena Berezhnaya** in the wake of the infamous Salt Lake City judging scandal in 2002.

RECORD BOOK: ICE DANCE

Britain's **Jayne Torvill** and **Christopher Dean,** who introduced a generation to the sport, won gold medals a decade apart: at Sarajevo in 1984 and Lillehammer in 1994. Even more prolific were the Russian pair **Marina Klimova** and **Sergey Ponomarenko,** who won bronze at Sarajevo in 1984, silver at Calgary in 1988, and gold at Albertville in 1992. Russians have dominated the event in recent history. North American medals include Canada's **Robert McCall** and **Tracy Wilson's** bronze at Calgary and a silver for America's **Tanith Belbin** (a hastily nationalized native Canadian) and **Ben Agosto** at Turin, 2006—the first U.S. ice dance medal since **Colleen O'Connor** and **James Millns** won bronze at the sport's Olympic introduction in Innsbruck, 1976.

NEXT STOP: PACIFIC COLISEUM

Location: Hastings Park, Vancouver, B.C.

Spectator capacity: 14,239

Elevation: 26 meters (85 feet)

Other events: Short-track speedskating

Medal ceremonies: B.C. Place Stadium

The revamped Pacific Coliseum and surrounding Hastings Park are no strangers to big crowds: This is the primary big-events center on the city's east side, and with its proximity to Highway 1 and major thoroughfares, it's well served by public transportation. The Coliseum is the current home of the Vancouver Giants junior hockey team, and Hastings Park is the site of the annual Pacific National Exhibition, the city's summer fair, which attracts up to 60,000 people a day.

Like its predecessor, the remodeled Palavela in downtown Turin, Italy, Pacific Coliseum will serve as a dual-role venue, hosting figure skating and short-track speedskating. That setup has worked well at previous Games, including the Turin Olympics. But the Coliseum, from a seating standpoint, will be nearly twice as large as the Palavela, which seated only 8,250 fans.

Vancouver's revamped ice stadium will continue to serve as a venue for hockey, ice shows, concerts, basketball, boxing, and trade shows after the 2010 Games.

Figure Skating 2010 Schedule

February 14: Pairs short program

February 15: Pairs free skate

February 16: Men's short program

February 18: Men's free skate

February 19: Ice dancing compulsories

February 21: Ice dancing original dance

February 22: Ice dancing free dance

February 23: Women's short program

February 25: Women's free skate

February 27: Exhibition

ICE HOCKEY

❄ ❄ ❄ ❄ ❄

It should never happen. But just in case:

If any doubt should ever arise as to the most memorable moment in the history of American sport—and perhaps in the history of the Winter Olympics—just do the following:

Go to Lake Placid, in upstate New York, a town of fewer than 3,000 people that somehow managed to successfully host the world's biggest winter sports event—twice.

Find, near the center of town, next to the ice oval where Eric Heiden's five-gold-medal performance is memorialized on the rink-side wall, the Olympic Center. Then make your way into the Lake Placid Olympic Museum, on the ground floor.

There, in the far corner, you'll hear the sounds and see the sight: A small, decidedly low-def television set, playing, on a VHS cassette loop, the "Miracle on Ice" game that unfolded on February 22, 1980, inside that very building.

The TV sits next to one of the actual goals that sat on the ice for that game. Inside the goal hangs an American flag, the one draped over the shoulders of goalie Jim Craig as he skated around

the ice in a sporting moment where time seemed to stand still.

Even now, nearly 30 years after the fact, it is impossible to hear Al Michaels' play call, see the young, underdog, red-white-and-blue-clad players scrambling, diving to block pucks, and generally leaving it all out on the ice, without stopping and getting sucked, once again, into the miracle.

It happens nearly every day at the museum, where you'll see fathers and sons and daughters perched on a bench, watching history remake itself in a stunning series of on-ice acts:

- Mark Johnson's improbable goal against legendary Soviet keeper Vladislav Tretiak as the first period expires, followed by coach Herb Brooks' menacing glance toward opposing coach Viktor Tikhonov, with his message unspoken but unmistakable: "It's on."

- Johnson's second goal, to tie the game at 3, six minutes into the second period.

- Team captain Eruzione's winning goal as he used a defender as a screen and put a shot past the right skate of the Soviet goalie and into the corner of the net from 20 feet.

○ The joyous countdown from a capacity crowd, followed by Michaels repeating the words now etched into the memory of successive generations.

Do we believe in miracles?

Hell, yes.

But it's worth remembering that we didn't always, in terms of either competing at the Winter Olympics—where, let's face it, the bulk of winners' medals had always hung around the necks of Europeans—or, it seems, national pride.

The 1980 "Miracle" game, with the United States achieving one of the great upsets in sports history by defeating the gold-medal-favored Soviet hockey machine 4–3, pulled America from a prolonged national doldrums, and thus will be viewed through the hindsight of history as much more than a simple hockey game.

It also inspired an entire next generation of young players—especially, and somewhat ironically, on the women's side. Cammi Granato, the first female American hockey star and the woman who would lead her squad to the first-ever women's hockey gold medal at the 1998 Nagano Games, recounted how she'd spent years re-creating the biggest moments of that historic game with her brother, future NHL player Tony, in their Chicago basement.

Eight years later, the Swedish women's team, stunning an American squad stocked with some of the same players, would stand in their locker room, beaming, as they credited the Disney movie *Miracle,* the Hollywood account of Brooks and the 1980 gold medal campaign, with inspiring *them* to beat the Americans—abruptly ending a decades-long period of North American domination of the women's game.

In 2008, when American sports network colossus ESPN polled its viewers and readers about the network's, and the nation's, greatest sports highlight, Mike Eruzione's go-ahead goal rated first among more than 230,000 voters. And that's a 30-year-old highlight competing against other great sports moments more fresh in the minds of fans.

Memories of the event, which turned the Winter Olympics in America from a curious sidelight to a mainstream event, are fading now. But the American Olympic movement will always owe a debt of gratitude to the 1980 squad composed of a group of overachieving, mostly East Coast–based, U.S. collegiate hockey players and Brooks, their plucky, irrepressible coach. Recognition would come, in a meaningful way, 24 years later, when the entire team was invited to light the 2004 Olympic Cauldron at the opening ceremonies in Rice-Eccles Stadium in Salt Lake City.

Much has been written, much of it eloquently, about the 1980 U.S. Olympic hockey team, in many cases by the participants themselves. We'll make no attempt to match those words here, except to emphasize the fact that the victory, followed by a come-from-behind win in the gold medal game against Finland, will forever stand as the moment that elevated Olympic hockey into the national consciousness of not only Americans, but fans of winter sport around the globe.

If you go to Lake Placid, make time for one of the tours of the building where it all went down, and if you're lucky, you might get, as a tour guide, Jim Rogers, a 1980 Olympic official, who will recount how the late Brooks, for whom the Lake Placid ice arena is now named, exhorted his players before the start of the third period of the gold medal match against Finland:

"You lose this game, and you take it to your [bleeping] grave. Your [bleeping] grave!"

Rogers explains that the hockey gold medal was an even grander occurrence then than it would be now, because the Games were so much smaller,

Members of the 1980 "Miracle on Ice" hockey team had the honor of lighting the torch cauldron in 2002.

simpler, and more approachable than they are now. The entire 1980 Olympics, he says, cost less to stage than the opening ceremony for the '06 Winter Games in Turin. The Lake Placid Games would also be the end of an era in Olympic ice hockey.

Four years after the United States shocked the world at Lake Placid, international hockey officials, who had long toyed with the definition of "professional" hockey players barred from the Olympics, allowed some pros into the Olympics for the first time. By 1988, all of them were technically allowed, although only a handful played because the NHL season coincided with the Winter Games. That obstacle vanished in 1998, when the NHL, for the first time, suspended its season for two weeks to allow stars to play for their respective national teams in the Nagano Olympics.

The impact was immediate: It undoubtedly drew far more NHL fans to Olympic hockey than ever before and it also evened the international playing field. It's now impossible that a team with as little international experience as the 1980 U.S. team could go up against, let alone beat, a steely bunch like the late-1980s Soviet squad, who, although they were professional players, were not considered so by the IOC, because they were paid by their government, not private hockey clubs.

The rule change is a good thing, in terms of

even competition. But it also has robbed the Olympic tourney of much of its charm, many would argue. And for the Vancouver Games of 2010, Olympic hockey will take another, perhaps even greater step toward mimicking NHL play: For the first time, games will be contested on narrower NHL-sized ice rinks, instead of the broader ice sheets that have always produced more open, fluid—and less physical—games in the Olympics, even with NHL stars on the ice.

Unless you're a huge fan of NHL hockey—and most Americans are not—that's too bad. Because it puts the game one step farther away from the simple, pure contest it was in 1980, when a scrappy bunch of Americans could take on the world's best and beat them fair and square. (It's worth mentioning that the women's game, still played largely by amateurs and without body checking, still retains some of that old charm.)

Bottom line: The reshuffled NHL roster-tourney that is today's Olympic men's hockey is more modern and, to some, more attractive. But it likely never again will produce moments as magical—and history making—as those in 1980, when events at the Olympics proved that the Games truly were capable of shaping the history not just of sport, but of the world.

Need proof? A full 25 years later, a former Soviet dignitary would wind up on one of Jim Rogers' tours at the Olympic Center. There he would stand and stare at the ice, reliving the moment when his nation's players stood in stunned disbelief at their defeat, and assess the long-term meaning of the 1980 Games to the once-proud Soviet Union.

"This," he said, "is where the slide began."

"And that," Rogers says, "is goosebump stuff."

SPECTATOR'S GUIDE

Hockey, an original Winter Games sport, has also traditionally been among its most popular. One reason: Unlike most other Winter Olympic sports, it's played professionally around the world, making it easy to understand by even the most casual fan of the Winter Olympics.

Field of Play

Traditionally, Olympic hockey has been played on an ice rink that's 4.1 meters (13.5 feet) wider than its modern counterpart in the National Hockey League and most other pro leagues. The larger, 61- by 30-meter (200- by 98.5-foot) rink created a faster and, many would argue, purer form of the game, which made Olympic competitions unique, even after the rules were changed to allow professional hockey players in 1988.

But Vancouver will introduce a twist: an Olympic tournament played on regulation NHL ice. This decision was born of practicality, not hockey philosophy nor, apparently, any attempt to gain a national advantage. The primary hockey facility for the Vancouver Games, Canada Hockey Place, is a preexisting (previously-named-GM Place) modern NHL arena. Retrofitting it to widen the ice by removing some rows of seats would have cost up to $10 million, and Games organizers appealed to the International Ice Hockey Federation, which makes such decisions, to allow NHL-sized ice for the 2010 Games. The group, quietly making a decision that likely won't draw much public attention until the Games begin, concurred, breaking a long tradition.

When hockey rounds begin in Vancouver, the sport thus will be that much closer to an NHL all-star tourney, with players shuffled up onto teams of their national origin. It's a regrettable turn of events if you're a fan of the more open Olympic hockey of yore. And it's likely to prompt coaches and national governing bodies to take a second look at how they choose athletes for their teams.

LEGEND OF THE SPORT

HAYLEY WICKENHEISER, CANADA, ICE HOCKEY

Born: 12 August 1978, Shaunavon, Saskatchewan
Olympics: Nagano, Sydney, Salt Lake City, Turin
Medals: 2 gold, 1 silver

Since Olympic women's hockey debuted as a medal sport in 1998, no player has provided more highlight-reel films than Canada's Hayley Wickenheiser, widely considered the greatest women's player of modern times.

A native of Saskatchewan, Wickenheiser first began chasing pucks at age 3 and played against boys for much of her youth. By 15, she was the youngest player ever selected for Canada's national team, where her size (5 feet 9 inches, 175 pounds), speed, and deft puck-handling skills quickly set her apart at forward.

Wickenheiser led Canada to five gold medals at the women's world hockey championships, a silver medal at the Nagano Winter Games, and gold medals at the Salt Lake City and Turin Olympics. She particularly shone in Salt Lake, leading her underdog Canadian team, which had lost eight straight pre-Olympics bouts with Team USA, to an upset 3–2 victory in the gold medal game. She tied America's Natalie Darwitz for top goal honors in those Olympics, with seven.

Her athletic prowess becomes evident in a deeper scan of her resume: Wickenheiser also was an elite softball player and played for Team Canada at the 2000 Summer Games in Sydney, making her a rare, summer/winter team-sport athlete.

As an adult, Wickenheiser has starred in women's professional hockey and later advanced to play with men in NHL training camps and European professional leagues. In January 2003, she became the first female hockey player to post a point in a men's professional game, playing for the Kirkkonummen Salamat of the Finnish Second Division.

Canada's Hayley Wickenheiser is a dominant figure in women's hockey, and has even cracked the ranks of the men's professional game.

She wasn't doing it to make history, she said—just to improve her game.

"I always try to challenge myself and play with guys who are better than me," Wickenheiser told the *Toronto Globe & Mail* before the Salt Lake Games in 2002. "I know if I don't train hard or keep on top of my game, that I won't be one of the best anymore. I love to play and I love new opportunities."

Her biography, *Hayley Wickenheiser: Born to Play,* by Elizabeth Etue, was published in 2005. But they might have to add some additional chapters.

To this day, more than 15 years after first playing in international competition, Wickenheiser, at 31, remains a force in the sport.

Says Karen Bye, a longtime opponent from Team USA, "When she's on the ice, everybody knows it."

Format, Rules, and Strategy

The Olympic tourney is a round-robin contest made up of twelve teams for men, eight teams for women. They're split into two groups for an initial round-robin, with each team facing the others in its group once. The teams with the best records advance to a single-elimination "medal round," with seeding determined by the round-robins.

Games consist of three 20-minute periods. In the medal rounds, in which one team must advance, ties are broken by a 5-minute sudden-death overtime period. In the gold medal game, the extra period is 20 minutes. If the overtime period produces no goal, it goes to a penalty-shot competition—a best-of-five matchup of individual skaters and the opposing team's goalie. If that still produces no winner, another sudden-death round of shootouts is launched. The game is decided when one team's shooter scores and the other team's does not. For better or worse, this white-knuckle "shootout" has loomed large a couple of times already in Olympic competition.

In terms of rules, Olympic hockey is very much like the hockey you're accustomed to watching. But if you watch hockey only every four years, a refresher course might be in order:

The ice is divided into three zones: each team's defensive zone, or the area behind its blue line, and the neutral zone, or the space between the two blue lines.

Teams skate six to a side—a goalkeeper, two defensemen, and a front line consisting of a center and two wingers. The players often make **shift changes** in the neutral zone at mid-ice during play, which explains why you'll see dozens of players on the ice at any one time—some coming onto the field of play, some exiting. In reality, hockey players usually play only in short bursts—ranging from about 45 seconds to 2 minutes—at a time, swapping off while the puck is at the other end of the ice.

Checking, or physically crunching an opposing player's body with one's own, is allowed in the men's game. It's not allowed in the women's game. In general, Olympic hockey tends to be called more closely and thus is not as prone to violence and fights as professional NHL hockey, where a job description for linesmen is to "break up fights."

LEGEND OF THE SPORT
VLADISLAV TRETIAK, USSR/RUSSIA, ICE HOCKEY

Born: 25 April 1952, Orudyevo, Russia
Olympics: Sapporo; Innsbruck; Lake Placid (1980); Sarajevo
Medals: 3 gold, 1 silver

He is likely the greatest hockey player of modern times never to don a pro uniform in the National Hockey League—and a legend in Olympic competition.

Vladislav Tretiak, a star in goal for the USSR, is considered perhaps the best goal-keeper of all time, leading his national team to global dominance, with gold medals in three Olympic Games and a silver in one other notable instance—the 1980 Lake Placid upset by Team USA.

His skills were first evident on the international stage in 1972, when he led his team to victory in Sapporo. But Tretiak didn't garner much attention from fans of professional hockey—then still a distinct entity from the Olympic game—until he shut down wave after wave of offensive stars from Team Canada in the 1972 Canada/USSR Summit Series.

Tretiak was among the first athletes to pioneer the now-predominant "butterfly" style of goalkeeping, playing with feet apart and knees bent. The position allows keepers, on low shots, to drop to their knees, using their legs to protect the goal. It also allows better side-to-side mobility than the old upright position, with feet close together.

The NHL took notice. Tretiak ultimately was drafted by the Montreal Canadiens in 1983 but was never allowed by his government to play professionally in North America.

Little wonder: The Russians wanted Tretiak all to themselves.

And Tretiak did not disappoint. He led Soviet teams to gold medals in Sapporo, 1972, and Innsbruck, 1976, setting the stage for the confrontation with the Americans in 1980. Mark Johnson's goal in the last seconds of the first period of the famous "Miracle on Ice" game prompted Soviet coach Viktor Tikhonov, shockingly, to pull Tretiak from the game, replacing

Vladislav Tretiak was elected president of the Russian Ice Hockey Federation in 2006.

him with Vladimir Myshkin. It ultimately would prove the undoing of Tretiak's long love affair with Soviet hockey.

Tretiak, in his autobiography, *Tretiak: The Legend,* said he never should have been pulled from the game, and suggested that Soviet officials in attendance pressured the coach.

"I had made so many mistakes already, I was confident my play would only improve," he wrote. Myshkin, he said, was "an excellent goalie, but he wasn't prepared for the struggle."

Tretiak led his squad to another gold medal four years later in Sarajevo, shutting out Czechoslovakia 2–0. He then abruptly retired at only 32 (with an amazing 1.78-goals-against average in 98 international games), reportedly frustrated over Tikhonov's coaching and his government's refusal to let him play professionally.

That might explain why some of Tretiak's most legendary performances came in exhibitions against NHL teams. His performance in a 1975 New Year's Eve contest against the Montreal Canadiens is considered one of the greatest of all time: The Russians were outshot by Montreal 38–13 but still left with a 3–3 tie.

Tretiak would leave a mark on professional hockey that remains to this day. After retiring, he worked as a goalie coach for the Chicago Blackhawks, for whom he remains a consultant, and he has shaped some of the league's top goalies, including Dominik Hasek, an Olympic star in his own right, and six-time NHL all-star Ed Belfour, who wore number 20 as a tribute to the Russian great and served as a backup goalie on Canada's 2002 gold medal squad.

Tretiak, elected to the Hockey Hall of Fame in 1989, also runs an elite goalkeeping school in Toronto and serves as president of the Russian Hockey Federation. He remains a stalwart ambassador for the sport.

Players pass the puck, made of hard rubber, to one another and score by getting the puck past the red line in the goal crease—not necessarily into the mesh net behind it. The puck must completely cross the line to count, meaning that space must exist between the puck and the back of the line. A goal judge flips on a red light behind the glass to the rear of the goal crease to indicate a goal. Players can, and often do, block shots with their bodies by falling onto the ice. Yes, it hurts. They also can knock a flying puck down to the ice with a gloved hand but can't catch it or move it backward or forward that way.

Penalties, defined as either major or minor, are assessed for tripping, hooking, slashing, and so on, with a player sent to a penalty box to serve his or her time (usually 2 minutes, although sometimes up to 10). In such situations, one team can find itself shorthanded by one, two, or even more players, giving the other team a **power play** opportunity until the penalty time is served.

Team penalties don't create penalty time but often result in a change of puck possession. Examples are **icing,** when a player on his own side of the center line fires the puck down the ice, across the other team's goal line (the line that runs through the goal crease), and **offside,** when a player on the attacking team crosses the blue line into the other team's zone before the puck does, or makes a two-line pass across any two of the three lines near center ice. These infractions result in a play stoppage and a **face-off,** or puck drop by an official between two opposing players, who battle to control it. The idea is to stop play and disallow any advantage gained by illegal passing. Note that offsides can be **waved off** by an official if attacking players acknowledge the mistake and leave the other team's zone, and that icing isn't called when a defending team is shooting the puck down the ice in an attempt to "kill a penalty" by intentionally draining time off the clock until the penalized player is let out of the penalty box.

Given all this, it's easy to see why teams develop defensive **penalty-killing** schemes and offensive power-play strategies, and why stats on both factors often prove key telling points to the outcome of any game.

Don't feel bad if you lose track of the puck during a game, especially a televised one (note: high-definition helps immensely!). Hockey is the fastest team sport in the world. Players can skate up to 37 mph (60 kilometers per hour), and the puck can come off a stick on a slap shot at up to 120 mph (193 kilometers per hour).

And don't be alarmed if one team winds up without a goalkeeper at game's end. The trailing team often "pulls the goalie" and replaces him or her with another attacker to gain a one-player advantage at the end of a game.

Training and Equipment

Ice hockey combines speed, intense lower body strength, endurance, and lightning-quick reflexes.

Most players spend more time on the ice, scrimmaging, than in weight rooms or other training facilities. Common aerobic training, using cycles and treadmills, and strength training also come into play. Equipment is rather bulky, befitting the high-contact sport it's designed for. Players wear helmets with face masks, shoulder and elbow pads, knee/shin pads, padded gloves, and loose-fitting jerseys and knee-length pants. Skates are molded boots with a blade that's upturned at the end to facilitate quick turns. Sticks, formerly carved from a single piece of wood, now are made of wood, composites such as Kevlar, aluminum, or some combination thereof. The blade of the stick, up to 14.5 inches (36.8 centimeters) long, can have an inward curve of up to a half inch (1.3 centimeters).

HISTORY'S HITS AND MISSES

Ice hockey in the Olympics is even older than the Winter Games themselves. By four years, in fact.

It was played at the 1920 Summer Games in Antwerp. Don't be thinking the Belgians were that far ahead of the rest of the world in refrigeration. The Summer Games that year took place in early April, when it was still cold enough to maintain an outdoor rink.

The winter sport in those Summer Games featured another Olympic oddity: seven men to a side. Canada won the gold medal, and by 1924, the year of the first official Winter Games at Chamonix, the rules had changed to the six men or women per side we're accustomed to seeing today.

A Stick by Any Other Name

The word "hockey" is derived from the French *hocquet,* or "stick." And while the Canadians may have perfected hockey, it's unclear whether the game as we know it today was actually invented in Canada.

Scotsmen are said to have brought a hockey-like game to North America, with soldiers based in Nova Scotia staging the earliest games in the late 19th century. Other sources credit Canadians with combining that game and lacrosse into a game resembling modern hockey in Halifax, Nova Scotia, and Kingston, Ontario, around 1840.

The game spread to Canadian colleges and, ultimately, south to America.

One other form of hockey whose roots are not in dispute: The record shall reflect that "leaf blower hockey" was invented by a bunch of guys with nothing better to do in Toronto in the early part of the 21st century.

Make Way for the Girls

Women's hockey didn't debut in the Olympics until 1998, but the sport actually has a long history. First played in the 1890s in—where else?—Canada, the game, played at first in wool skirts and sweaters, peaked in popularity in the 1930s, reemerging after World War II. It still was far from the mainstream, however. In 1956, a nine-year-old Ontario girl lost a Supreme Court decision challenging the "boys only" policy in her local junior league.

But the womens' version picked up momentum in the 1960s and by 1982 had become popular enough to spawn a national tournament, sponsored by the Ontario Women's Hockey Association. By that point, women in the United States and Europe had taken up the challenge, and women's hockey quickly grew to be a popular college sport in the States. The first international championship tournament was in 1987 in Ontario—an invitational. By 1990, the sport was exploding in North America, and the world championships became a regular feature, organized by the International Ice Hockey Federation. The sport was approved for the Olympics in 1992 and recognized by the NCAA in 1993.

Inclusion in the Olympics sent a few select players all the way into the men's game. In 2003, Team Canada Olympic star Hayley Wickenheiser, playing in the Finnish Second Division, became the first woman to record a point in a men's professional hockey game.

O, Canada!

The record reflects that the early decades of Olympic hockey were a showcase for Team Canada. But the nation's complete domination isn't evident until you start looking at the scores. From 1920 to 1952, Canada went 37–1–3 in Olympic tournaments, outscoring opponents 403–34.

One shining example of Canada's early superiority is the Toronto Granites club, which competed for Canada at the first Winter Games in Chamonix in 1924. That squad won its first two games over Czechoslovakia and Sweden by scores of 30–0 and 22–0 and then beat Switzerland 33–0 and a British squad manned mostly by Canadian players 19–2. They won the gold medal game 6–1 over an American squad that had similarly waltzed through the opening rounds.

Canada's dominance would end, however, starting with the 1956 Cortina d'Ampezzo Games, the first appearance of the well-oiled USSR hockey juggernaut. The Soviets' easy victory in the Cortina Games was particularly noteworthy considering that, unbeknownst to most of the world, nearly its entire squad had been killed in a plane crash in 1950, Olympic historian David Wallechinsky notes.

Miracle on Ice: The Prequel

Although many people remember intricate details of America's dramatic 1980 "Miracle on Ice" performance in Lake Placid, few remember even the outcome of a similar underdog performance by a much-maligned U.S. squad at the 1960 Squaw Valley Olympics.

Like the 1980 team, the '60 squad came into

the tourney as huge underdogs, having lost embarrassing Olympic warm-up matches to American collegiate squads. But they found their game at Squaw Valley, beating Czechoslovakia, Australia, Sweden, and Germany before nipping archrival Canada 2–1. The squad then faced the defending champ, the heavily favored USSR, whom they beat 3–2 on strong performances by two pairs of brothers, Bill and Roger Christian of Minnesota and Bob and Bill Cleary, of Harvard fame.

Just as the 1980 players would twenty years later, the 1960 team had one more game to play for the gold medal, against a lesser opponent, the same Czech team the United States had already beaten. The Americans fell behind early, but rallied—reportedly after infusing themselves with some fresh bottled oxygen to combat fatigue—to win 9–4.

The game, although nationally televised, was early in the morning and not seen by most Americans, who issued a relative yawn.

Canada's Therese Brisson is taken out from behind by the USA's Shelley Looney (right) behind the U.S. goal during the gold medal match at the 1998 Nagano Games.

Onward Christian Soldiers

Bill and Roger Christian of Warroad, Minnesota, one of the pairs of brothers of Squaw Valley fame, contributed in their own way to the corresponding Miracle repeat on home ice 20 years later. Bill's son, Dave, played for the victorious 1980 U.S. team, providing a blood link to its overachieving predecessor. He provided a key assist in the gold medal game against Finland.

They weren't the only direct link between the 1960 and 1980 squads. The last player cut from that 1960 Olympic team was a guy named Herb Brooks.

That Golden Goal

Any student of Olympic hockey must—*must*—be well versed in the particulars of the 1994 gold medal game at Lillehammer, which will live as an Olympic classic.

On the ice at Hakon Hall: Team Canada, which had dominated the Olympics in the early years but hadn't won a gold in 42 years, and Sweden, which had never won a gold medal. The two teams played a crunching back-and-forth match, skating to a 2–2 tie at the end of regulation.

A 10-minute sudden-death overtime followed, with neither team notching a goal. At its conclusion, the referees—to the surprise of even some of the players—signaled for a game-deciding shootout. The shootout, understand, hadn't been used in Olympic competition before, having been approved by the IOC only two years before, in 1992.

The Sweden–Canada game would become the first gold medal game ever decided this way, which is thrilling if you're a fan of the shootout, but a disgrace if you're a traditionalist who believes that no hockey game fought to a draw for 70 minutes by two complete teams should come down to one-on-one, made-for-TV gimmickry between two players.

The rules of the shootout are simple: Each team sends out five skaters to go one on one with the goalie. The team with the most scores in five attempts wins. If it's still a tie, it becomes sudden death, where a goal by one team that is not matched by the other decides the game.

As it happened, the '94 medal game, on February 27, 1994, would be decided by two youngsters, Peter Forsberg, 20, of Sweden and Paul Kariya, 19, of Canada—likely the most talented players in the world not already serving in the NHL (remember, this was before NHL stars took over the Games in 1998).

The shootout already had been through its opening round of five shooters, with the two teams tying 2–2—including goals by Kariya and Forsberg. Sudden death, again, was in the air.

The first two shooters in the sudden-death round missed. Then Forsberg, the seventh shooter for Sweden, put a move on Canadian goalie Corey Hirsch that will long live in hockey lore. (He later would reveal that he copied it from a move Swedish star Kent Nilsson made in the 1989 world championships.) Skating to Hirsch's right with the puck on his stick, Forsberg, in a confrontation that seemed to lapse into slow motion, made a series of quick "dekes," or fakes—left, right, then left again. At the last possible instant before skating past the goal, he reached wide to his right with his stick and, with a soft backhander, slid the puck smoothly past Hirsch, who was fully extended on the ice and couldn't quite reach it. (Watch the replay on YouTube and see for yourself; it's worth the time just to hear the Swedish broadcasters erupt when Forsberg scores.)

Kariya, shooting for Canada, put a shot high into the right corner of the Swedish goal, only to see it deflected by goalie Tommy Salo. Pandemonium ensued, with Sweden winning 3–2 to claim its first gold medal.

An artist's rendering of Forsberg punching the puck past Hirsch made it onto a Swedish postal stamp, which remains a valuable collector's item today.

Both Forsberg and Kariya would go on to great exploits in the NHL, with Forsberg leading two Stanley Cup teams for the Colorado Avalanche and helping Sweden to a second Olympic gold medal in 2006 at Turin.

But no part of his illustrious career ever outshone his performance on the fateful day that served as the punctuation mark for the '94 Lillehammer Games.

A Lucky Loonie

The 2002 Salt Lake City Olympics were the scene of Canada's return to hockey glory. Gold medals were won both by the men's team, with the program now shepherded by the Great One, Wayne Gretzky, and by the women's team, which avenged its 1998 loss to the United States by beating Team USA on its home ice.

Little known at the time, but much ballyhooed later, was Canada's "home ice" advantage in those games. The ice engineer at the E Center, the primary hockey venue, was Trent Evans—a Canadian from Edmonton. As the story goes, Evans, as the ice was being installed, dropped a Canadian dollar coin, or Loonie, onto the floor to mark center ice. It then was covered in ice, and lay buried for the remainder of the Olympics, until he melted it out with warm water and retrieved it later.

Gretzky showed off the Lucky Loonie to the world's media, and it now resides—where else?—in the Canadian Hockey Hall of Fame in Toronto.

North America Loses Its Grip

From its inception as an Olympic sport in 1998, women's hockey has been dominated by the United States and Canada, one of which has won every world championship and, entering the Turin Games, every gold medal. But that dominance didn't last long once the rest of the world was ex-

posed to the game. In Turin, a U.S. squad widely believed to be on its way to yet another gold medal match against Canada was caught by surprise by Sweden, which beat the Americans, 3–2, and went on to claim the silver medal after being edged by Canada in the gold medal game. Team USA settled for bronze.

RECORD BOOK: MEN'S ICE HOCKEY

In the early years, Canada reigned supreme. Maple Leaf Nation, in fact, won a gold medal in Olympic hockey before Olympic hockey was a Winter Games sport: Canadians brought home gold from the 1920 Antwerp Summer Games, beating the United States and launching a North American rivalry that exists to this day.

Canada would go on to win six of the first seven Olympic ice hockey tournaments, through the 1956 Cortina d'Ampezzo Games, with only a win by Great Britain's team (loaded with Canadian players) in 1936 breaking the streak. That dominance faded, however, as more and more of Canada's best players joined the ranks of the National Hockey League, which made them professionals who were ineligible to play. At the same time, the USSR began fielding teams of professional players who weren't considered pros because they were paid by their government rather than private clubs. That tipped the balance against North America, which was none too pleased. Canada, in fact, didn't send a team to the 1972 or 1976 Games, sitting out much of the era handily dominated by the Soviets, who captured gold at seven of ten Olympics between 1956 and 1992 (once as the Unified Team after the breakup of the USSR).

By 1998, with the NHL agreeing to suspend its season for the Olympics after the IOC declared

Mario Lemieux (center, waving) takes a victory lap with Team Canada after defeating the U.S. 5–2 for the men's gold medal in hockey at Salt Lake.

players eligible, Canada was back in the game but far from on top, and the Czech Republic was a surprise gold medal winner at Nagano.

In 2002, with the reins of the franchise handed over to Wayne Gretzky, Canada reclaimed its throne with a gold medal at Salt Lake City, in a stirring victory over Team USA that complemented the first gold medal performance of Canada's women's team, also over the United States.

American success in hockey is widely viewed in terms of what happened in Lake Placid: a silver-medal performance in the 1932 Games and then 1980's "Miracle on Ice" shocker. But the United States has fared better than most nations in hockey, also winning silver medals in 1920 at Antwerp and 1924 in Chamonix, bronze in 1936 at Garmisch-Partenkirchen, silvers in 1952 at Oslo and 1956 at Cortina d'Ampezzo, gold at home in Squaw Valley in 1960, silver at Sapporo in 1972, and silver in the 2002 Salt Lake Games.

Still, it's a far cry from Russia, which, competing either as the USSR, the Unified Team, or Russia, has won 12 medals (eight of them gold) in 14 Olympic appearances.

The other most successful nation on Olympic hockey ice? Sweden, with nine men's medals, including the gold at Lillehammer in 1994 and at Turin in 2006.

OLYMPIC FLASHBACK
NAGANO GAMES

Feb. 17, 1998

Reported by Ron C. Judd for The Seattle Times

NAGANO, Japan—Everybody cried.

Players cried. Coaches cried. Trainers cried.

Reporters, for Pete's sake—battle-hardened journalists from Miami and Washington and Boston and Frankfurt and Seattle—got downright misty-eyed when that gold medal went around Cammi Granato's neck, signifying the ascension of women's hockey into the sporting big time.

Everybody waited for someone to tell them it was too CBS to be true. That this hard-work-pays-off-for-U.S.-college-gals tale wasn't as magic as it felt. That Team USA's hard-fought, 3–1 victory over Peace Arch–rival Canada was something less than poetic.

Surely Shannon Miller, the abrasive Calgary cop who patrols the sidelines as head coach of Canada, could throw some cold water on this quickly escalating women's hockey lovefest.

"There's no question there's a feeling of emptiness," Miller said, grimacing in defeat after leading her squad to Canada's first big-game defeat at the hands of the U.S.

Now we're getting somewhere. Let hatred ring, Coach.

"But interestingly enough, when they showed Cammi Granato's face on the big screen, and an Olympic gold medal going around her neck, my feelings changed very quickly inside me," Miller said.

Huh?

"I had a feeling of joy go through my body, because what I realized was an Olympic gold medal was being hung around a female hockey player, and I couldn't believe the impact it had on me."

And there you had it. Sometimes, even journalists are forced to admit the obvious.

Dreams came true on this night.

For Granato, who used to reenact the final moments of Team USA's stunning upset of the Soviet Union at Lake Placid in 1980 with her brothers in their suburban Chicago basement, it was Miracle on Ice, Book Two.

Was the real thing—an upset victory over Canada, which had taken the U.S. over its knee in every important match in women's hockey's short history, as good as the dream?

"It was better," said Granato, the first U.S. player to be awarded a medal at center ice in the Big Hat, Nagano's hockey rink. "All you had worked for your whole life has paid off at that moment," she said later. "At that point, it hit me—what we've accomplished."

What they will have accomplished in the long term won't be fully realized for a decade or more, when a generation of young Cammi Granatos and Sarah Tuetings and Laurie Bakers and Allison Mleczkos grow up believing, for the first time, that the Winter Olympics has room for women who want to skate, but not in tutus.

But what they've already accomplished at the Nagano Games is as clear as the ice in the M-Wave.

On a cold, snowy night in Nagano, when the alpine skiers were put to bed, the curlers sent home to curl up and the snowboarders . . . well, we hesitate to speculate, women's hockey became The Story in Nagano.

Heroes were born on this night. Not the NHL-promoted, beer-sponsored kind. The real kind.

Look at the play-by-play and memorize their names.

Forward Shelley Looney, 26, Northeastern University graduate and closet figure skating fan, was in the right place, as usual, at the right time when a perfect pass came from teammate Sandra Whyte with nine minutes remaining.

She knew where to put it. U.S. 2, Canada 0.

Defender Colleen Coyne, 26, whose philosophy of life includes "collecting as many hugs as possible," was the only defender back when Canada's most prolific scorer, forward Hayley Wickenheiser, broke loose at the blue line and bore down on an out-of-position goalie.

Zero hesitation. Head-first dive. Brilliant stick check. Threat averted.

Goalie Sarah Tueting, 21, former cellist in the Dartmouth Symphony Orchestra, was in a crouch, with that all-alone feeling that only a goalie and perhaps Bill Clinton can know, with her team ahead 2–1 and Canada's Jayna Hefford streaking toward her on a breakaway.

Wrist shot. Skate save.

They're the kind of Olympians you want to send e-mail home about. The kind who train hard, play hard, earn little, and win with grace.

Twenty years from now, will they be remembered as the Founding Mothers of women's hockey?

"I think we've created a wonderful opportunity for many young women to play," said their coach, Ben Smith. "But I'm not a visionary."

Some of his players might be.

"Women's hockey has kind of grown up in the dark," Mleczko said after the game, gold medal clutched in one hand. "It's . . . not a mainstream sport. It's still not a mainstream sport. But it's coming out, coming into focus."

For the record, Mleczko, soon to appear on a TV screen near you, isn't going to Disneyland. She's going back to Harvard. Carrying a medal and a memory of something as historic as it was fun.

"It's so moving," Mleczko said. "I've never felt so patriotic in my whole life."

Women's hockey was born on this night, and the parents deserve to be proud.

The 1998 U.S. Women's hockey team sings the "Star Spangled Banner" after capturing the first gold medal awarded to women in that sport.

RECORD BOOK: WOMEN'S ICE HOCKEY

It was a grand moment for Team USA when its women's team captured the first-ever women's gold medal at Nagano in 1998—and something of a national embarrassment to Canada, which had long dominated the women's game at the international level.

That pecking order was turned upside down—or upside right, if you're a Canadian fan—in 2002 at Salt Lake City, where Canada stunned the host nation and captured the women's gold, which it successfully defended in 2006 at Turin. At those same Games, a Swedish team stocked with players who had trained and competed at American universities shocked the United States by capturing the silver medal, with the United States settling for bronze.

NEXT STOP: CANADA HOCKEY PLACE AND UBC THUNDERBIRD ARENA

Location: Vancouver, B.C.
Spectator capacity: Canada Hockey Place, 18,630; UBC, 7,200
Elevation: Canada Hockey Place, 8 meters (26 feet); UBC, 90 meters (295 feet)
Other events: UBC: Sledge hockey, Paralympics
Medal ceremonies: B.C. Place Stadium

As is usually the case with the modern Winter Games, ice hockey's large numbers of games command two arenas. Thus, hockey will be split between two venues, one existing, one rebuilt for the Games.

The main building, formerly known as GM Place but, for the duration of the Games going by Canada Hockey Place, in downtown Vancouver, was built in 1995 and is home to the NHL Vancouver Canucks. A massive stadium that seats 18,630, it is centrally located on the city's public transit grid.

It will play host to all the medal-round games.

The secondary building, home to preliminary-round games and much of the women's hockey tournament, is the **UBC Thunderbird Arena,** a remodeled facility on the University of British Columbia campus on the city's west side. With a seating capacity of 7,200, the Arena replaces the college's existing Thunderbird Winter Sport Complex, at the same time preserving a notable historical link: The project retains the original 1963 Thunderbird Arena, where Father David Bauer trained the 1964 and 1968 Canadian Olympic hockey teams.

After the Olympics, the new venue will serve as a multiuse sports arena for the campus, with a downsized seating capacity of 5,500. Construction work consisted of a wholesale renovation of the existing facility and construction of two ice sheets, one for the competition arena and one to be used in the future for training. VANOC contributed $38.5 million to the $48 million renovation.

One thing is certain: Neither of these buildings is likely to mimic their predecessors at the 2006 Turin Games in game-time environment and attendance. At Turin, many early-round games were played before sparse crowds. In Vancouver, Canada Hockey Place and UBC Thunderbird Arena will be long sold out and rocking—the epicenter of fan enthusiasm at the 2010 Olympics. Vancouver is a hockey-crazy town, the westernmost port in a hockey-crazed nation. Tickets to ice hockey will be the most hotly sought in all the Games. And both buildings should be well up to the task.

Vancouver routinely moves 18,000 fans into and out of Canada Hockey Place for sold-out Canucks Games, and the expanded arena at UBC is similarly well situated for public transit and general access.

Thanks to all this, hockey is likely to play an even more prominent role than usual in these Winter Games.

Ice Hockey 2010 Schedule

Canada Hockey Place

February 13: Women, 1 game

February 16–21: Men's round-robin, 3 games per day

February 22: Women's semifinal, 2 games

February 23: Men's qualification playoff, 3 games

February 24: Men's quarterfinal, 3 games

February 25: Women's medals, 2 games

February 26: Men's semifinal, 2 games

February 27: Men's bronze medal, 1 game

February 28: Men's gold medal game

UBC Thunderbird Arena

February 13–18: Women's round-robin play

February 20: Women's playoff, 2 games

February 22: Women's playoff, 2 games

February 23: Men's qualification playoff

February 24: Men's quarterfinal, 1 game

The Thunderbird Arena at the University of British Columbia will be home to much of the hockey action at the 2010 Vancouver Winter Games.

SPEEDSKATING

❄ ❄ ❄ ❄ ❄

It's agony.

About halfway through speedskating's 10,000-meter event, your legs start to give out. Your quads freeze in place, your glutes start to scream. Your eyes roll back in your head, and you ask yourself out loud: Why am I doing this?

And that's just how those of us watching in the stands feel.

Can you imagine actually doing it?

That's what I was telling a friend one day as we sat in the back row of the Oval Lingotto in Turin in February 2006, watching a pair of Europeans toil on the track for what seemed like forever, waiting for one of that day's biggest stories—indeed, one of that Olympic Games' biggest stories—Chad Hedrick, to take his turn on the ice.

Speedskating, to be sure, can be a thrilling spectator sport. It's just that the 10,000 meters is long. *Twenty-five laps* long. And the problem is, they race only two at a time. So when you've got a full field of international, sausage-casing-suited speedskating superstars waiting their turn, this is one event that can go on. And on. And on.

Which is why, if you're a sportswriter, you gradually learn from experience. First Olympics: You're there for the race an hour ahead of time. The last pair skates about 4 hours later. Three hours after that, you've filed your story and you're done.

Sixth Olympics: You watch the first pair skate on a monitor at the press center and note that the event has begun. You then go shopping, take the train to Milan for dinner, return, prepare your next year's tax return, write a screenplay, go through an entire sudoku puzzle book, and defrag your hard drive, then walk over to the ice oval and catch the action about midway through.

And so on.

The point, again: If covering this race is that arduous, can you imagine actually doing it? All bent over like that? Breathing that hard? The 10,000 meters, skated only by men—women, we can only surmise, are too smart—is nothing short of grueling. It ranks, in fact, among the top one or two gut-check events in all the Winter Olympics, a setting that's no stranger to brutal tests of strength and endurance (see, for example, cross-country skiing).

America's Joey Cheek, who donated cash bonuses for winning two medals to charitable organizations for children, was selected as U.S. flag-bearer for the 2006 Turin Games closing ceremony.

Its best practitioners clearly must possess a masochistic streak. There's no other way to explain the training they endure to function at a stage of near anaerobic bust for the 13 minutes it takes the sport's über-racers to run this race—and the 15 to 18 minutes it takes more mortal souls with only slightly above average lung capacities and pain tolerances.

Bottom line: Speedskating is hard. Damn hard. And unless you're a distance racer in the Netherlands or a sprint star in Norway, there's not a lot of glamour attached to it, either. This probably goes a long way toward explaining why the sport has produced, over the years, more than its relative share of athletes of unusually impeccable character. Something about making all those training laps around that oval eventually makes you . . . well, just better.

Speedskating, in fact, is a sport that's been dominated by some of the Winter Games' most interesting and graceful participants—people who use feats of glory on the ice to better the lives of those off of it. They are gold medalists who also happen to be great humanitarians.

The competition at the Turin Olympics was a grand example. The ice at the Oval Lingotto presented many moments of glory, but few as memorable as the night when America's Joey Cheek, a 26-year-old speedskater from North Carolina, took to the ice in the 500 meters.

It wasn't so much what happened on the ice that will live on in our minds—Cheek, the recent world sprint champion, skated a pair of flawless races (the 500 meters is the only speedskating race at which you get two cracks), finishing with a combined time of 1:09.76—more than a half second faster than the nearest competitor, Dmitry Dorofeyev of Russia. It was what happened afterward.

Cheek, literally grabbing a microphone in the post-race news conference, seized the spotlight he'd seen firsthand by winning a bronze medal in Salt Lake in 2002—and exercised a carefully conceived plan to put it to good use.

"I have a pretty unique opportunity here, so I'm going to take advantage of it while I can," Cheek told reporters.

He went on to explain that he'd been inspired, as a 14-year-old watching the Lillehammer Games on TV, by Norwegian speedskating hero Johann Olav Koss, who famously set three world records on the way to three gold medals in his home nation. The achievement drove young Cheek to switch from his love, inline skating, to ice skating, purely so he could pursue an Olympic medal dream.

As it turned out, Koss, who had used his own fame to establish the Right to Play organization, a charity designed to bring sports, and improved living conditions, to the world's neediest children, had inspired Cheek in grander ways as well.

Cheek announced that he would donate the night's proceeds—the $25,000 cash bonus awarded all U.S. gold medalists by the U.S. Olympic Committee—to Right to Play. Specifically, he wanted his money to benefit refugees in Chad.

"It's my hope that I can assist some people and maybe walk in his large shoes," Cheek said of Koss.

Then he kept walking.

Days later, he won another medal, a silver, in the 1,000 meters. The bonus check for that medal, $15,000, also went to Right to Play.

His generosity soon spread.

Short-track speedskater Yang Yang (A) of China donated her gold medal proceeds, about $10,000, to Right to Play. And speedskater/cyclist Clara Hughes of Canada, another Right to Play volunteer, donated her own $10,000 (Canadian athletes don't receive cash rewards for medals; she gave her own money) and challenged her teammates to do the same.

All the athletes challenged their sponsors, and other companies, to match or better their donations. When all was said and done, the effort had raised some $650,000 for charity.

All because one athlete had the uncommon wisdom to see how lucky he'd been, and how badly he wanted to extend those same opportunities to those less fortunate.

Maybe it's a speedskating thing—the kind of battle-honed character you get only by skating until it hurts—and then skating some more, with nobody there to cheer you on. Speedskaters trade a lifetime of preparation for a few minutes of fame, assuming they're one of the lucky ones.

Whatever the reason, Cheek was one of those rare athletes able to keep his sport in perspective relative to the world revolving outside it.

Since retiring from the sport after the Turin Games—his moment in the spotlight well spent—Cheek has lived up to his pledge to keep the need for humanitarian assistance front and center. It likely will be his legacy long after his speedskating exploits are forgotten.

"What I do is great fun," Cheek said in Turin, making it clear that most people in the world aren't so lucky. "I've seen the entire world and I've met amazing friends. But it's honestly a pretty ridiculous thing. I mean, I skate around on ice in tights, right?"

In the athletic world, it's a rare sense of self-awareness. And it's the very spirit that occasionally makes the Olympic Games truly special.

SPECTATOR'S GUIDE

As a spectator sport, speedskating can range from thrilling, usually in shorter races, to painfully long, in the case of endurance races such as the 10,000 meters. But in every case, it's a lively event at the Olympics, thanks to the hordes of mostly European—predominantly Dutch—speedskating fanatics who treat the sport like a religion.

Field of Play

Speedskaters compete on an ice oval measuring 400 meters (1,320 feet) around. (For reference purposes, think of a standard running track around a football field at your local university. It's the same distance.) Lanes are 3 to 4 meters (9.8 to 13 feet) wide.

Skaters, like runners, go counterclockwise. Don't ask; that's just the way it is. This gives rise to jokes among skaters that all they ever do in life is turn left, turn left, turn left—and to the reality that many skaters walk around with one leg, the left one, looking much bigger than the right.

Racers compete at varying distances: The sprint races are 500 and 1,000 meters. Intermediate races are 1,500 and 3,000 meters. Grueling distance races are 5,000 and 10,000 meters. Finish times range from 35 to 40 seconds in the 500 to a full 12 minutes for the 10,000. Thus, most skaters specialize in short, middle, or long-distance races—except for the few true human freaks of nature, such as America's Eric Heiden.

Here are the races and their corresponding numbers of laps:

- 500 meters: 1.25 laps
- 1,000 meters: 2.5 laps
- 1,500 meters: 3.75 laps
- 3,000 meters (women only): 7.5 laps
- 5,000 meters: 12.5 laps
- 10,000 meters (men only): 25 laps

Format, Rules, and Strategy

Skaters compete in pairs, and in all races except the 500 meters skate in designated inside and outside lanes until they reach the "crossing straight" on the track's back straightaway—a zone in which they swap lanes, once per lap, to negate the distance advantage gained from skating the inside lane the entire way. Sometimes these crossings can get tricky, but the skater crossing from the outer lane to the inner lane always has the right-of-way should the competitors be even. Racers wear armbands—white for the inner lane and red for the outer—to help officials keep track of who started where. Collisions and obstructions can disqualify a skater and give the fouled skater a chance for a reskate.

If you fall, you can get back up and continue in longer races. But the race is usually lost the instant you start to go down.

The way you win in speedskating is not necessarily as it appears. Although skaters are paired head to head, time is the decision maker. The fastest time posted by any racer, no matter who his opponent was or how he fared, wins the event. That said, skaters prefer to race against fast opponents—a tight contest gets the adrenaline flowing and almost always produces faster times.

Although all the other events are single races, the 500 meters, at least since the Nagano Games of 1998, is run as two heats, with the lowest combined time winning. The reason is that the racer in the inside lane has a small distance advantage.

One exception to the formats described above is the team pursuit, a new event added to the lineup as of the 2006 Turin Games. It's conducted like a professional track-cycling race: Two national teams of three skaters each begin on opposite sides of the track. Men race for eight laps, women six, and the last team member across the finish line marks the finishing time. Strategy, obviously, includes drafting off teammates and switching lead skaters to maximize time and efficiency. And you have to watch out for that other team.

Training and Equipment

Given the unnatural body positions, held under great stress for such long periods of time, the sport looks painful and difficult, even for its best practitioners. The truth? It is. No matter how good a skater gets at it, winning an Olympic medal against the world's best is always going to require digging down deeper, crossing a pain threshold he or she probably never knew existed.

Sprint medalist Jennifer Rodriguez of Miami, asked what it's like to cross the finish line in an elite-level race, said she really can't say: Usually, she is so spent that her body is running on instinct, her oxygen level so depleted that she's literally blacking out and can't really see where she's going.

Bottom line: Speedskaters don't get those sculpted bodies simply by being naturally gifted. It's the result of long, long hours of training, followed by recovery techniques such as full-body ice baths that few of us would likely endure once, let alone day after day for years.

Their tight-fitting speed suits, including hoods, are designed to minimize drag and save the precious fractions of a second that often determine placing. The suits are fitted with friction-reducing fabric under the armpits and inside the upper thighs. They also wear lightweight goggles to keep the wind out of their eyes—in full sprint, a speedskater can reach speeds in excess of 40 mph, making this the fastest human-powered sport of all. With the graceful, fluid movements of speedskating, it's often easy to forget that the skaters are traveling at near-highway speeds.

Speedskates are ankle high, for improved mobility. The uppers are made of plastic or carbon fiber. Their blades are long and straight, up to 46 centimeters, or just over 18 inches long, and about 1 millimeter wide. They're made of steel and extremely sharp. A fairly recent innovation, the "clap skate," has improved skaters' times by keeping the full length of that sharp blade on the ice for longer periods of time. Unlike earlier skates, in which the blade was fixed front and back on the boot, the clap skate blade is hinged under the forefoot, allowing the heel of the skate boot to lift off the blade. It increases the efficiency of each push-off stroke and also prevents stumbles late in races when skaters tire and become susceptible to digging their blade tips into the ice.

The clap skate debuted at the 1998 Nagano Games, and the result was striking: five world records were set, and new Olympic records were established in all eleven events.

Unlike their short-track skating cousins, long-track speedskaters do not wear helmets or other protective headwear, except for that hood.

Speedskating Technique

Speedskating, perhaps more than any other winter sport, is all about precise form. When you're in it, you're a rhapsody on ice, flowing like the wind. But when you fall out of it, it's painfully obvious to you, your Aunt Marla, and about 4 billion people watching on satellite around the globe. What's good form? It's all about gaining as much propulsion from each skate stroke as possible. In a straightaway, skaters are bent forward at the waist, head low, looking up just high enough to see forward, with their torsos

Speedskaters race in pairs in separate lanes, but their real enemy is the clock.

almost parallel to the ice. They make long, powerful strokes with their glutes and quads, arms thrusting in perfect rhythm and staying in close contact with the torso. For much of the race (except in sprints), skaters will skate with one arm behind their back to reduce wind drag.

Watch the top racers carefully and see how much glide they wring out of every stride—and how they know instinctively when to stop riding that skate and begin a new stride before the momentum begins to wane.

Racers are almost constantly turning, with only a dozen or more strides on straightaways before that next big left. Cornering is key: Racers enter the turn still bent at the waist for a low center of gravity, with their inside arm tucked behind

them. They swing the outside arm as a counter to centrifugal force, to fight the natural tendency to drift away from the turn—all the while making crossover steps, which are exactly what the name implies, to turn more sharply and efficiently.

It looks very difficult to bring all this together, especially when it's the 25th turn you've made in the same race. And it is.

The only place where speedskating form differs dramatically is the start. Racers stand, one skate blade flat, the other on its front tip at the start line, arms cocked in skate-stride position, waiting for the starting gun. They then sprint on both skate tips, arms pumping, until they reach a speed suitable for skate strides. It looks quite awkward, but quick reflexes and powerful running strides here are crucial, especially in shorter races, where a bad start can leave a skater doomed from the get-go.

In longer-distance races, pacing is every bit as crucial as in a distance race in track and field. Racers usually decide beforehand how fast they plan to skate every lap and even how many strides they should take per lap. That plan sometimes goes out the window if they make a mistake by stumbling or falling—fates that can befall even the best skaters.

HISTORY'S HITS AND MISSES

Ice skating, legend has it, dates all the way back to the Vikings. Archaeologists say they've unearthed (un-iced?) crude versions of skates with iron or bone blades dating back to A.D. 200 or 300.

We know that the northern people of Finland, Sweden, Norway, and Holland were the first big ice skaters—and, in many respects, still are.

Speedskate racing took flight in the Netherlands, first on frozen canals, with skaters racing full-out in a straight line for long distances. The invention of the iron skate blade in Scotland, around 1572, sent the sport leaping forward. The first recorded speedskate race took place in England in 1763 and measured 24 kilometers (15 miles). A century later, skating clubs were found throughout northern Europe, and skating on measured tracks was more common.

A new invention, the steel skate blade, developed in America in 1850, was a major boon. The first world championships were hosted by the Dutch in 1889. The sport began to take its current form in around 1892, when the birth of the International Skating Union led to standardized rules (such as the 400-meter track and most of the common distances raced today) and an organized world championship series.

Japan's Hiroyasu Shimizu leans into a turn on his way to an Olympic record in the 500-meter race at the 1998 Nagano Games.

LEGEND OF THE SPORT
ERIC HEIDEN, USA, SPEEDSKATING

Born: 14 June 1958, Madison, Wisconsin
Olympics: Innsbruck, Lake Placid (1980)
Medals: 5 gold

Even today, all these years later, it's impossible to skate out onto the ice of the Olympic Oval in Lake Placid and not see, feel, and hear the spirit of Eric Heiden.

Granted, that billboard-sized "Legends of the Oval" sign above the first curve might have something to do with it.

"Eric Heiden, 1980, Five Gold Medals," it reads. "Winner of all distances."

This is holy land for the speedskating aficionado, a sacred space even for moderately afflicted Olympiphiles. It's where a 21-year-old from Wisconsin went out and did the seemingly impossible in February 1980.

"Winner of all distances."

Think about the power of those four words. Heiden's Olympic five-fer—a gold medal sweep in the 500, 1,000, 1,500, 5,000, and 10,000 meters—over nine days at Lake Placid was astonishing, not just because it was unprecedented, but because of the remarkable athletic versatility it required. Speedskating is a specialized sport; few skaters adept in the sprint races (500 and 1,000 meters) could even be competitive at longer distances, such as 5,000 and 10,000 meters. Only a select handful can actually win at such diverse endeavors. And only Heiden was able to win each of them in a single Olympics.

Think of it in track and field terms.

"*Every* race," says U.S. speedskater Casey FitzRandolph. "That's like Maurice Greene or Michael Johnson lacing 'em up the next day to go out and *win* the Olympic marathon. It just doesn't happen."

Bottom line: It's a pretty good week and a half at the office, no matter where you work.

The man truly had ice in his veins— perhaps because he didn't realize until after it was all over exactly what fame and craziness his accomplishment would bring.

Eric Heiden set a mark no speedskater has equaled, winning all five of his events at the 1980 Lake Placid Games.

His methodical pursuit of the impossible illustrates both his demeanor and mastery of the sport:

Heiden, who competed in the 1976 Olympics at Innsbruck as a 17-year-old and then won world titles from 1977 to 1979, could have fallen off the perfection bus right from the start. His weakest event was the 500 meters, a race in which he'd been beaten only a week before by a teammate at the world sprint championships.

On February 15, he was matched, in the first pair, with world record holder Yevgeny Kulikov of Russia. Heiden took full advantage of the chance pairing, nipping the Russian, who stumbled on the final turn, at the finish line for gold medal number one, skating an Olympic record time.

"The last turn of that race is really what won it for me," he said in an interview with the U.S. Olympic Committee years later. "You hope that you never have to finish on the inner on the 500 meters, but that was the lane that I had drawn. I went into that corner and didn't hold anything back, and the training paid off."

The next day, in the 5,000 meters, Heiden, setting another Olympic record, beat Kai Arne Stenshjemmet of Norway by more than a second, for his second gold. Heiden: "I consider myself lucky to have won that. It was a slim margin, a very slim margin."

On February 19, in the 1,000 meters, Heiden posted yet another Olympic-record time of 1:15.18 to win his third gold. His closest competitor, Gaétan Boucher of Canada, finished in 1:16.68. Two days later: Same story in the 1,500, gold medal number four: Heiden, 1:55.44, Olympic record; Norway's Stenshjemmet, the world record holder, 1:56.81. And this with a stumble from Heiden after slipping on a groove in the ice.

Heiden recalls, "The thing that stands out is I had a big slip about 600 meters into that race. It looked bad when I had a chance to have a look at the video after that. I'll tell you, it never entered my mind when it happened that something bad had happened. It was just one of those things where the subconscious must have taken over and I had a slip and gosh, it never fazed me."

The fifth victory, in the 10,000 meters, was classic Heiden. Having attended the gripping U.S./USSR "Miracle on Ice" hockey match the night before, Heiden says he overslept, crammed down three slices of bread for breakfast, and arrived at the track late. He calmly took to the start line, matched with world record holder Viktor Leskin of the USSR. At the midpoint of the long, grueling race, it looked as though Leskin would play an all-time spoiler role.

But this was all part of the strategy laid down by Heiden's coach, Dianne Holum.

"Physically, I was certainly up to it. Mentally, though, I was starting to be very fatigued," Heiden recalled. "Before the race, I sat down with my coach and we decided that I was going to have to skate a time near world record time. In the middle of the race, he (Leskin) took off. I remember Dianne being very adamant about me staying on my schedule and not chasing him. At some point he was probably 150 meters up the track.

"Caught him, passed him, and never saw him again."

Heiden had, indeed, bettered the world record time—by 6.2 seconds.

As the first person to win five gold medals in individual events in the same Games,

Heiden quickly became an international superstar. Everyone wanted an interview or autograph; women swooned over his measurements—the famous 31-inch waist and 27-inch thighs that filled out every available inch of his (what else?) golden speed suit.

Add in the bronze medal in speedskating won by Eric's sister, Beth, in the same Games, and the Heiden family took home exactly half of the total medals won by Team USA that year.

But fame didn't sit well with Heiden at the time, and he never seemed to get used to it.

He was a godlike figure in northern Europe, where speedskating reigns supreme, but he knew that his fame would be passing in America, where speedskating was then, and still is, a peripheral sport. He believed American sports fans, in particular, placed too much emphasis on the Olympic Games.

"Heck, gold medals, what can you do with them?" he once said. "I'd rather get a nice warm-up suit. That's something I can use. Gold medals just sit there. When I get old, maybe I could sell them if I need the money."

Always an extremely reluctant hero, he retired the same year as he made history, telling reporters, "I really liked it best when I was a nobody."

Later, he would take up cycling, riding with the 7-Eleven Cycling Team and competing in 1986 on the first U.S. team in the Tour de France. He suffered a frightening fall and failed to finish.

Heiden earned B.S. and M.D. degrees from Stanford and began practicing as an orthopedic surgeon. He served as a TV commentator for the Olympics and as team physician for the U.S. Speedskating Olympic teams in 2002 and 2006. (Ironically, it was Heiden who would sew up the slashed leg of short-track speedskater Apolo Anton Ohno after a crash at the Salt Lake Games; Ohno in the Turin Games of '06 would become the first U.S. man to equal Heiden's mark of five Winter Games medals.)

Heiden now operates a sports-medicine practice in Murray, Utah, and still downplays those nine days in 1980.

"I have known Eric for many years, and sometimes I'm not even sure that he knows how incredible his accomplishments were/are," speedskater Dan Jansen told reporters in 2005, at a celebration of the 25th anniversary of Heiden's feat. "He never talks about how good he was or what he did. He is a doctor now and his skating life was just part of his past."

But the legend lives on. Heiden's exploits in Lake Placid have inspired succeeding generations of Olympians. And even those who've brushed up against his level of success still defer to the master.

"I never dreamed I would have had the success I did, or even be mentioned in the same breath as Eric Heiden," Bonnie Blair said at the Heiden anniversary celebration. "But like I have said before, he won his five golds in one week. It took me three Olympics and six years. What he accomplished in Lake Placid will never be done again."

Jansen, who knows more about Olympic pressure than perhaps anyone alive, sums up Heiden's performance thusly: "I have always felt that it is the single greatest feat in the history of sports."

Men's speedskating was conducted at the first Winter Games in Chamonix, in 1924; women, who had been racing in ISU-sanctioned events since the 1930s, joined at the 1960 Games in Squaw Valley, which also were the first Olympic races conducted on manmade ice.

Controversy—Right Out of the Starting Block

History will record that the first-ever Winter Olympics medal was awarded to Charles Jewtraw, of Lake Placid, New York, at the 1924 Chamonix Games. But history will also record that the Norwegians in attendance that day went to their graves insisting their guy, Oskar Olsen, got robbed.

They contend that the timer flat-out got it wrong. The thing is, it's possible. Back then, races were timed by hand—by cold, frozen hand—on stopwatches. And the 500 meters is such a short race that slow trigger fingers by race officials could dramatically alter the finish. This remained a problem in the sport for decades, until the inception of electronic clocks during the 1960s.

The Race That Wasn't

In spite of a world record performance in long-distance speedskating in 1927, Irving Jaffee, a young Jewish speed skater—likely the first—from New York City, was almost left off the 1928 Olympic team because he was a Jew, according to Harold U. Ribalow and Meir Z. Ribalow's *The Jew in American Sports*. But he was named as a last-minute addition and, once at the Games, made history.

Almost.

Jaffee finished fourth in the 5,000 meters, the best American finish in the race at the Olympics. Later, in the 10,000 meters, he was matched against defending world champion Bernt Evensen of Norway. In a dramatic, come-from-behind finish, Jaffee nipped Evensen by the slimmest possible margin,

one tenth of a second, apparently claiming a dramatic gold medal victory. But after only six racers had completed their laps in the long, 18-minute event, the head race official, a Norwegian, decided the ice had warmed too much, and called the race "no contest."

A long argument ensued, with Jaffee subsequently declared the winner by the IOC and the ISU then overturning the decision and ordering a rerace. In the meantime, the Norwegian skaters, tired of waiting for a committee decision, had packed up their stuff and left. The event was declared canceled, leaving a gaping official hole in the Olympic record book—and a firestorm of protest played out at the officials' hotel in St. Moritz and in newspapers around the globe.

In a stellar display of sportsmanship, Evensen, saying he was beaten fair and square, publicly insisted that Jaffee was the rightful winner of the gold medal—one he never received.

Talk About a Home Ice Advantage

Organizers of skating events at the 1932 Lake Placid Games apparently abided by that old golden rule of competition: He who hosts the Games makes the rules.

That's how it appeared, anyway, when the world's skaters learned that, in a radical departure, speedskating events would feature "pack-style" starts—something the Europeans had little experience with. The howls of protest were so loud that the world's top skater, defending world champion and five-time Olympic gold medalist A. Clas Thunberg, stayed home in Finland in disgust.

This did little to faze the Americans, who proceeded to dominate the speedskating events, with Lake Placid's Jack Shea winning the 500 meters on the Games' opening day and then winning the 1,500 meters days later, and teammate Jaffee, finally getting his due, winning the gold in the 5,000 and 10,000 meters. Canada won five medals, all silver and bronze. Only two medals, in fact, went to European racers. Americans and Canadians also swept the three women's races, which were held as demonstration events.

The change in starting procedure wasn't the only irregularity at those Games. During one heat of the 1,500-meter event ultimately won by Shea, judges suddenly stopped the race, accused the competitors of "loafing," and ordered a restart. The 10,000 meters turned even more bizarre: Officials, reports Olympic historian David Wallechinsky, in *The Complete Book of the Winter Olympics,* added another new rule requiring skaters to do their fair share in setting the pace for the long race (with a winning time that year of more than 19 minutes). At the end of the first of two qualifying heats, three skaters, including heat winner Alex Hurd, were disqualified for not being responsible pace setters.

Later, after a controversy over skating interference in the second heat, it was decided to rerun the two races the next day. But the resulting eight finalists were the same, and Jaffee, skating a slow, deliberate pace with Norway's Ivar Ballangrud and Canada's Frank Stack, broke into a finishing sprint and then dove across the finish line on his stomach to nip them both. As he lay there, exhausted but jubilant, state troopers rushed to the ice to help him, thinking he was injured.

The three racers were happy to take their medals and get out of there before another new rule came down the pike.

Irving Jaffee—Hard Luck Circles Back Around

Unfortunately, not all of the '32 Games medalists wound up keeping their treasured medals. Jaffee learned the hard way during the Great Depression that Olympic gold doesn't pay the bills.

"There was some talk of professional racing, but nothing came of it," Jaffee told the *New York Post.* "I got $450 from Wheaties and $600 from Gillette. . . . I gave exhibitions at the hockey games between periods, skating around the rink five times for $25. I had no commercial outlet and I had no job. I had to bring some money home to my family."

So he gathered all his skating medals—more than 300 of them, including the two Olympic golds—and pawned them at a Harlem pawn shop for $3,500. Later, with a job on Wall Street, he returned to buy them back, only to find the building torn down. He never saw the medals again.

Jaffee was done with the Olympics but not with speedskating. In 1934, although he had never skated more than 10,000 meters before, Jaffee, working at a resort in the Catskills, smashed a 30-year-old world distance record by skating 40 kilometers (25 miles) in 1:26.01.

Melting Ice, Part Two

Modern speedskaters don't have a sense of what their forefathers and foremothers went through in the early years—not only in speedskating, but in figure skating and ice hockey as well. Then, skate competitions were conducted on natural ice, outdoors, where wind and weather conditions played a huge role—as did the sun, even after the advent of refrigerated tracks.

At the 1968 Games in Grenoble, U.S. sprinter Terry McDermott, the defending champion in the 500 meters, drew the 24th and last starting spot for the race. By the time he started, the ice was sloppy and soft. He finished second by a mere two tenths of a second, and the winner, Erhard Keller of Germany, conceded that McDermott would have won if not for the (bad) luck of that draw.

Triple Your Fun

The 1968 Grenoble Games produced a rare event in the women's 500 meters—a three-way tie for second. In a race won in 46.1 seconds by Lyudmila Titova of Russia, America's Jennifer Fish, Dianne Holum, and Mary Meyers tied at 46.3. Each was awarded a silver medal.

Ahead of His Time

He almost became Eric Heiden before Eric Heiden—at least in terms of Olympic performance. Adrianus "Ard" Schenk of Holland dominated speedskating at the 1972 Sapporo Games unlike any man before him. A silver medalist in the 1,500 meters at the previous Olympics in Grenoble, Schenk went into the Sapporo Games as the reigning world record holder at that distance, as well as in the 5,000 and 10,000 meters. Schenk, racing through a snowstorm, won the 5,000 meters by a whopping 4.57 seconds. In his next race, the 500, he stumbled and finished 34th. That race would be the only blemish on his record. Schenk won the 1,500 and 10,000 meters handily, then swept all four events at the world championships only two weeks later. He's such a hero in his homeland that a flower, *Crocus chrysanthus 'Ard Schenk,'* has been named in his honor.

For Jansen, the Eighth Time's the Charm

Very few athletes have come as close to grasping an Olympic medal—and failed so many times—as American Dan Jansen, the hard-luck skater whose triumphant performance at Lillehammer was the highlight of the 1994 Winter Games. A seven-time World Cup overall champion, multiple world record holder, and two-time world sprint champion, Jansen had to be wondering—just as the rest of the world was—what else could go wrong when he stepped to the line to race the 500 meters, his favored event, in Norway.

His career medal chase over the years could only be viewed as star-crossed and tragic: In 1984, as an 18-year-old, he had finished fourth at Sarajevo, narrowly missing a bronze. In 1988, Jansen, the race

favorite, was devastated as his youngest sister, Jane, lay near death from leukemia. She died the morning of his 500-meter final. Jansen raced that night in spite of the news, but fell and finished out of the running. In 1992, Jansen again underperformed, finishing fourth in the 500 meters. Attempting to recover and grab another medal, he went out too strong in the 1,000 meters, fading to an embarrassing 26th place.

The Lillehammer Games were his last shot, and the world knew it, as did the wildly enthusiastic speedskating fans of Norway, who began rooting for the American to cap his Olympic career with a medal. He seemed, even more than usual, poised to do it. Since the previous Games, Jansen had become the only man to break the 36-second barrier in the 500 meters, reaching the mark four times. But the old Olympic hex descended on him once more in Lillehammer, where he finished eighth—six years to the day after his sister's death.

"I'm finished," he told his coach, Peter Mueller. "I just want to go home."

The 500 meters appeared to have been his last, best hope. Jansen's times in the 1,000 meters, his only other race at Lillehammer, barely rated in the top half-dozen in the world. He went into his eighth and final Olympic race as a major underdog.

But somehow on that day, the stars above Dan Jansen all, at long last, aligned. He shot from the start line at a pace that shocked everyone. By midway, he was on a world record pace, and the crowd sensed history in the making—or else another notable Jansen bonk about to happen. The latter fate appeared inevitable when, on his penultimate turn, Jansen slipped and put a hand to the ice. But this time he stayed up, stayed in bounds, and stayed on task, blasting to the finish line with a world record time of 1:12.43. The crowd went crazy. Competing skaters all around the oval stopped what they were doing to hail the American. Olympic fans watching around the world did the same.

At his medal ceremony, Jansen paid homage to his late sister, then took a victory lap around the ice with his young daughter, Jane, named after her.

There's nothing like a hard-luck-guy-does-good story to warm hearts, and nothing like the Olympic Games to put the story on a stage for all the world to see. Jansen's triumph will go down in history as one of the Games' great feel-good moments.

Jansen was inducted into the United States Olympic Hall of Fame in 2004. He went on to work as a TV commentator and skating coach for the Chicago Blackhawks.

Make Way for the Inliners

During the 1990s, the ranks of speedskating suddenly began to be filled by a new breed of athlete—skaters who had cut their skating teeth on inline roller skates. Among the first of the group were K. C. Boutiette, a distance specialist from Tacoma, Washington; and a young middle-distance phenom from Miami, Jennifer Rodriguez, who later would become Boutiette's wife.

Other inline upstarts—among them, Seattle's Apolo Anton Ohno—were making their mark in short-track speedskating. The trail blazed by those athletes inspired others to follow. One, Derek Parra, of San Bernardino, California, would become an unlikely—and triumphant—gold medalist.

Parra, perhaps the world's most decorated inline skater, had made a run at the 1998 Nagano Games, and qualified to race there in the 5,000 meters—he thought. He later was told that his admission as the last skater in the event had been the result of a clerical error. So he continued to train for Salt Lake City in 2002, seeking one shot at a Winter Games medal.

There, Parra, who grew up under tough circumstances in California to excel as an athlete, was selected by his peers to carry the shredded World Trade Center flag, a relic of the recent September 11, 2001 terror attacks on New York City, into Rice-Eccles

Stadium for the opening ceremony. The emotion from that chilly evening stayed with him the next day, when Parra stunned the world in the 5,000 meters, setting a world record time that, amazingly, was 15 seconds better than his previous personal best. (Parra's best finish in this event previously in international competition had been ninth.) He could only stand by and watch in wonder, however, as Dutch skater Jochem Uytdehaage skated out a short time later and obliterated Parra's time, shaving another 3.5 seconds off the world record and taking the gold.

Parra, thrilled with the silver in an event in which he'd never been expected to medal, wasn't finished. He met Uytdehaage on the Kearns, Utah, oval again in the 1,500 meters 10 days later, and this time he turned the tables: Parra, skating after Uytdehaage had set another world record in his early pairing, broke the record himself by 0.62 second, becoming the first Mexican-American to win a Winter Games gold medal.

Can't We All Just Get Along?

When Parra won that gold medal at Salt Lake that day, another inline skater, Chad Hedrick, aka "The Exception," was watching—on TV, from a Las Vegas casino. He vowed on the spot to hang up his roller skates, slap on the blades, and pull off the same switcheroo for himself. He thus began a relentless campaign to claim a gold medal at the next Olympics, in Turin, 2006.

His conversion and ascension in the sister sport was rapid, and historic. Within two years, Hedrick stunned the ice skating world by winning the 2004 world all-around speed skating championships, in the process setting a new world record for accumulated points. But the following year, still building for Turin and still posting record times, he was knocked off that all-around world championship medal perch by another American with a nontraditional speedskating background, Shani Davis of Chicago.

America's Shani Davis, a crossover from short-track speedskating, was a U.S. star at the 2006 Turin Games.

Davis was a converted short-track speed-skater, and the first great African-American skater in either sport. As the Turin Games approached, it looked to be a medals bonanza for U.S. speed-skating: Davis was a favorite in the 1,000 and 1,500, and Hedrick was versatile enough that he was widely believed to be a medal threat in all five events. Indeed, he told reporters before the Games that he was capable of equaling Heiden's stunning five-gold-medal performance from Lake Placid.

With all that combined talent, the United States also seemed a lock for a medal in a new event, the team pursuit.

Alas, as is often the case, all of that potential led to divisions within the U.S. "team" at Turin. Hedrick won a gold medal in the 5,000 meters, but carping quickly began between him and Davis, who had announced early in the Games that he would not participate in the Team Pursuit heats. Hedrick seized on this to imply that Davis was selfishly more concerned with his own medal haul than with the success of the U.S. team as a whole. Multiple days of sniping ensued between the two, with the media as a conduit, casting a cloud over what turned out to be a successful U.S. effort in Turin. When it was over, Davis had won gold in the 1,000 and silver in the 1,500; Hedrick took gold in the 5,000, silver in the 10,000, and bronze in the 1,500; Joey Cheek, as detailed earlier, won gold in the 500 and silver in the 1,000. As for the team pursuit? The hometown Italians stunned the world and took gold, Canada took silver, the Dutch claimed bronze, and the bickering Americans failed to place.

Like a Red Flame

No speedskater in modern times has left a more lasting impression than Johann Olav Koss, the Norwegian legend who continues to inspire athletes on and off the field of play. Koss began his Olympic career by winning a gold medal in the 1,500 meters at Albertville—a week after passing a gallstone in a hospital. Koss, wearing a flaming red bodysuit, later added a silver in the 10,000 meters. Four years later, he dominated the Lillehammer Games, breaking his own world record in the 5,000 meters, doing the same in defending his 1,500-meter title, and again bettering his own world record—the third of the Games—by nearly 13 seconds in the 10,000 meters, which he won by 18.7 seconds, the second-largest margin in Olympic history.

Koss then went on to do something almost as remarkable off the ice. Striving to make a difference for disadvantaged youth, particularly in Africa, he founded a humanitarian group, Olympic Aid. He auctioned his famous skates from the Lillehammer Games to get the organization off the ground. Although it proved successful, Koss dropped the "Olympic" label when he learned that that connection came with a price—bureaucratic meddling by the International Olympic Committee.

The group then became Right to Play, a nationless charity that went on to finance relief projects in Africa, Asia, and the Middle East.

His skating exploits, and his nonskating humanitarian work, have inspired many other athletes, such as Canada's Clara Hughes and America's Joey Cheek, to follow the path he so selflessly laid out.

RECORD BOOK: MEN'S SPEEDSKATING

Men's events in recent years have been dominated by skaters from the two speedskating hotbeds, Denmark (particularly in the grueling long distances) and Norway, with Russia producing its own healthy share of medalists. But Americans have begun to reassert themselves in a sport that they dominated in its infancy.

The first official event of the first official Winter Olympics—at Chamonix in 1924—was the 500 meters, and it was won by an American, **Charles Jewtraw** of Lake Placid, New York. Jewtraw's gold medal currently resides, on loan from the Smithsonian, at the Olympic Museum in Lake Placid, not far from Mirror Lake, where Jewtraw and his father worked at the local speedskating rink.

Other American medal moments: **John Farrell** won bronze in the 500 at St. Moritz, 1928. **John "Jack" Shea,** only hours after reciting the Olympic Oath at the opening ceremonies, took gold in the 500 at Lake Placid in 1932 in front of an ecstatic hometown crowd. He later would win gold in the 1,500 meters. Shea's son, **Jack,** and grandson, **Jim,** would go on to compete in the 1964 Innsbruck and 2002 Salt Lake City Olympics, with Jim winning the gold medal in skeleton. Fellow American **Irving Jaffee** won the 5,000 and 10,000 meters at the same '32 Games, and teammate Edward Murphy captured silver in the 5,000. **Leo Freisinger** won the 500-meter bronze in 1936 at Garmisch-Partenkirchen.

LEGEND OF THE SPORT
BONNIE BLAIR, USA, SPEEDSKATING

Born: 18 March 1964, Cornwall, New York
Olympics: Sarajevo, Calgary, Albertville, Lillehammer
Medals: 5 gold, 1 bronze

As a young kid, Bonnie Blair learned how to skate ahead of the pack. A real pack, as it were: As a youth, she was an ultracompetitive short-track skater.

You could say it was in her blood. As the story goes, her father, Charlie, whose brood of five children were heavily into skate racing, took the kids to a skate meet in Yonkers, New York, while mom was in the hospital giving birth to Bonnie, whose arrival was announced on the arena public-address system.

Not everyone believes that. "But it's true," Blair told ESPN.com. "In those days husbands really weren't allowed in the delivery room. So dad figured instead of waiting for me to be born, since mom had been through this five times before, that he'd take the rest of the kids to a skating meet. . . . So I was just a few hours old when I got my first loudspeaker announcement."

Blair, who grew up in Champaign, Illinois, began skating as a tot but didn't start skating the nonbruising long-track style until age 16.

To learn the ropes, she embarked on a crash-course educational tour in Europe—an endeavor financed largely by a $7,000 donation from the Champaign Policemen's Benevolent Association. She caught on fast, winning multiple U.S. titles in the mid-1980s. At her first Olympics, competing as a 19-year-old in Sarajevo in 1984, she finished eighth in the 500 meters.

Four years later, she was back and on the medal stand, claiming gold in the 500 meters at the 1988 Calgary Olympics.

Only then did the true dominance of Blair, a plucky 5-foot-4, 130-pound brunette, become evident. She won the world title in 1989 and remained in the top three for several years, entering the 1992

Bonnie Blair was golden at the Calgary, Albertville, and Lillehammer Games.

Albertville Games as a medal contender in the sprints. Quickly becoming a favorite among American fans for her friendly, upbeat, unpretentious demeanor, she won both the 500 and 1,000 meters. Her fan club, the "Blair Bunch," was there en masse from her hometown, cheering Blair on and serenading her to "My Bonnie Lies Over the Ocean" as she skated onto the ice.

The same year, she won the Sullivan Award, granted to the United States' top amateur athlete.

At the 1994 Lillehammer Games, Blair went out in style, once again taking the gold in the 500. In a sport where no woman had won consecutive 500-meter races at the Olympics, Blair had taken three straight.

Blair then skated further into history by repeating her victory in the 1,000 meters. That race was memorable not just for its historic significance—it was her fifth gold medal, the most ever for any American female athlete in the Summer or Winter Olympics—but for her dominating performance. Blair, skating 1:18.74, won by 1.38 seconds, the largest margin of victory in the history of the event.

A month later, skating in Calgary, Blair became the first woman to skate the 500 meters in less than 39 seconds.

The skating legend retired after another notable achievement on her 31st birthday: establishing a personal best and U.S. record in the 1,000 meters, 1:18.05.

After retiring, Blair married a skating teammate, Dave Cruikshank. She now works as a motivational speaker and remains active in charity through the Bonnie Blair Foundation, and in U.S. Speedskating, the sport's American governing body. She was elected to the U.S. Olympic Hall of Fame in 2004.

In an oddity at the 1948 St. Moritz Games, **Kenneth Bartholomew** and **Robert Fitzgerald** of the U.S. and Norwegian **Thomas Byberg** were awarded silver medals in a three-way tie in the 500-meters behind **Finn Helgesen** of Norway. America's **Kenneth Henry** won the gold in the 500 meters in Oslo, 1952, with teammate **Donald McDermott** taking silver; **William Disney** took the silver in the same race at Squaw Valley in 1960.

Richard "Terry" McDermott was an upset winner in the 500 at the 1964 Innsbruck Games. He repeated the feat in 1968 at Grenoble. At Innsbruck in 1976, **Peter Mueller** won gold in the 1,000 meters; **Daniel Immerfall** took the bronze in the 500 meters.

At the 1980 Lake Placid Games, **Eric Heiden** posted one of the most impressive Winter Olympic performances by any athlete in any sport, sweeping the gold medals in the 500, 1,000, 1,500, 5,000, and 10,000 meters in a nine-day period.

At the 1988 Calgary Games, **Eric Flaim** won silver in the 1,500 meters. In the 1994 Lillehammer Games, **Dan Jansen** won a memorable gold in the 1,000 meters. At the 2002 Salt Lake Games, **Casey FitzRandolph** took gold in the 500, while teammate

Chad Hedrick, a former inline skater, didn't quite live up to his own hype at the 2006 Winter Games.

Kip Carpenter captured bronze; **Derek Parra** won gold in the 1,500 and silver in the 5,000; and **Joey Cheek** took a bronze in the 1,000.

At the 2006 Turin Games, Cheek took gold in the 500 and silver in the 1,000; **Chad Hedrick** won gold in the 5,000 meters, silver in the 10,000, and bronze in the 1,500, while **Shani Davis** took gold in the 1,000 and silver in the 1,500.

Canada's medal contributions: **Alexander Hurd** took bronze in the 500 meters at Lake Placid, 1932. Teammate **William Logan** won bronze in the 5,000 meters the same year. **Gaétan Boucher** won gold in the 1,000 meters at Lake Placid in 1980 and also won gold in the 1,000 and 1,500 meters and bronze in the 500 meters at Sarajevo in 1984; **Jeremy Wotherspoon** and **Kevin Overland** combined to win the silver and bronze, respectively, in the 500 meters at Nagano in 1998.

RECORD BOOK: WOMEN'S SPEEDSKATING

Women's speedskating, added to the Games in 1960, is yet another Winter Games sport long dominated by Germans. The best of them:

Karin Enke, a converted figure skater (at 5 feet 9 inches, she was deemed too tall) from Dresden, whose career on the track made her the first woman in Olympic history to win eight medals in individual events: gold in the 500 in 1980, gold in the 1,500 and 1,000 and silver in the 500 and 3,000 in 1984; and silver in the 1,000 and 1,500 and bronze in the 500 in 1988, when she competed as **Karin Kania.** After that final 500-meter race, Kania stood on the podium with teammate Christa Luding-Rothenburger and America's Bonnie Blair, both of whom bettered the previous world record in the race. Kania finished only 0.14 second out of first.

Gunda Niemann-Stirnemann, who would soon equal Enke's monumental eight-medal achievement. She won the 3,000 meters by almost 3 seconds and the 5,000 meters by more than 6 seconds at Albertville, where she also won a silver in the 1,500 meters. She added a silver in the 5,000 and bronze in the 1,500 at Lillehammer, then shone again at the 1998 Nagano Games, winning the 3,000 meters and earning silver medals in the 1,500 and 5,000 to finish her career with eight medals.

Claudia Pechstein, who did them both one better: Competing in five Winter Games, she medaled at least once every time, earning a complete set of medals in the 3,000 meters and an amazing three consecutive gold medals and a bronze in the 5,000 meters. She retired with a total of nine medals won in five consecutive Winter Olympics.

No single Games have been dominated on ice by a woman, however, the way Russia's **Lidiya**

Skoblikova dominated the 1964 Innsbruck Games. Having won gold in the 1,500 and 3,000 meters at the 1960 Squaw Valley Games, she was favored in every race except the 500-meter events at Innsbruck. But she led a Russian sweep in that race and then went on to win the 1,000-, 1,500-, and 3,000-meter races—on successive days, no less—duplicating her sweep of the 1963 world championships in Japan. She was the first person to win four gold medals in a single Winter Olympics and remains the only woman in history to win six gold medals in individual events. She is considered by many to be the greatest female speedskater of all time.

Two other female speedskaters stand out in the record books: Canada's **Clara Hughes** won a pair of bronze medals in cycling at the 1996 Summer Games in Atlanta, then raced again in Sydney but failed to medal. She then retired from cycling and resumed the sport of her childhood, speedskating, in 2001, and after less than two months of training, she made the Canadian Olympic Team for the Salt Lake City Games. There she finished 10th in the 3,000 meters and third in the 5,000 meters, claiming a bronze medal. In the Turin Games of 2006, she won a silver medal in the new event of team pursuit, then captured gold in the 5,000 meters in a dramatic race against Claudia Pechstein of Germany. Hughes thus became the second person in history to win multiple medals in both the Summer and Winter Olympics. **Christa Luding-Rothenburger** of Germany is the other, also winning in track cycling and speedskating. Rothenburger remains the only person to have pulled off the double in the same year: 1988, at Calgary and Seoul.

America's female medalists: **Jeanne Ashworth** won gold in the 500 meters at Squaw Valley in 1960; **Barbara Roles** won bronze in the 500 and bronze in the individual. At Grenoble in 1968, **Jennifer Fish, Dianne Holum,** and **Mary Meyers** completed a rare three-way tie for the silver in the 500; Holum would win bronze in the 1,000 at Grenoble and go on to win the 1,500 while skating an Olympic record, then win a silver in the 3,000 meters at Sapporo in 1972. Her teammate, **Anne Henning,** won the 500 meters at Sapporo.

At Innsbruck in 1976, **Leah Mueller** won silver in the 1,000, with **Sheila Young** grabbing the bronze; Young also won gold in the 500 and silver in the 1,500. At Lake Placid in 1980, Mueller again won silver in the 1,000 and the 500; **Beth Heiden,** sister of a somewhat famous speedskater, took bronze in the 3,000 meters.

Calgary in 1988 brought the medal-stand debut of **Bonnie Blair,** who watched **Christa Luding-Rothenburger** of East Germany break the world record in the 500 and then went out and beat it by two hundredths of a second. She also would claim bronze in the 1,000 meters. In 1992 at Albertville, Blair defended her 500 crown and added a gold in the 1,000 meters. In 1994 at Lillehammer, she again won the 500 and 1,000, with her margin of 1.38 seconds in the latter race standing as the largest margin in the event's history. Her six Winter Games medals are the most for an American woman, and her five golds leave her tied for third among all women at the Winter Games.

At Nagano in 1998, **Chris Witty** won bronze in the 1,500 and silver in the 1,000. At Salt Lake City in 2002, Witty won the 1,000, with **Jennifer Rodriguez** winning the bronze.

For Canada, **Petra Burka** won bronze in the individual at Innsbruck in 1964; **Cathy Priestner** took the silver in the 500 at Innsbruck in 1976; **Susan Auch** was second behind Bonnie Blair in the 500 meters at Lillehammer, 1994; **Catriona Lemay-Doan** won bronze in the 1,000 meters and gold in the 500 at Nagano in 1998; Auch won the silver in the 500. At the Salt Lake 2002 Games, Lemay-Doan won the 500, **Clara Hughes** won bronze in the 5,000, and **Cindy Klassen** took bronze in the 3,000.

Klassen then dominated the 2006 Turin Games, winning five medals—gold in the 1,500, silver in the 1,000 meters and team pursuit, and bronze in the 3,000 and 5,000 meters, making her Canada's most decorated Winter Olympian, with six career medals. She was the first Canadian to win more than three medals in a single Winter Games. Also in Turin, teammate **Clara Hughes,** the multisport athlete who had medaled in track cycling, won the 5,000. Klassen and Hughes combined with teammates **Kristina Groves, Christine Nesbitt,** and **Shannon Rempel** to win silver in the inaugural Olympic team pursuit, in which Germany took the gold.

NEXT STOP: RICHMOND OVAL

Location: Richmond, B.C.
Spectator capacity: 8,000
Elevation: Sea level
Other events: None
Medal ceremonies: B.C. Place Stadium

Spectators will drive or take the train to the Richmond Oval, in Richmond, B.C., 25 minutes south of Vancouver's Olympic Village, on the banks of the Fraser River. The brand new, 33,750-square-meter (111,000-square-foot) building is an impressive structure. The roof, which seems to flow in a wave shape, is built with arched trusses and rafters made of British Columbia timber—some of which apparently was installed before being suitably dried, leading to substantial and costly repairs in mid-2008.

But skaters will be more concerned with what lies underneath that roof. The moment the doors open, the question is likely to be: Will the Richmond Oval put the brakes on Olympic speedskating's rocket-booster speeds?

It has a lot to do with science.

At the Salt Lake Games of 2002, records fell left and right as skaters zipped across the ice in the

Olympic Oval at Kearns that bragged of the "fastest ice on Earth." The claim had some scientific backing: In addition to all the building's whiz-bang high-tech ice-making attributes, the 2002 Oval sits at an elevation of about 1,372 meters (4,500 feet)— almost a mile above sea level. Air at that altitude is thinner, and ice is drier and harder. Thus, times are lower, as skaters feel less resistance, in terms of both wind and ice drag.

Richmond, by contrast, sits barely above sea level. Will the times increase at an equal rate, or have speedskaters simply gained so much speed and strength through refined training techniques that it really won't matter?

Only time—and that first starting gun for the Olympic 500 meters—will tell.

But however fast the ice proves to be, speedskaters and fans should be in good hands with suburban Vancouver's spanking new Oval.

The facility, which seats 8,000, is part of a

Speedskaters at the 2010 Vancouver Winter Games will compete in the sprawling Richmond Oval once it is completed.

larger Richmond Oval Project that also includes a new waterfront plaza for the city. Built by the City of Richmond, the total price tag was $178 million (Canadian).

After the Games, the Oval will remain in use as an ice rink and training facility, as well as hosting community events on its indoor ice, hardwood, and track surfaces.

Speedskating 2010 Schedule

February 13: 5,000-meter men
February 14: 3,000-meter women
February 15: 500-meter men
February 16: 500-meter women
February 17: 1,000-meter men
February 18: 1,000-meter women
February 20: 1,500-meter men
February 21: 1,500-meter women
February 23: 10,000-meter men
February 24: 5,000-meter women
February 26: Team pursuit qualifying, women and men
February 27: Team pursuit finals, women and men

SHORT-TRACK SPEEDSKATING

❄ ❄ ❄ ❄ ❄

The entire arena was in bedlam. And I was deaf, dumb, and blindfolded.

Not literally. But I might just as well have been.

Usually, one of the advantages of being a sportswriter is that you get a good seat. Hence, *Best Seat in the House,* the title of an autobiography by Christine Brennan, a fellow Olympic writer.

But it's not always the case at the Olympics, where a Winter Games typically draws about 10,000 journalists from around the globe, half of whom might want to see, let's say, the 1,000-meter men's short-track speedskating final, all at the same time.

Thus, large sections of the arena—in this case, Salt Lake City's Delta Center—are reserved for media types. And not all seats are as good as all others, a fact that you might not realize until it's too late. Like when a race has ended in chaos and several rows of journalists perched in front of large TV monitors in front of you block your view of the finish line.

So there I stood, on a tight deadline, with a prewritten story about Seattle's Apolo Anton Ohno winning his first gold medal on my computer screen, waiting to hit the Send button and impress everyone back home by filing a complete story only minutes after the race, to be followed by a longer, more navel-gazing piece later on, complete with context and quotes from the athletes.

But reality, as it often does, intruded—this time in spectacular fashion.

Everything had looked great only seconds earlier, when Ohno, 19, headed down the last straightaway in the lead, heading for home and, it seemed, a sure gold medal.

It was all as advertised: Ohno, a Federal Way, Washington, native and convert from inline roller skating, had been billed by broadcaster NBC and others as the likely breakout star of the 2002 Salt Lake Winter Games. He was the only medal favorite on a U.S. team facing more powerful, deeper squads from South Korea, China, and Canada. Yet he was still expected to waltz into his first Olympics and win—repeatedly. If that wasn't pressure enough, Ohno was largely expected to boost his sport, a relative newcomer to the Winter Games, into national prominence in the United States for the first time.

All of which he had handled with grace beyond his years, with a Zenlike unflappability, a winning smile, and looks that made preteen girls from Seattle to Seoul swoon.

At that moment, with the world watching on TV, all he needed to do was deliver the goods and grab at least one gold medal. As he raced across that backstretch, all that remained between him and the top rung of the podium was one final turn and a final dash to the line—about 15 seconds of skating.

Then it happened. Even from my seat—may it be consigned to hell forever—I could see things start to go bad. Chinese skater Li JiaJun, making a last-minute charge, tried to fight past Ohno on the outside, causing their skates to tangle and Li to fall.

Ohno, thrown off balance, careened into young speedster Ahn Hyun-Soo of South Korea, sending both of them sprawling, a flailing skate slicing a gash into Ohno's thigh in the process. Canada's Mathieu Turcotte, riding both their bumpers, went down with them.

Bodies were strewn across the ice. Everyone, it seemed, was down. Everyone, that is, except Steven Bradbury, a gangly, bleached-blond skater from Australia who had been trailing the entire field by half a lap—on purpose, he later revealed—hoping against hope that the other four skaters would find a way to wipe themselves out, leaving him a clear lane to victory.

Which, history will record, is precisely what happened. As the other skaters scrambled to regain their feet, Bradbury picked his way through the carnage and crossed the line first, raising his arms in stunned triumph in a race that would make him a legend, complete with a title: the "accidental medalist."

The crowd of 15,000 people stood, stunned, mouths agape, not knowing whether to cheer, cry, or laugh out loud. It was as if someone had sucked all the oxygen from the arena. Did they just see what they thought they saw? And what in the world,

I was wondering to myself, had they just seen and I'd missed?

Somehow, amidst all this, Ohno had the presence to stumble to his feet and stagger the last dozen meters to the finish line, finishing second. Turcotte, seeing him move, instinctively followed suit and crawled across third.

And the entire world buzzed in nervous anticipation, waiting for the referee's decision. It's not unusual in short track for a postrace disqualification to change the order of finish, or even to determine that a race should be rerun.

But remarkably, these results stood. Replays were watched, officials consulted, and Li, who had finished out of the running, ultimately was disqualified. But none of the leaders—least of all Bradbury, who had come into contact with nothing but the ice beneath his skates for the entire race—was found guilty of anything except being in the wrong place at the wrong time, with a couple billion people looking on.

Hence, the result became official. And one confused journalist from Seattle, who hadn't been able to see the finish line and was forced to piece all this together later from replays, had to spike his cleverly prewritten story about the newest hometown hero and start completely from scratch.

As a result, we didn't get the story we wanted in the first edition. But that short-term setback paled in comparison to the broader picture. Short-track speedskating—albeit in a way no one had expected—had finally achieved dining-room-conversation status in the United States.

The Ohno race was replayed thousands of times that night. And the postrace news conference proved to be one of the most hilarious moments we're likely to ever enjoy at an Olympics.

Bradbury, with a surfer's 'do and a charming Aussie glint in his eye, made no bones about it: His strategy, not only in this race but in two preceding qualifying races that got him there, had been to ride

Apolo Anton Ohno, Canada's Mathieu Turcotte, and Korea's Ahn Hyun-Soo crash on the final turn of the 1000 meters at Salt Lake City. Ohno recovered to crawl across the line for a silver medal.

in the back and hope for accidents, collisions, and so on, he reiterated to the world's assembled media.

"Those were my tactics," Bradbury said, still shaking his head. "And they worked like a charm."

"When I came across the finish line," he deadpanned, "I was like, 'Oh. Hang on. This can't be right. I think I won!'"

A hero was born. Bradbury became the patron saint of hanging in there and hoping for a bit of random luck. It was the first time any athlete from the Southern Hemisphere, let alone an Australian, had ever won a Winter Games gold medal. And it might be the last.

"I don't take this gold medal as (an award for) a minute and a half of skating," said the three-time Olympian, who had never finished higher than eighth in an individual event. "I'll take it as a reward for the last decade of hard work."

Most people expected Ohno, the favorite, to be downcast when he was wheeled into the postrace press conference in a wheelchair—a medical precaution, as he'd just been stitched up. He looked, instead, like a cat who'd just eaten the canary. This high degree of unpredictability, we learned that night, really was a part of the sport that Ohno thrived on.

All he could do was smile, shrug, and repeat the official speedskater's post-disaster mantra: "That's short track!"

He'd raced as fast as he could and had been taken out in a collision that couldn't be avoided, he said.

"My quest, my journey, is not about winning four golds," Ohno said. "It's about coming to the Olympics and performing my best, regardless of the medal outcome."

It sounded cornball, but as time would tell, he really meant it. He still had other races, such as his specialty, the 1,500 meters, to come, he noted.

"Maybe next time," he said with a grin, "I need to be a little further out in front."

As it turns out, he wasn't. But in the upside-down world of short-track logic, he was right where he needed to be to win that race. A few nights later in the 1,500 meters—with even more eyes on the ice, both inside the arena and on television sets around the globe—Ohno was the one coming from behind, attempting a final-lap bull rush to pass rival South Korean Kim Dong-Sung.

The pass was thwarted when Kim appeared to edge slightly into Ohno's path, prompting the younger skater to throw up his arms, either in frustration or to avoid a collision—in either case, a move that visibly slowed his pace.

Kim, by all appearances, had held off Ohno's charge, winning the gold medal. He grabbed his nation's flag and was skating at center ice in triumph when the fateful announcement was made on the arena intercom:

"Ladies and gentlemen, we have a disqualification."

Kim was disqualified for cross tracking, or blocking the attempted pass by Ohno, who was awarded the gold medal.

It was a night that still lives in the memory of short-track fans, many of whom trace their interest in the sport to that night. Ohno's frustrated arm thrust on that last lap became a source of lasting national angst in South Korea, a nation whose many short-track fans to this day see it as playing—successfully, if that's the case—to the officials to win a battle he couldn't win on the ice.

The rest of the world saw it much differently. The U.S. skater's sincere postrace joy, coupled with his good sportsmanship following the earlier crash in the 1,000 meters, made an international star of Ohno. Context was a big part of this: Ohno's demeanor was a breath of fresh air at an Olympics plagued by scandal, from doping cheats in cross-country skiing to the shame of the judging scandal in the pairs figure skating contest.

And so it was that in the United States, short track become synonymous with Ohno, the sport's first true national star. This has been a good thing for the sport, because many young fans drawn to the action by the soul-patched Seattleite ultimately fell in love with the action itself. Ohno's rise to stardom—expanded beyond the realm of athletics by his participation in, of all things, a cheesy TV show, *Dancing with the Stars,* in 2007—has created new legions of fans of short-track racing.

They've learned what fans in many other nations—particularly South Korea, China, and Canada—have known for much longer: Short-track speedskating is inarguably one of the greatest pure spectator sports in all the Olympics, summer or winter.

It has all the elements: Speed, with skaters careening around a tight, oval course at upwards of 30 mph (48 kilometers per hour). Drama, with many apparent victories turning to losses via disqualifications. Athleticism, with skaters propelled by incredibly powerful bodies clinging to the ice on razor-edged skates. And, like any good speed sport, frequent carnage, as skaters lose their grips and go flying, like bodies shot from a cannon, into the sideboards, rebounding off foam pads with a thud that can be felt all the way up in the cheap seats.

On television, short track also provides a bit of hotly contested, head-to-head action, a relative rarity at any Winter Olympics, at least in the days before snowboard and skier cross.

But in person, as is often the case, it's an even greater thrill. The speeds seem faster, the falls seem nastier, and, with the benefit of being able to hear, see, and feel the action firsthand, short-track races are as exciting as anything you're likely to see under the five rings.

Short track is usually one of the first events to sell out in pre-Games ticket sales. And the races often provide some of the more memorable moments of any Winter Games. Thus, one of the Winter Games' youngest sports has also proved one of its more popular.

But it hasn't lived up to expectations in every way.

A lot of short-track insiders in the United States expected Ohno's skyrocketing popularity to translate into increased interest—and increased success—by a new generation of young American skaters. Ohno's post–Salt Lake performances only fueled this expectation: He repeated as overall World Cup champion, then won three more medals at the 2006 Turin Games, giving him five overall and tying him with Eric Heiden for the most by any male U.S. Winter Olympian.

But that expected wave of new talent hasn't materialized yet. At this writing, Ohno, in spite of great promise shown by a handful of junior racers, remains the U.S. team's only serious World Cup contender and its only solid Olympic medal favorite for Vancouver. My advice: Set the TiVo. Every time he races, something crazy happens. And every time something crazy happens, short-track Olympic speedskating gains a few million more fans.

SPECTATOR'S GUIDE

Short-track racers wear the same types of uniforms and similar skates, at least to outward appearances, as their long-track speedskating counterparts. But the similarities end there. Where long track is a graceful, fluid pursuit of speed in a race against the clock, short track is a raucous, short-strided race around a relatively tiny oval. Skaters are turning at extreme angles much of the time, and body contact, while limited by rules, is a constant part of the sport. Crashes are frequent. In long track, skaters occasionally fall, but when they do, it's usually due to their own misstep. In short track, a racer can do everything right and still get taken out in a collision by being in the wrong place at the wrong time. The sport often lives up to its billing as "NASCAR on ice." That constant, on-the-edge uncertainty is challenging for the athletes, but for spectators, it makes short track one of the most thrilling of all Olympic winter sports.

Field of Play

Short-track races unfold in the middle of what usually doubles as a hockey rink, on an oval course that's 111.12 meters (364.57 feet) around. The course is marked by small rubber pylons placed on the ice. The ice rink is ringed by thick, foam pads, designed to blunt the impact of racers who lose an edge in a turn and hurtle at high speeds into the sideboards.

Format, Rules, and Strategy

Olympic short-track racers compete in 500-, 1,000-, and 1,500-meter individual races, as well as a 5,000-meter team relay for men and a 3,000-meter relay for women. A longer individual race, the 3,000 meters, is sometimes run at the World Cup but, as yet, not in the Olympics.

Competitors are given a standing start and then race counterclockwise (skaters turn only left) in a pack around the course. The course is always the same size—only the number of laps changes with longer races.

The 500-meter sprint is only 4.5 laps long, placing greater emphasis on the start. The 1,500 meters is 13.5 laps. In that race, competitors typically lollygag off the start line, racing around slowly while measuring up the competition and jockeying for position until a sprint to the finish over the final few laps. Time is kept, but it's irrelevant: First skate across the line wins—a judgment that's sometimes not made until an instant replay can show, with a freeze frame reminiscent of a photo finish in a horse race, who got there first.

Ironically, however, the person crossing the finish line first in short track often is not the official winner. Referees can—and frequently do—penalize skaters for having interfered with or "impeded" another at some point in the race. Disqualifications are common and are a source of great frustration to racers who think they've trained for and won an Olympic gold medal, only to see it snatched away by what clearly is a judgment call.

The sport often is compared to roller derby and auto racing, but in truth, only light contact is allowed. Most of the time, skaters are crouched, sprinting down straightaways and then shifting into nearly horizontal turn positions, their knife-edged skates clinging to keep them upright as they drop a hand on the inside of the turn for balance. It's legal to place a hand down on the ice inside the course pylons while turning. It's also legal to skate outside your imaginary "lane" on the straightaways, as long as you get back in position at the start of the next turn. There, you're supposed to maintain your lane and not cut people off.

Skaters often nudge the rubber-pylon turn markers at the corners, sending the markers scur-rying across the ice, to be replaced by officials before the skaters make another lap. That's not illegal, but crossing inside the pylons with a skate is forbidden.

Spectacular falls are part and parcel of this sport. Not surprisingly, given the close distances maintained while racing, one skater losing an edge and tumbling out of a turn can cause chaos, drawing most of the rest of the pack into the same crash. Speedskaters who blow a turn are carried with huge amounts of force into the ice rink sideboards, creating an audible "WHUMP!" as their bodies are propelled into the foam padding.

Once down, a skater can get up and resume racing, but by then, it's usually too late. Normally, only in long races such as relays is it possible to recover from a fall to finish in medal position.

Because of the speed, centrifugal force, and ultrasharp steel skate blades, slashing injuries also are common. Most veteran speedskaters bear a number of scars; a few times cuts during races have caused serious injury, not to mention a fair amount of blood pooling up on the ice.

Skaters also have received serious spinal injuries from crashing into the boards. At least one has been permanently paralyzed.

All of this is simply considered part of the allure—and challenge—of the sport to competitors.

Team Relays

One of the most exciting races to watch—and one of the greatest spectacles in all of Winter Olympic sport—is the short-track team relay: 5,000 meters for men, 3,000 meters for women. At first glance, it's complete chaos: Four (and occasionally five) teams of four skaters each circle the ice, with only one designated skater from each team actually "racing" at a time. That person hands off the racing duties by skating up behind the succeeding skater, who will have mirrored the first skater's progress along the course infield for about one lap. The new skater then is literally shoved forward, from behind, by the previous skater, giving him or her a burst of speed to start a new leg of the race.

The team's other two skaters, meanwhile, mill about in the infield, awaiting their turn. The result is skaters moving all over the ice at the same time, with only four moving at top speed at any given moment. Spectators who take their eye off the leader at any point often lose track of who's ahead of the pack, as skaters tend to spread out and even lap some other teams during the long race (45 laps, in the case of the men's contest).

This is another one of those Olympic sports best watched live: A TV view gives you no real appreciation of all the activity spread across the ice rink at any given time.

Training and Equipment

Short-track racers appear suited up for battle: They wear skintight stretch suits, helmets, goggles, gloves, and skates with extremely long, razor-sharp blades canted to the left. They are intensely trained all-around athletes, employing the usual battery of aerobic and resistance training, with added emphasis on lower-body strength. To get it, short trackers

Korea's Jeon Da-Hye falls in the first turn of the 3,000-meter relay at the 2006 Turin Games.

will undergo training many other athletes would consider torturous, such as hopping up mile-long flights of steep steps on one leg or the other, to the point of exhaustion. Skaters also need lightning-quick reflexes to adjust to the unpredictable spills and turns of sport.

HISTORY'S HITS AND MISSES

Short-track speedskating is still one of the newest Winter Games sports. Although a previous form of "pack" speedskating around a long course found its way into the Games as early as 1932, the modern form of short track was first a demonstration event at the Calgary Olympics in 1988. It earned medal status for the first time in 1992 at Albertville, where only the men's 1,000 meters and 5,000-meter relay and the women's 500 meters and 3,000-meter relay were run. The schedule reached its full present complement of eight medal events at Salt Lake City in 2002.

A Real-Life International Incident

Apolo Anton Ohno's much-ballyhooed gold medal by default in the Salt Lake Games set off bad blood between South Korea and the United States that continued to simmer for years. Ohno received online death threats in the wake of the event. In the skittish climate of the Salt Lake Games, coming, as they did, only months after the September 11, 2001, terror attacks, the result was an immediate security clampdown: Ohno speaks of being placed under constant guard for the remainder of the Games.

At the same time, angry Korean fans flooded Olympic websites with so much Ohno ire that the servers crashed for several days.

The scandal, which went nowhere, officially, after a South Korean protest was declined by authorities, continued to burn in Korea the next year. It spilled over publicly at a World Cup soccer match

the next June, when Korean players, after fighting to an upset draw with the United States in Taegu, celebrated by aping speedskater motions, a reference to the Ohno scandal.

Koreans also were irked the following year, when Ohno declined to attend a Korean World Cup event because of security concerns. When he did return to the nation for a World Cup meet in 2005, he described being greeted at the airport by a phalanx of security police called in to protect him. Thankfully, it all proved to be overkill. Ohno was largely treated politely by fans, won two events at the World Cup meet, and seemed to win over local fans, who appreciated his raw ability.

The hatchet appeared to be buried, finally, in Italy. On the final night of short-track racing at the Palavela in Turin, Ohno surprised everyone by winning the 500 meters—not his strongest race—by leading from start to finish. Hours later, the United States finished third in the team relay, a race won by South Korea. At the medals ceremony, members of the Korean squad embraced their U.S. competitors—Ohno included.

Some fans were surprised, but they probably shouldn't have been. Most of the rancor directed at Ohno from Korea was generated by fans of the sport, not competitors, all of whom know that officials' calls routinely change the outcome of short-track races. Even on the big stage of the Olympics.

Nailing the Start

In that 500-meter race in Turin, Apolo Ohno leapt into the lead, which he never lost, with what appeared to be a perfect start—perhaps too perfect. Replays suggested that Ohno, who left the line like an arrow shot from a crossbow, might have taken off a fraction ahead of the start gun. If he did, he got away with it, claiming his fifth overall Winter Games medal, leaving him tied with Eric Heiden for the most by an American man.

Apolo Anton Ohno reacts to winning a gold medal in the 500-meters race at the 2006 Turin Games.

China's Meng Wang celebrates her gold medal in the 500 meters at the 2006 Turin Games.

"I was just waiting for him to make even just one mistake—a little one," said Francois-Louis Tremblay of Canada, the eventual silver medalist. He's still waiting.

Remarkably, because of his previous history of races decided by referees' decisions, it was the first time five-time medalist Ohno had ever actually crossed the finish line first in an Olympic race.

Blood on the Ice

The aforementioned Steven Bradbury of Australia is legendary in short-track circles, and not just because of his improbable gold medal at Salt Lake City. In Salt Lake, he described for reporters a 1994 World Cup race in Montreal, where he was in a three-skater pileup on the boards that launched him into the air and then dropped him down atop a competitor's knife-sharp skate. "Impaled" is the word he uses to describe it.

The accident left him with 111 stitches—and a literal brush with death.

"I lost four liters of blood—of the six liters I have," he said. "I guess I was very lucky to be alive. It was a very scary moment in my life."

One Too Many Yangs

When your nation is home to more than a billion people, all sorts of seemingly mathematically improbable stuff can happen. Like: You wind up with two star short-track speedskaters, both named Yang Yang, on the same national team. Coaches, to keep them straight, placed designations after their names. Thus, the Yang Yang who would go on to become China's first Winter Games gold medalist by winning the 500 meters in Salt Lake City was dubbed Yang Yang (L), which stood for "large," because she was older than her namesake, who was dubbed Yang Yang (S), for "small."

Yang Yang (L) reportedly balked at the implication of going through life with a supersize designation. So she changed her calling card to Yang Yang (A), which she's kept ever since, even after the retirement of Yang Yang (S). For the record, Yang Yang (A) was never large. Just fast. She is one of three Chinese women to achieve the feat of winning five career Olympic medals in short track.

A Long-Forgotten Scandal Shapes Two Olympic Careers

Ironically, the Ohno escapades might never have happened if an arbitrator's decision had gone another way early in his career.

At the December 2001 short-track Olympic trials in Utah, Ohno was on top of his game. By the time the qualifying race for the 1,000 meters came along, Ohno had won every race he entered and had long ago qualified for his first Olympics, where he was considered a favorite in three events.

The last race will live in his mind for a long time. In it, close friend Shani Davis, who stood eighth going into the event, needed not only to win the race but also to beat his close friend, Ohno, and teammate Rusty Smith, who also had already qualified for the Olympics. If he did so, he could earn the sixth and final spot on the Olympic team and thus make history

as the first African-American skater to do so.

Davis wound up winning the race and qualifying for the team. But only, charged competitor Tommy O'Hare, who was bumped from the Olympic team because of Davis's surprise finish, because Ohno and Smith intentionally sandbagged the race, trailing happily along behind Davis and letting him win. Referees on the scene were quoted as saying they believed the race was fixed. Veteran journalists familiar with the sport at an international level agreed: Ohno had mailed it in, never attempting to win. Another skater even reported Ohno telling Smith "Don't pass" once Davis took the lead.

By rule, referees who believe a race is fixed have the right to order the race rerun. But they didn't do so.

O'Hare filed a complaint with the speedskating federation. An arbitrator, one month before the Olympics, ruled that there was insufficient evidence to support his charge that the race was fixed. The matter was dropped, and Ohno—who finally admitted that he'd held back in the race, but said he did so only to avoid collisions, and thus injury—became a star in Salt Lake.

To this day, it's unclear what Ohno's motivations were. It may be that he was, indeed, simply trying to help a friend but never considered the possible consequences until after the fact. Had the arbitration gone the other way, Ohno could have been left off the Olympic team himself, and American speedskating history would have been forever altered.

Davis went to Salt Lake as a member of the short-track team, essentially as an alternate, but never set foot on the ice in competition. He left before the Games ended to compete in the world junior long-track championships in Italy, where he won the 1,500 meters and began to chart his new course.

Never accused of being part of, or even aware of, any conspiracy to wrongfully place him on the Olympic team, Davis nonetheless was stung by the "cheater" implication and later said that he used the controversy to motivate himself. He continued to train for short track, but quickly proved to be the rare athlete who could compete at an elite level in both short- and long-track skating.

The latter proved to be his calling. By the time the 2006 Olympics rolled around, Davis had set numerous long-track world records but still attempted to qualify for the Turin Games as a short-track racer as well. He failed, but lived up to his billing on the long track, winning a gold in the 1,000 meters and a silver in the 1,500 meters in Turin, and removing any doubt that he was, and likely still is, one of fastest humans alive on the ice.

RECORD BOOK: SHORT-TRACK SPEEDSKATING

If there is an official Big Book of Olympic Short-Track Medals, it's kept under lock and key somewhere in Seoul. With brief and notable incursions from the United States, Canada, and China, South Korea has owned short-track speedskating at the Olympic Games, mirroring its dominance of the fast-action sport on the World Cup level.

When the final tallies from Turin were made in 2006, South Korea was left with 29 overall medals—17 golds, seven silvers, and five bronze. Tied for second place were China and Canada, with 20 overall medals, followed by the United States with 12. From there, it drops off precipitously, to France's four overall medals.

Men's Short-Track Record Book

On the men's side, South Korea's **Kim Ki-Hoon** got his nation off to a big start, repeating as gold medalist in the 1,000 meters at both Albertville in 1992 and Lillehammer in 1994. He was followed at the top of the podium by countryman **Kim Dong-Sung,** who captured gold in Nagano in 1998.

None of them, however, compare to South

Korea's **Ahn Hyun-Soo,** who was shut out as a youngster at the 2002 Salt Lake Games but returned four years later to claim four medals at the Turin Games: gold in the 1,000 and 1,500 meters and the 5,000-meter team relay, and bronze in the 500 meters. South Korea's **Lee Ho-Suk** is another three-time medalist, claiming gold in the team relay in Turin and silver in the 1,000 and 1,500 meters at the same Olympics.

China's most medaled skater is **Li JiaJun,** with silvers in the 1,000 meters at Nagano and the 1,500 meters in Salt Lake City and bronze in the Nagano and Salt Lake relays and the 1,500 meters at Turin.

America's **Apolo Anton Ohno,** competing in just two Olympics, has already claimed five medals. He won gold in the 1,500 meters and silver in the 1,000 meters at Salt Lake City in 2002, and gold in the 500 meters and bronze in the 1,000 meters and team relay at Turin in 2006. Longtime teammate **Rusty Smith** has two medals: bronze in the 500 meters at Salt Lake City and bronze in the relay in Turin.

Canada has produced its own multimedalists: **Marc Gagnon** leads the pack with five: gold in the relay in Nagano and in the relay and the 500 meters in Salt Lake, bronze in the 1,000 meters at Lillehammer in 1994 and in the 1,500 meters at Salt Lake City. Gagnon was his nation's most decorated Winter Olympian until 2006, when Canadian long-track speedskater **Cindy Klassen** won her sixth medal in Turin. **Eric Bedard** is a four-time medalist, with golds in the relay at Nagano and Salt Lake City, silver in the relay at Turin, and a bronze in the 1,000 meters at Nagano. **François-Louis Tremblay** claimed gold in the team relay at Salt Lake and bronze in the 500 meters and team relay in Turin. **Mathieu Turcotte** has a gold (team relay, Salt Lake City), silver (team relay, Turin), and bronze (1,000 meters, Salt Lake City). **Jonathan Guilmette** won gold in the relay in Salt Lake and silver in the relay and the 500 meters in Turin.

Women's Short-Track Record Book

On the women's side, America's **Cathy Turner** led the U.S. women's parade—and a short one it proved to be—by winning consecutive gold medals in the 500 meters at Albertville in 1992 and Lillehammer in 1994. Her teammate **Amy Peterson** won bronze in the 500 meters at the 1994 Games.

China's **Chun Lee-Kyung** is a five-time medalist, with four golds and a bronze at the Lillehammer and Nagano Games. Matching the feat more recently was **Yang Yang (A),** with golds in the 500 and 1,000 meters at Salt Lake City, silver in the relay at both Nagano and Salt Lake City, and bronze in the 1,000 meters at Turin. Her teammate and namesake, **Yang Yang (S),** is another five-time medalist, with four silvers and a bronze at the Nagano and Salt Lake Games. **Meng Wang** won gold, silver, and bronze in the 500 meters, 1,000 meters, and 1,500 meters, respectively, at Turin.

South Korea's **Jin Sun-Yu** starred in her country's overpowering performance at Turin, winning three gold medals—in the 1,000 and 1,500 meters and the relay—at the same event. Her teammate **Choi Eun-Kyung** is a four-time medalist, with gold medals in the relay at Salt Lake City and Turin and silvers in the 1,500 meters at both of the same Olympics.

Stocky, powerful **Evgenia Radanova** of Bulgaria is a rarity—a three-time medalist from Europe, having won silver in the 500 meters at both Salt Lake City and Turin and bronze in the 1,500 meters at Salt Lake.

Short-track speedskating and figure skating will share the remodeled Pacific Coliseum in Vancouver for 2010 Olympic competition.

NEXT STOP: PACIFIC COLISEUM

Location: Hastings Park, Vancouver, B.C.
Spectator capacity: 14,239
Elevation: 26 meters (85 feet)
Other events: Figure skating
Medal ceremonies: B.C. Place Stadium

See the Figure Skating chapter for a description of this venue.

Short-Track Speedskating 2010 Schedule

February 13: 500-meter women, qualifying
February 13: 3,000-meter relay, women, qualifying
February 13: 1,500-meter men
February 17: 1,000-meter men, qualifying
February 17: 5,000-meter relay, men, qualifying
February 17: 500-meter women, finals
February 20: 1,500-meter women
February 20: 1,000-meter men, finals
February 24: 1,000-meter women, qualifying
February 24: 500-meter men, qualifying
February 24: 3,000-meter relay, women finals
February 26: 500-meter men, finals
February 26: 1,000-meter women, finals
February 26: 5,000-meter relay, men, finals

Opposite: Austrian ski legend Hermann Maier cuts a turn in a race at Beaver Creek, Colorado.

PART TWO

SNOW SPORTS

ALPINE SKIING

❄ ❄ ❄ ❄ ❄

You know they're going fast. You know they're turning sharp. You know they're hanging it all out there. But you really don't appreciate *how* fast or *how* sharp or *how* far out there until you're on the snow next to them.

That's a lesson my friend and fellow ringhead (Olympic journalist) Elliott Almond and I learned one day long ago on the slopes of Mount Hood.

It was a sunny day in July in 1997, and skiers were making tracks all over the Palmer Glacier high on the side of the mountain. Thanks to its high elevation and cold temperatures, the alpine ski venue is open all summer, and on this day, it would serve as a launching pad for Picabo Street, recovering from a crash at Vail, Colorado, that basically destroyed her knee.

She was, I noted at the time, at risk of becoming just an asterisk in U.S. ski history. Yes, she'd won nine World Cup downhills and consecutive downhill titles, not to mention a silver medal at the Lillehammer Games. And sure, she was the solitary flare shot up from the sinking ship that was the U.S. ski team in the long dry spell of the post–Phil Mahre era.

But her most impressive asset—an ability to hurtle down mountainsides at 90 mph with absolutely no fear, in spite of a couple of horrendous injuries—was now at risk. Ski racers who run the speed events, downhill and super-G, know only one speed: borderline reckless. The best of the best can hang their chin right out over their ski tips and simply fly, shutting off that primeval part of the brain that says, "Stop or you're gonna die."

At some point in their careers, most of them suffer the dreaded knee blowout. And only a few of them make it all the way back. Physical recovery is difficult. The mental part is even tougher, the body having this quaint thing about not wanting to repeatedly flirt with death.

So Elliott and I were here to watch the legend get back on skis for the first time and see how she looked. We were there to check in on the legend, to proclaim it alive and flying or dead on arrival.

We got there a little early, rode up the Palmer Glacier lift, and stood in the shadow of a lava rock, shivering. Street showed up in a red wool "A-Squad" ski-team vest, said a few words to us and a

TV crew attempting to stand there on the slope, and then did what Picabo does when you put her on the side of a mountain.

Disappeared.

We watched her big Rossignols point toward Timberline Lodge, make a couple of quick turns, and then point straight downhill. She was gone before we could look at each other. I stood there for a second, stunned. This wasn't a ski racer in top form. It was a top ski racer just getting off her sickbed.

When you see it live, the speed carried by downhillers is phenomenal. When they pass close by at full pace, you actually feel the suction they create by slicing through the wind, their skis issuing a thrilling *pfffft!* as they cross the snow at jet speed.

At the bottom, Picabo declared her first runs back a success, saying it felt good, and then she started talking about the World Cup and cut to the chase: "I want my title back."

She was serious, and she went for it. Alas, the World Cup crown was never again in the cards for Picabo, the Triumph, Idaho, daughter of hippie parents who captured the world's attention when she came from nowhere to win a medal in Lillehammer.

She competed strongly at the World Cup that season but was not a favorite to repeat her medal performance at Nagano, only 14 months after her potentially career-ending injury. So all she did was go out and win a gold medal in the super-G.

Watching Street's recovery, her unforgettable gold medal run, and then her resiliency as she overcame injuries from another, even more destructive, crash a year later, turned a lot of people into fans of Picabo Street—and, by extension, of ski racing.

Once you get up close and personal with the sport, it's easy to see why alpine skiing is the signature snow sport of any Olympics, and why the downhill is perhaps its marquee event.

It's spectacular for spectators, with full-camera coverage on race courses bringing the astonishing

Picabo Street exults over her gold-medal performance in the super-G at the 1998 Nagano Games.

speed and strength of alpine racers into viewers' living rooms. It's also extremely user friendly: No complicated rules to understand. No French judges to be bribed by corrupt Russians. Just the fastest one down the hill wins.

It's also downright dangerous.

Alpine skiing is a sport with little margin for error. It's a knife-edge balance between being just in control and just out of it, the latter condition often leading to severe injuries and, in rare but persistent cases, even death.

The greatest practitioners of the sport are equal parts precise and maniacal, the results often unforgettable.

I think back through many years of covering ski racing, and the epic heroes of the slopes—and, especially, their performances under the Olympic rings—leap to mind: Street shocking the world in Nagano. Austrian superman Hermann Maier going airborne in the men's downhill at Hakuba during the same Games, then coming back three days later to win the super-G.

The graceful, resilient, and all-time clutch performances of Norway's Kjetil André Aamodt as he notched eight medals at four Olympics. The class and spark of Croatian phenom Janica Kostelić, whose Salt Lake Games medal four-peat stands alone as the greatest 10 days of skiing by any alpine skier, anywhere, anytime.

It is one of those sports that I usually offer up

A World Cup skier nears the finish on the Olympic super-G course at Whistler, British Columbia.

as an answer when fans ask about the don't-miss events to witness in person at a Winter Games. You simply cannot relate to the speed, daring, and thrill of the event by watching it on TV.

Most people are afraid to drive at 90 mph. Alpine skiers go that fast on wisps of metal, plastic, and wood, with only a thin speed suit separating them from trees, cliffs, rocks, and possible paralysis.

Alpine racing is as keen a test of mettle as you'll find in winter sports. And it's an undeniable cornerstone of any Winter Games.

Medals are won on ice rinks, curling sheets, skating ovals, and bobsled tracks. But it is in the mountains where legends are born.

SPECTATOR'S GUIDE

Modern alpine ski events in the Olympics mirror those of the World Cup, a winter-long series of races organized and controlled by the International Ski Federation, or FIS. The races are the downhill, slalom, giant slalom, super-G, and alpine combined.

Field of Play

One of the allures of downhill skiing is its great diversity of venues. No single ski race is ever the same from one locale to another, simply because they're competed on mountainsides, each of which is unique. Ski races typically unfold on the slopes of established ski areas: A giant swath of the ski terrain is essentially roped off, from top to bottom. From there, course setters—often former ski racers well versed in the sort of turns, jumps, and terrain transitions skiers can physically make—choose a path down the mountainside, marking it with "gates," made of fiberglass poles inserted into the snow. Placement and distance between the gates varies widely depending on the type of race.

In addition to the wild-card element of varying topography, weather and snow conditions play perhaps a larger role in ski racing than in any other winter sport.

Weather can change dramatically during a race. An approaching warm front can turn a fast, icy course to soft and mushy between the time the first racer and 20th racer take the course. Visibility also can change quickly and dramatically.

Sometimes, where you start (in a race starting order is determined by a draw; second runs are usually run in reverse order of finish from the first run, with the fastest first-run competitors skiing last) may be every bit as important as how you perform: Conditions conducive to very fast times for early starters might become impossible to match later on. This is the crapshoot element of this and other alpine sports. Unlike their ice-based rivals, snow sports remain firmly under the control of the elements.

Format, Rules, and Strategy

The downhill and super-G are known as "speed" events, while the slaloms fall into the "technical" skiing category. Combined is a mixture of both. Most skiers excel at one category or the other. Only the choicest few can lay down winning times in both disciplines. And they become the masters of the international ski-racing universe.

The **downhill,** one of the most gripping events in alpine skiing, has become a signature competition for the Olympics, thanks to some memorable performances. It's one of the true gut-check events in competitive sports, with skiers hurtling at speeds approaching 90 mph (145 kilometers per hour), often barely under control, down mountainsides for long distances.

It's also one of the easiest races to follow for spectators: It's one run only, and the fastest one down wins. Races are timed to within one hundredth of a second, and that's sometimes the margin of victory over a course that takes more than 2 minutes to run. Tiny mistakes, needless to say, are magnified, and can mean the difference between gold and a bottom-20 finish.

LEGEND OF THE SPORT
JANICA KOSTELIĆ, CROATIA, ALPINE SKIING

Born: 5 January 1982, Zagreb, Croatia
Olympics: Nagano, Salt Lake City, Turin
Medals: 4 gold, 2 silver

She looked for all the world like Pippi Longstocking in a race suit.

That's the first impression, seared onto my brain, of the Croatian Sensation, Janica (pronounced "Yah-NEET-sa") Kostelić.

It came during an America's Opening World Cup race at Park City in 1998. Kostelić, an unknown 16-year-old at the time, started in 53rd position in her first World Cup slalom and proceeded to carve up the Park City course, finishing third and landing her first trip to the podium of her young career. Race officials were caught so off guard that they didn't even have a Croatian flag to raise in honor of Janica's war-ravaged nation. She pulled one from her own ski bag for the medal ceremony.

Janica Kostelić of Croatia turned in one of the Winter Games' all-time great performances by winning four medals at the 2002 Salt Lake Olympics.

After the race, Kostelić, red-headed and pig-tailed, was bubbling over with glee. You could see the sparks fly in her eyes when she talked about ski racing, her greatest passion. She had that magical aura of a star on the rise, a young athlete who had all the magic, but none of the pretense, of a superstar.

And it was a wonder she was there at all.

As a kid growing up in Zagreb, Janica's entire national-ski-team support system consisted of her dad, Ante (a former handball coach), and her brother, Ivica, who would go on to become a world-class skier as well. The skiing family traveled around Europe to races while sleeping in their car and living on salami-and-pickle sandwiches. They scraped by, and Janica credits an Olympic scholarship, awarded by the IOC when she was 13, with making her career possible.

As I noted in a *Seattle Times* column during the Salt Lake Games:

The Kostelićs didn't have a national training center, like the Swiss, Germans, Americans, Austrians, Norwegians, and other self-impressed ski nations do. They didn't have physical therapists, sports psychologists, or loaner GMC Yukons.

They barely even had a country.

From 1945 to 1991, Croatia was part of the Soviet-bloc Republic of Yugoslavia, which included Bosnia, Herzegovina, Slovenia, Montenegro, Serbia, and Macedonia. While political turmoil swept through the region, Kostelić, growing up in a new nation of 4.6 million people, honed herself into a ski racer.

She started skiing at age nine, progressing by age 14 to the top junior racer in her region. At 16, she skied all the alpine events in the 1998 Nagano Games, posting an impressive eighth place in the combined.

The following season, Kostelić was ripping up the World Cup, winning slalom races by unheard-of margins. A potentially career-ending crash in 1999 at St. Moritz derailed her, tearing four ligaments in her right knee. But after a long, strenuous rehab, Kostelić won seven straight slaloms and her first World Cup overall title in 2000–2001, at the age of 19.

She seemed to compile injuries as readily as medals. In 2001–2002, recovering from yet another knee surgery, she skied through the World Cup season leading up to the Salt Lake Games and posted not a single victory. Then she arrived in Salt Lake and rewrote the record books.

Back at the site of her first World Cup podium finish, Kostelić, then 20, literally took over the women's alpine ski program. From my dispatches at the time:

Kostelić, on a gimpy knee, came to Utah's vaunted steep, deep slopes—and pared them like a laser knife through meringue. Nothing, it turned out, could stop the dynamo from Zagreb.

Kostelić has skied on all types of snow in all kinds of weather on four courses against 100 opponents—and destroyed them all.

She began the Games by winning the alpine combined (slalom and downhill), one of the true tests of a skier's overall ability. She won the super-G under sunny skies, then plowed through heavy, wet crud to win the slalom under impossible conditions at Deer Valley.

Yesterday, as she laid down another of her trademark smooth, powerful runs in springlike conditions at Park City Mountain Resort, Kostelić entered the Olympic history books, just ahead of a couple of legends. The grand slalom gold medal was her third gold and fourth medal of the Games—unprecedented for an alpine skier. Jean-Claude Killy of France and Toni Sailer of Austria were the only other skiers to win three golds in a single Olympics.

"I didn't have any pressure," she said, explaining her performance and beaming with a grin that can light up a train tunnel. "Maybe that was it, because I felt really relaxed—especially after my first medal."

I've never seen an athlete, in any sport, in more of a groove. I concluded:

After this magical week, Janica Kostelić's name will be branded forever across the Wasatch Front. Remember it: Here, for two sweet weeks, one of the world's great skiers took on some of the world's great mountains.

It wasn't even close.

And Kostelić wasn't close to being done. After winning the World Cup title again in 2003 and suffering yet another knee injury in 2004, Kostelić got up off the canvas again to win the gold medal in the alpine combined and silver in the super-G in Turin's 2006 Games, retiring from Olympic competition as the Games' most medaled female skier (six), the only woman to win four golds in alpine skiing, and the only woman to win four alpine medals at the same Olympics (no other woman has yet won three).

The icing on the cake: Brother Ivica won a medal of his own, a silver in the combined, at the same Turin Games.

For Janica, all that, and three World Cup titles, from the most humble beginnings imaginable. And until the last day, she still had that sparkle in her eyes whenever she clicked out of her bindings.

Injured once again, Janica retired from active racing in 2007. The sport really hasn't been the same since.

She is perhaps the best skier I've ever seen, and one of the greatest Olympians—in the true sense of the word—I've ever met.

I still wonder what's taking them so long to make the movie.

Gates for downhill courses are spaced far apart, creating wide, sweeping turns to accommodate the speed of the racers. Most courses have at least one jump, where skiers fly long distances through the air while remaining in a tucked position. As if all this weren't difficult enough, downhill offers an additional challenge: Because the courses are so long and cover such a wide range of altitudes, snow conditions can vary greatly from one part of the course to the next within a single racer's run. Skiers have to adjust their balance quickly and repeatedly to accommodate for very icy or very grippy snow.

It's notable that the downhill, because it's so dangerous (racers have been killed in spectacular crashes on the World Cup circuit), is the only alpine ski event for which training runs are allowed.

The other speed event, the **super-G** (short for super giant slalom) is similar to a downhill, except that the gates (minimum number of turns is 35 for men, 30 for women) are placed closer together and the overall course is shorter. It's also a single-run event: the fastest time wins.

In the **giant slalom,** on a course even shorter than a super-G with more closely bunched gates (alternating blue and red), skiers make more rapid, rhythmic turns down two different courses on the same slope. Typically, one run is held in the morning, the other in the afternoon, with the top 30 finishers from the first run advancing to the second. The lowest combined time of the two runs is the winner.

The **slalom,** run on a short course with gates very close together, is ski racing's most technical—that is, quick-turning—race. Slalom skiers are constantly turning between closely bunched gates (55 to 75 for men, 45 to 65 for women), usually crashing through them with their shins and forearms. As long as their skis go around the gate poles, it's all legal. But if you miss a gate, you have to go back up and around it, which means you'll be out of the

running. Slalom thus is a bit of a game of chicken with the spring-loaded gates: You want to cut as close to their base as you can, but cut it too close and you're all done. Like giant slalom, the slalom is run on two different courses on the same slope, on the same day. The lowest total time wins.

The **super combined** is a hybrid event, combining one run of downhill followed by two slalom runs, usually the following day. The times are added together, with the lowest total time winning. It's a true test of total skier ability; even those with the very fastest downhill times can't win the super combined without posting better-than-respectable times in the slalom, and vice versa.

Training and Equipment

Training for alpine racing, not surprisingly, is intensely lower-body oriented. Ski racers undergo leg-strength training that borders on brutal: everything from intensive weight and resistance training to cycling and performing nonstop, two-footed hops over tall obstacles to the point of exhaustion. Endurance is also critical, creating the need for constant aerobic work as well. The fastest racers are those who have the strength to stay in perfect form—that tight-ball tuck position at the end of the downhill is more difficult to maintain than you can possibly imagine—all the way to the finish line.

Equipment also plays a crucial role—perhaps more so than in any other Olympic sport. Fast skis—those "tuned" perfectly for the conditions by sharpening and dulling edges and using the proper type of wax—are essential. Not even the world's best skiers will win on a day where they've chosen the wrong boards for their run.

Most skiers thus travel with entire truckloads of skis suited for all manner of conditions, and the top-level racers have their own personal ski technicians, usually provided by one of the ski manufacturers signed on as sponsors. Note that ski technology has changed radically in the past 15 years. With the advent of wider, "shaped" skis that are broader at the tips and tail than the old straight-arrow skis of yore, most competitive racers are skiing on shorter skis than ever before. Whereas long racing skis of up to 215 centimeters were the norm through the 1980s, most racers are running on skis as short as the 180-centimeter range in "speed" events today, and slalom racers will be found on skis as short as 160 centimeters.

HISTORY'S HITS AND MISSES

Ask any downhill speed freak: Alpine skiing is just a natural evolution from crossing the flats. Humans figured out how to ski across flat surfaces—no doubt somewhere in Norway—thousands of years ago. But only in the past 150 years or so has that pursuit evolved into downhill skiing, using wider skis with sharp edges to gain a foothold while, in essence, making a series of quick, underfoot traverses down a steep slope.

Downhill skiing first caught on in the Alps of Europe, spreading to North America in the 1920s and 1930s when European ski instructors began emigrating to America to spread word of the "Arlberg technique" of modern, linked turns, developed in the Alps. The invention of ski lifts—modeled after banana-crane pulleys in Central America—in the late 1930s vastly increased the popularity of the sport: no more "upclimb" to get you on the "downhill."

The concept of racing on downhill skis popped into the minds of skiers just about as soon as there were enough of them to race and has been going strong ever since. The first widely recognized international downhill competition, the Roberts of Kandahar Cup, was launched in Switzerland in 1911. The first international slalom contest was held in Switzerland in 1915.

The Olympics were a logical next step. Alpine skiing was added to the program for the 1936 Garmisch-Partenkirchen Games, with an alpine combined (downhill plus slalom) for both men and women. More events were added in subsequent Games, with the first full slate of alpine events appearing in the 1948 St. Moritz Olympics. (Interestingly, alpine combined, the inaugural event, would disappear from the schedule that same year, as soon as individual slalom and downhill were added to the schedule. It did not reappear as a combined event until the Calgary Games of 1988, when the super-G was also added for the first time.)

Thrice as Nice: The Jean-Claude Killy "Shadow Man" Controversy

If you're looking for the guy who had the best single Olympics on the slopes, maybe ever, look no further than French legend Jean-Claude Killy, who won gold in the downhill, giant slalom, and slalom, all on the home slopes of Grenoble in 1968.

And it came with Killy under the sort of intense pressure only an Olympic athlete who is a prohibitive favorite in the host nation can feel. Killy, in 1968 a wiry 24-year-old Val d'Isere native—and playboy of some repute—had competed in Innsbruck in 1964, his best finish being a fifth in giant slalom. But going into the Grenoble Games, Killy had won 12 of the 16 previous seasons' World Cup races and was widely favored to capture the fabled "alpine sweep," which only Austrian Anthony "Toni" Sailer had accomplished before (in 1956 at Cortina d'Ampezzo).

Killy, whose multiple lucrative sponsorship contracts had drawn the ire of IOC officials and put his status as an amateur in jeopardy, put on bib number 14 and captured the downhill first, beating countryman Guy Périllat by eight-hundredths of a second. The second race, the giant slalom, was easier, with Killy beating Switzerland's Willy Favre by more than 2 seconds in the first Olympic grand slalom to tabulate the results of two separate runs.

The third gold, in the slalom, was and always will be controversial. On a foggy day at Chamrousse, near Grenoble, Killy, skiing 15th, led the field after the first run, only to see the fog thicken. Skiing first in the second run, he led again until a Norwegian skier finally bettered his time. Then, a miracle: The Norwegian was disqualified for missing two gates.

Only Killy's closest rival, Austria's Karl Schranz, remained a threat. But Schranz, skiing through the thick fog, pulled off the course midway through his run, never appearing at the fog-shrouded finish line. He insisted that he had seen a mysterious, shadowy figure cross his path. He was granted a second run, which was picture-perfect and 24 hundredths of a second faster than Killy's.

French fans were in an uproar as Schranz enjoyed the spoils of victory, including a center-stage spot at the postrace press conference. Hours later, however, a jury of appeal voted 3–1 to disqualify Schranz for missing two gates before the alleged man-on-the-course incident, ruling that he should not have been granted a second run. Killy was declared the winner, and Austrians, who insisted that some Frenchman really had interfered with Schranz, throwing off his timing and causing him to miss the gates, are ticked off to this day.

Schranz, accused by the French of making up the mystery-man story after missing a gate, not only didn't win but didn't get a medal. (He later insisted that he was "hypnotized" by the shadowy figure, and indeed might have missed a gate.) It ruined what would have been a rare podium sweep for Austria, as Schranz's countrymen, Herbert Huber and Alfred Matt, captured the silver and bronze that day.

Killy, of course, went on to international fame and fortune, signing dozens of global endorsement contracts and becoming the most famous ski racer in history up to that time. The Frenchman would

Jean-Claude Killy of France skied to fame— and controversy—at the 1968 Grenoble Games.

go on to serve as copresident of the organizing committee for France's next Winter Games, in Albertville in 1992, and also as an adviser to the organizers of the Turin Games, just across the Alps in Italy, in 2006.

Toni Sailer's Alpine Sweep

Austrian superstar Toni Sailer's unprecedented three-gold "alpine sweep" in 1956 will long be remembered not only because it was a first, but for the spectacular distance the Kitzbuehel native put between himself and the rest of the field in the process. Sailer, known as the "Blitz from Kitz," covered Cortina's 71-gate giant slalom course on Tondi di Faloria an astonishing 6.2 seconds faster than countryman Andreas Molterer—still the largest margin in Olympic alpine skiing history.

LEGEND OF THE SPORT
KJETIL ANDRÉ AAMODT, NORWAY,
ALPINE SKIING

Born: 2 September 1971, Oslo, Norway
Olympics: Albertville, Lillehammer, Salt Lake City, Turin
Medals: 4 gold, 2 silver, 2 bronze

Note atop the official Turin Olympics biography of Kjetil André Aamodt: *"Due to the especially long list of major performances for this athlete, some of the results are not displayed."*

It was an image of unbridled joy I'll always remember.

At the base area of the Kandahar Banchetta course above Sestriere, alpine ski base for the 2006 Turin Games, a half-dozen coaches, trainers, and teammates are throwing a man in a speed suit high into the air, whooping loudly, catching him in their arms, and then launching him upward again.

Up, down. Up, down. Whoop! Whoop!

The man is wearing a red racing suit and old-style blue Lange ski boots that look as though they've been around the block—and back. Clutched in his two hands are the top corners of the red, white, and blue Norwegian flag, which flutters in the breeze as he comes down into the arms of teammates.

He's wearing the kind of smile you get to wear only when you realize you've just entered the realm of Olympic immortality.

I remember thinking: It's very likely that some skier, somewhere, has been better in short stretches of time. But nobody has been as good for as long as Kjetil André Aamodt.

The Norwegian ski sensation, who actually lives on the Riviera in Monaco, retired from the full-time ski biz at age 35, months after that victory celebration for winning the super-G at the 2006 Turin Games.

The medal was the capper on an Olympic ski career not likely to be equaled anytime soon.

Teammates toss Norway's Kjetil André Aamodt in celebration after his stunning performance in the Mens Super-G Alpine Skiing Final at the 2006 Winter Games.

He is the only alpine skier on the planet with eight Olympic medals, the only one with four medals in one event (super-G), the first to win four golds.

Even more remarkable is his longevity: Aamodt is both the youngest (age 20) and the oldest (age 34) alpine skier to win an Olympic gold medal.

And that's just what he does *between* World Cup seasons. Over his World Cup career, Aamodt notched 21 career victories and earned 12 world championship medals. In spite of winning the overall title only once (1994), he stands first in the Marathon (cumulative points) ranking, with 13,252 points posted between 1989 and 2006. He also ranks as one of only five skiers to have won a World Cup race in each of five disciplines.

Each of his Olympic victories has its own story, but for history's sake, it's important just to post the tally:

Gold in super-G and bronze in giant slalom at Albertville, 1992. Silver in downhill and combined and bronze in super-G at Lillehammer, 1994. Gold in the super-G and combined at Salt Lake City, 2002. And then that gold in the super-G at Turin, 2006, where he edged out longtime rival Hermann Maier of Austria.

When he finally announced his retirement on Norwegian national TV, where he was receiving an award, Norway mourned. But the nation also paused to celebrate one of its greatest national heroes.

Aamodt, born in Oslo, said he grew up idolizing the great Ingemar Stenmark of Sweden, the all-time World Cup leader. Skiing ran in his family's blood: His father, Finn Dag, was a noted ski instructor, and his son was a prize pupil at a young age.

Aamodt won a junior world championship in 1990 and by 1989–90 was skiing on the World Cup circuit alongside his idol.

A key to Aamodt's success was the company he kept: He grew up racing and training with countryman Lasse Kjus, another superstar on the World Cup circuit and himself a four-time Olympic medalist. Both excelled at being versatile skiers able to race in all five alpine events, a skill few skiers possess, particularly in the modern era, where specialization is more the norm.

Asked in Salt Lake City why more skiers don't attempt it, Aamodt just smiled.

"It's hard," he said.

"It's just been that way since we started skiing World Cup when we were 18 or 19," Aamodt told CNN/*SI*. "It's difficult to say why. But I love skiing and I always try to push myself."

Many of his exploits at the Olympics came under improbable circumstances. Three months before the Albertville Games, his first Olympics, Aamodt was in the hospital with mononucleosis. Exhausted and somewhat emaciated, he returned to training within eight weeks and went on to win his first medal, in what would become his signature race, the super-G.

Likewise, his last medal came in true Aamodt bounce-back fashion. At Sestriere, Aamodt had sprained ligaments in his left knee while landing a jump awkwardly in the downhill, where he still finished fourth. The injury prevented him from defending his Olympic title in the alpine combined. Many of his fans feared the end, but in spite of the knee problem, Aamodt laid down a perfect run in the super-G—a fitting cap to a remarkable, unparalleled career.

It's one that hasn't escaped notice by the handful of younger skiers following in Aamodt's five-event footsteps.

"If you're talking about ski racing and medals, you'd have to say he's the best athlete in the world," America's Bode Miller told reporters in Salt Lake City. "I think ski racing is one of the hardest sports there is to be good at, and be good at for a long time. There are only a few guys in the history of the sport who can stay on top for that long."

Aamodt, as always, ended his career with a display of class.

"This sport has given me a lot of opportunities, and I'm very grateful for that," Aamodt told reporters. "I love this sport. I have since I was four or five years old."

Someone asked him about the key to his longevity.

"If you work hard over a long period of time, and really focus, good things will happen for you," he said.

It's just that simple. And just that hard.

Two days later, he won the slalom by 4 seconds and then took on the downhill, which almost proved his undoing. Moments before the race, Sailer broke a ski-boot strap and couldn't find a replacement until an Italian team trainer lent him his own. Then, at the top of an icy course that sent eight other skiers off on stretchers, Sailer nearly crashed, landing a jump on the tails of both skis but pulling off a split-legged recovery that kept him on course and sent him into history, winning by 3.5 seconds. He reportedly gave one gold medal to each of his parents, saving the third one for himself.

Franz Klammer:
The Banana-Suited Blur

To this day, it remains the greatest Olympic downhill run of all time.

Hometown favorite Franz Klammer of Austria, skiing before an Innsbruck throng estimated at 60,000, nipped defending champ and favored racer Bernhard Russi of Switzerland with a harrowing downhill run during which he appeared to be out of control much of the time and, a number of times, actually was.

Footage of the now-famous run—by ABC, which provided the first-ever top-to-bottom coverage of an Olympic downhill—shows the banana-yellow-suited Klammer careening all over the 3,020-meter (9,960 feet) course, posting only the third fastest split time of the day at the midway point—nineteen-hundredths of a second slower than Russi.

At that point, Klammer, in one of the great win-or-perish finishes in Olympic history, simply poured it on, taking chance after chance in a classic example of hanging it all out there and then some.

He nearly bit it near the end. On the course's final left-hand turn, Klammer went airborne and came down awkwardly on the tails of both skis at the same time. Somehow, he willed himself through the turn, and went on to make up time on the bottom of the course to nip Russi by a third of a second.

Russi, who had the top time before Klammer's run, recalled years later that, feeling the energy of the crowd in the finish area, he was torn between rooting for Klammer and for himself while the Austrian ripped down the mountain.

Klammer's honest assessment of his run? "I thought I was going to crash all the way."

Russi was the first to congratulate Klammer, aka "The Kaiser," who became such a national hero in Austria that when he was left off the national ski team four years later, a contrite team manager had to explain the decision on national television.

Flashes in the Pan—Brilliant, but Still Flashes

Alpine skiing in general—and the downhill in particular—has been a European-dominated event. But two breakout performances by Americans will long live in the world's collective ski memory.

Approaching the 1984 Sarajevo Games, the name Bill Johnson was really on no one's radar screen. What attention was paid to U.S. skiing at the time was all devoted to the Mahre twins, Phil and Steve, competing for medals in the slalom. No American man had ever won an Olympic slalom, and nobody expected that record to change in Sarajevo.

But Johnson, who had won his first World Cup downhill at Wengen, Switzerland, several weeks before the Olympics, actually posted the fastest training times on the long, mostly straight course at Mt. Bjelasnica, prompting him to boldly predict a victory. After several weather delays, Johnson went out and backed up his words, winning the downhill in true Joe Namath fashion. Johnson would never

win another major race. Attempting a comeback at age 41 in 2001, he suffered a major crash that left him in a coma and seriously injured. He recovered, but continues to battle long-term physical damage from the crash.

Equally shocking was Alaskan Tommy Moe's gold medal run in Lillehammer in 1994, especially coming, as it did, immediately after race leader and hometown hero Kjetil André Aamodt's then-first-place run. Moe won the gold by four hundredths of a second, then captured a silver in the super-G. Like Johnson, he would never again win a World Cup or Olympic race.

The Mahre Twins

By the time the Sarajevo Olympics rolled around, Washington natives Phil Mahre, the three-time World Cup champion (and, at that point, unquestionably the greatest U.S. skier of all time), and twin brother, Steve, were at the twilights of their careers. They began the Olympics poorly, finishing out of the running in the giant slalom and prompting Phil to get into a nasty tiff with U.S. journalists, who questioned how hard he was trying and, in at least one case, urged him to simply go home.

They got their revenge in the slalom, where Phil captured gold and Steve, making an all-out effort to best his brother's time and win a gold medal on his second run, hung on for second place. Later, the twins learned that they'd captured their medals while Phil's wife, Holly, had given birth to the couple's first son.

Someone asked him which was more important, the medal or his son.

"I basically told them it was a ridiculous question."

That son, Alex, went on to become an accomplished ski racer as well. The twins retired in 1985 at age 26 and today run a ski-race clinic at Deer Valley, Utah. Phil can often be found skiing at White

Pass, his home mountain near Yakima, Washington, or at Timberline on Oregon's Mount Hood.

At this writing, Phil was attempting to make a ski-racing comeback—at age 50, explaining simply, "I'm a competitor. I still have a passion for skiing."

Greene Reign

When most people think of blazing fast alpine skiers from Canada, those "Crazy Canucks" come to mind: Ken Read, Steve Podborski, Dave Irwin, and Dave Murray, who unexpectedly rose to prominence on the World Cup circuit in the mid-1970s to early '80s, posting 107 top-10 World Cup finishes from 1978 to 1984.

But of that group, widely credited with putting Canadian alpine skiing on the map, only Podborski

Canada's Nancy Greene celebrates a victory at the 1968 Grenoble Games.

would win an Olympic medal—a bronze in the downhill at Lake Placid in 1980.

The fact is that Canadian alpine skiers had been on the map for a long time, thanks to Nancy Greene. A native of Rossland, British Columbia, Greene was Canada's first great ski racer, winning gold and silver medals in the giant slalom and slalom at Grenoble in 1968 and overall World Cup titles in 1967 and 1968. She posted 13 World Cup victories in her career—still a Canadian record.

In 1999 Greene was named Canada's female athlete of the century. Today, she and her husband operate a lodge at Sun Peaks, near Kamloops, B.C., where visitors with good timing might find themselves on the chair lift next to a true skiing legend.

The Hermannator Returns from the Dead

Long after he fades from the scene, Hermann Maier, the former bricklayer from Flachau, Austria, will be the subject of many a tall tale told around an après-ski bar. "The Hermannator," as he is widely known in Europe, dominated the World Cup for three seasons in the late 1990s, winning three overall titles and ruling the circuit like no one before him, or since.

But he'll be remembered most for his performance at the Nagano Games of 1998, where Maier, in a single week, wore the cloak of both the agony of defeat and the thrill of victory.

The agony came first—in an incident now known in Austria simply as "the Sturz" (the crash). In the downhill at Hakuba, Maier came around a turn too fast (as usual) and simply went airborne. With his arms circling cartoonishly, his body seemed to just keep gaining altitude as he soared sideways down the steep slope—about 60 yards in the air—turning completely upside down in the process.

He eventually landed, with a sickening impact, on his left shoulder and head, then tumbled tail over

Hermann Maier, a legend around the world, fought back from a near-fatal motorcycle accident to win the World Cup overall title.

heels, his skis flying off, before crashing completely through two mesh crash fences.

Some people in the crowd, watching on a video monitor, feared he was dead. But Maier immediately popped up from the crater his body had created, clicked back into his skis and went down the hill, seemingly ready to race again. Three days later, he raced in the super-G and not only finished but won, by more than a half second over Didier Cuche of Switzerland. Three days after that, the patched-up Maier took to the hill again and won his second gold medal in the giant slalom.

Said Austrian teammate Hans Knauss, "He is for sure not one of us."

After a 2001 motorcycle accident that nearly destroyed one of his legs and could have killed him, Maier made another amazing recovery. He narrowly missed the 2002 Salt Lake Games, but 18 months after the crash, skiing with a foot-long titanium rod in his leg, he resumed the World Cup circuit and, incredibly, won his fourth overall World Cup title the following year.

He was on the Olympic medal stand again in 2006, claiming a silver in the super-G and bronze in the giant slalom at the Turin Games.

MEN'S RECORD BOOK: ALPINE SKIING

For North American ski racing fans, occasional standout performances by home athletes tend to obscure the fact that downhill skiing, as an event, is virtually owned by western Europeans, at least in terms of Olympic medals. This is true across all the disciplines but is even more glaring in signature events such as the men's downhill, where France, Switzerland, Austria, Germany, Italy, and Norway have combined to claim 45 of 49 total medals. The notable exceptions: A bronze by Canada's **Steve Podborski** at Lake Placid in 1980; American **Bill Johnson's** gold at Sarajevo in 1984; American **Tommy Moe's** 1994 gold at Lillehammer; and Canadian **Ed Podivinsky's** bronze the same year.

The same Euro-dominance pervades slalom, except for some notable breakout years by North Americans: In 1964 at Innsbruck, Americans **Billy Kidd** and **Jimmy Heuga** took the silver and bronze; **Phil Mahre** finished second behind the legendary **Ingemar Stenmark** of Sweden at Lake Placid in 1980 and then won, with brother **Steve** grabbing the silver, at Sarajevo in 1994.

Giant slalom has also been a European affair, with legends such as **Stein Eriksen** (Oslo, 1952), **Jean-Claude Killy** (Grenoble, 1968), **Ingemar Stenmark** (Innsbruck, 1976), and **Alberto Tomba** (Calgary, 1988, and Albertville, 1992) wearing the gold medal. **Bode Miller's** silver in Salt Lake City, 2002, was the first—and so far the only—U.S.

Slalom king Alberto Tomba helps kick off the 2006 Winter Games in his home nation of Italy.

silver in Salt Lake City, 2002; teammate **Ted Ligety** captured gold at Turin in 2006, in a race that defending Olympic champion and World Cup combined leader **Kjetil André Aamodt** of Norway sat out with a knee injured in the downhill.

Norway's **Lasse Kjus,** Aamodt, and **Harald Strand Nilson** swept the podium for the combined at Lillehammer in 1994—a rare feat for any alpine discipline. Aamodt stands as the most-decorated Olympic skier in history, with eight overall medals: gold in the super-G at Turin; gold in the super-G and combined at Salt Lake City; silver in the combined and downhill, and bronze in the super-G at Lillehammer; gold in the super-G and bronze in the giant slalom at Albertville. After winning his sixth in Salt Lake City, the affable Norwegian was asked which medal means the most. His response: "The next medal is always the nicest one." Italy's Tomba, who made history by winning the giant slalom at consecutive Olympics, is the closest male runner-up for medals; he has five.

WOMEN'S RECORD BOOK: ALPINE SKIING

In the 16 times the women's downhill has been run it has been won 13 times by a skier from Austria, Switzerland, or Germany, the only breakout performance by a North American being **Kerrin Lee-Gartner's** gold for Canada at Albertville in 1992—by six-hundredths of a second over America's **Hilary Lindh** on a course considered by many to be the longest and most difficult ever raced by women.

In the super-G, **Diann Roffe** won gold at Lillehammer in 1994, and **Picabo Street** repeated the feat at Nagano in 1998. **Karen Percy** of Canada won bronze in Calgary, 1988.

North American women have had considerably more success than the men in slalom, although none of it recently: America's **Gretchen Fraser** won the inaugural event at St. Moritz in 1948, becoming the

medal in the event. Miller, a medal favorite in three races at Turin after becoming the first U.S. male since Phil Mahre to win the World Cup overall title, finished with no medals in 2006.

In the men's combined, American Miller won

nation's first alpine skiing gold medalist. She also captured silver in the alpine combined. **Andrea Mead-Lawrence** kept the crown for America at the 1952 Oslo Games. Subsequent U.S. and Canadian slalom medalists: Canada's **Anne Heggtveit** won gold in Squaw Valley, 1960, with a silver to America's **Betsy Snite** the same year; America's **Jean Saubert** won bronze at Innsbruck, 1964; Canada's **Nancy Greene** claimed silver at Grenoble, 1968; and America's **Barbara Cochran** took the gold at Sapporo, 1972.

In the giant slalom, America's Lawrence took the gold at Oslo in 1952; **Penny Pitou** claimed silver at Squaw Valley in 1960; **Jean Saubert** won the silver at Innsbruck in 1964; and Canada's Greene won the gold at Grenoble in 1968, posting a time 2.64

seconds faster than the field for the greatest margin of victory in Olympic history. America's **Debbie Armstrong** and **Christin Cooper** finished first and second at Sarajevo in 1984, America's **Diann Roffe** won silver in Albertville, 1992, and Lake Tahoe's **Julia Mancuso** won silver at Turin, 2006.

The most-decorated female skier is **Janica Kostelić** of Croatia who captured six medals, remarkably at only two Olympics. Germany's **Katja Seizinger,** a consecutive World Cup downhill title winner (1992–1994) is the only person to win the downhill at consecutive Olympics—Lillehammer in 1994 and Nagano in 1998. Seizinger and slalom specialist **Vreni Schneider** have collected five Olympic medals apiece.

In 2006, America's Bode Miller dominated the World Cup but fizzled in the Olympics.

NEXT STOP: WHISTLER CREEKSIDE

Location: Whistler, B.C.

Spectator capacity: 7,600

Elevation: 610 meters (2,000 feet) at the base; 810 meters (2,657 feet) at the top

Other events: Paralympic skiing

Medal ceremonies: Whistler Village Celebrations Plaza

The Courses

You can forgive the alpine ski world for reacting with mixed emotions to the news that the 2010 Olympic alpine events would be run on courses at the Whistler Blackcomb resort.

Not that the mountains lacked panache or steepness, or that Whistler Village—consistently rated as the top alpine ski town in North America—might not be up to the task. The mountain had hosted a series of World Cup races, run on courses at Whistler, over the years.

That was part of the problem. Skiing's World Cup abandoned Whistler after 1995, after the latest in a long string of event washouts. Literally. Whistler's World Cups fell prey, over and over, to inclement weather, in the form of either rain, warm weather, or one of Whistler's other persistent challenges—blinding fog.

But those races came early in the World Cup schedule—in November or December, when solid, racing snow is always an iffy proposition at the resort, which sits squarely in a moist coastal, maritime weather pattern due to its low elevation—only about 610 meters (2,000 feet) at the base—and its proximity to salt water.

Opposite: A skier races for the finish line at Whistler Creekside, site of the alpine ski events for the 2010 Winter Games.

The Olympics, which come around in mid-February, are at a time in the winter when ample snow is a safe bet. Weather can still be problematic—or perfect, as was the case with a February 2008 World Cup test event. That week, a men's and women's race with slaloms, a super-G, and both a men's and a women's downhill—went off without a hitch, under sunny skies and mostly firm snow.

The courses for those races were the same as the ones to be used at the Olympics. The men's downhill course is Whistler's traditional Dave Murray Downhill, named after the noted Canadian ski racer of the 1970s. The women's course is an all-new route that basically follows Franz's Run from a start below Roundhouse Lodge.

Both courses wind up in a new finish area just above Whistler's Creekside development. Super-G and slalom races will take place on lower slopes of the same routes.

After the test event, skiers had nothing but good things to say about the course.

"It's going to be sweet," ski racer Steve Nyman of Utah said of the Olympic downhill and super-G courses. "It's going to be a rad hill."

U.S. coach Phil McNichol agreed, saying the courses are steep, fairly technical, and challenging. The women's course, in fact, is considered one of the steepest in the world—and one of the best.

"Pretty much every single coach in the world loved the downhill," said U.S. women's downhill coach Alex Hoedlmoser. "It's challenging, it's technical, there's not too much gliding . . . there's jumps, there's terrain, there's banked turns."

But everyone's still a bit on edge about Whistler's weather reputation, deserved or not.

Race organizers say plenty of wiggle room will be built into the schedule, and they point out—correctly—that weather changes are a fact of life at any Olympics. But Whistler clearly will be the lowest-elevation finish, by a lot, for any Olympic alpine venue. So a little luck may well be in order.

In any case, the '08 test run was the only one racers will get before the Games. The World Cup won't return to Whistler before the Olympics, and no races of any kind will be run on the men's downhill course.

Fans gather beneath a ski lift at Whistler Creekside to watch the world's best downhillers on a nearby course.

That's unusual. Because the race is so dangerous, race organizers usually like to give athletes a chance for a trial run on a downhill course before an Olympic Games. Some World Cup skiers suspect that in this case, the Canadian hosts are taking their vaunted Own the Podium medal-accumulation program a bit too far. Even one of Canada's top prospects, downhiller Eric Guay, didn't deny it.

"It's to give us an advantage—for once," he said, referring to the training edge usually enjoyed by European racers on their home courses.

Other officials, including former Canadian ski racer Steve Podborski, who lives in Whistler and is on the Olympic Organizing Committee, said the lack of preparatory races on the Dave Murray Downhill was just a coincidence.

Either way, the pressure will be on the Canadians to own the hill at Whistler come February 2010.

The Venue

Old-timers might remember Whistler Creekside as a patch of grass that was Whistler's first lift station as you entered the village on Highway 99. It's not recognizable as such anymore. Since the old lift at Creekside was replaced by a gondola, a mini-village has sprung up around it, with a bevy of million-dollar ski-out homes dotting the hills above it.

For the Games, this will be alpine central. Creekside, 6.4 kilometers (4 miles) from Whistler Village proper, is a fairly confined, compact area, with not a lot of elbow room. Even more challenging is the fact that the finish line and spectator bleachers are not actually at Creekside, but about a half mile, and a couple hundred vertical feet, up the hill.

Access to that area will be highly restricted—to ticketholders, race officials, and the media, all of whom will be bused there either from Whistler Village or park-and-ride lots elsewhere, such as in the town of Squamish.

American skier Lindsey Vonn, a medal favorite for the Vancouver 2010 Games, chats with reporters at the Whistler Creekside finish area after a 2008 World Cup race.

Those without tickets but fortunate enough, for whatever reason, to be inside the secured-access zone that is likely to be Whistler (locals "will be able to drive to Whistler Village," Podborski deadpans, "but they might not be able to stop") can watch the action unfold from Whistler Village itself, where large TV screens are likely to be installed.

Either way, you'll always be able to say you were there—just like the other 5.5 million people who won't be but will lie about it later.

My advice: If you're fortunate enough to have a race ticket, get there early, and bring your patience and a sack lunch. Seating will be in portable bleachers, which should accommodate about 7,600 race fans. Cowbells are mandatory, not optional.

Alpine Skiing 2010 Schedule

February 13: Men's downhill
February 14: Women's super combined
February 16: Men's super combined
February 17: Women's downhill
February 19: Men's super-G
February 20: Women's super-G
February 21: Men's giant slalom
February 24: Women's giant slalom
February 26: Women's slalom
February 27: Men's slalom

CROSS-COUNTRY SKIING AND BIATHLON

❋ ❋ ❋ ❋ ❋

If you win your nation's first cross-country skiing medal at the Olympics, and no one is there to see it, did it really happen?

That's the question Vermont native Bill Koch must have been asking at Innsbruck in 1976. Naturally, a lot of fans of cross-country skiing were on hand to witness the race that day, won by Sergei Saveliev of Russia, with Koch taking silver.

But not a single American reporter was on hand to record the scene. None. No writer, no columnist. No Jim McKay, no Lucky Pierre Salinger, not even a spare TV camera from ABC. And this was 1976, when the Winter Games were a fairly big story in America—not the media dark ages.

Later in the day, embarrassed journos had to beg Koch to put his ski suit back on and get on his skis, just for pictures.

What did it say about America's attention span when it comes to slow, plodding endurance sports like those favored by northern Europeans?

Everything.

America, a country that doesn't like to admit it's not very good at something, is decidedly not very good at cross-country skiing or biathlon, the sport's rifle-toting stepsister. Aside from that one day at Innsbruck, they never have been.

No other Winter Games sport has served up humble pie so often, and so piping hot, as the Nordic pursuits. And that poor record isn't limited to the United States. Canada, a northern nation in its own right, had a similar record of futility until the 1990s, when upstart biathlete Myriam Bédard captured three medals for Maple Leaf Nation, becoming something of a media darling. More recently, Canadian cross-country racer Beckie Scott claimed a gold medal in Salt Lake City, and teammate Chandra Crawford won another in Turin, where Scott and partner Sara Renner combined to win another silver.

But as far as North America's time on the Nordic medal stand, that's it. Period. And the grandest cross-country medal of that lot, Scott's, was won by default when the top-finishing pair of Russians was disqualified for doping. All this came long after Bill Koch's first tentative ski tracks into the snow of international greatness.

That probably explains why, on that fateful day

in '76, nobody in the main press center got on the bus to the cross-country ski venue in Seefeld. As someone who's been there, done that, I can easily imagine the conversation with editors back home:

"Okay, for tomorrow, there's the men's downhill, with Franz Klammer and Bernhard Russi and 60,000 screaming maniacs. And there's women's speedskating, with Sheila Young. Oh, and this skinny kid from Vermont is racing in cross-country skiing, a sport where the last great moral victory for America was a 15th place back in the Lake Placid Games of '32."

Use your imagination, and guess in which direction the herd moseyed on that day.

Oh, sure, we love a winner, and when a North American pulls off a breakthrough, it's big news. Too big, probably, for Koch, who, once word got out, became an instant celebrity, and the most sought-after interview in Innsbruck.

It might even have been partly responsible for his subsequent undoing.

"Suddenly, there was pressure from all sides," Koch told *Time* magazine. "Every time I competed, people expected me to win. Becoming a top contender, I soon realized, had been easy compared to staying on top."

It all took a toll on Koch. After many months of hype, Koch, who had radically changed his style and increasingly suffered from exercise-induced asthma, struggled in Lake Placid, finishing 15th in the 50-kilometer race.

He was only 24, and his career was far from over. In fact, it hadn't completely blossomed yet. Koch would go on to win the overall Nordic World Cup title—a greater achievement, for sure, than an Olympic medal—in 1982. He persevered in the sport long enough to carry the American flag at the opening ceremonies of the 1992 Winter Olympics in Albertville.

But he never won another Olympic medal, and

Bill Koch blazed trails in cross-country skiing that no other American has been able to follow.

cross-country—in spite of Koch's bold prediction about reporters: "They'll be there next time"—was pushed once more to the North American back burner.

Why?

Over the years, various experts and observers have counted the reasons. But in my mind, it really boils down to three things, each obvious if you think about it long enough:

- ◉ Nordic sports don't have the history in North America that they do in northern

Europe. In Norway, Sweden, Finland, and Russia, the predominant medal-winning nations, these sports go back 5,000 years.

- Thanks—or no thanks—to America's diversity of youth sports, there's far too much after-school competition here for any snow sports, let alone the challenging, solitary pursuits of Nordic racing, to compete. Which leads me to the biggest reason of all, namely:

- Nordic sports are too hard. We North Americans don't mind vigorous training, mind you. Nobody ever said two-a-day summer American football workouts were easy. But there's difficult and then there's mind-numbing, body-defeating, soul-crushing difficult. And the Nordic pursuits, especially the truly masochistic ones, such as the 30-kilometer (women's) and 50-kilometer (men's) distance races, are off the charts.

Something in our very constitutions—and perhaps in the national constitution itself, if you read enough of the fine print—just doesn't sit well with that. The same holds true for spectators. For whatever reason—and how this squares with the success of *American Idol* we will never know—we don't like to pay to watch people plod and suffer. And that's what athletes do in the distance events in cross-country and biathlon, not to mention other sports wildly popular in northern Europe, such as long-distance speedskating.

The Dutch literally go crazy over the latter, filling stadiums, dressing up in costumes, and fielding their own play-along oompah-loompah bands to go with the competition. Here? Not so much.

It's a Zen sport. Most of us are not Zen people.

"There is something very spiritual about cross-country skiing," Koch once said. "It really moves me. Sometimes I see it as an art form."

It's not a stretch to say he's a touch out of the mainstream on that point.

Which is why what Koch, Bedard, Scott, Crawford, and Renner accomplished is all the more remarkable. And also why we shouldn't be all that surprised that few North American athletes have followed in their footsteps. In Europe, the sport's popularity is such that an athlete can make a decent living doing it. Here, it's a solitary, thankless—and often penniless—pursuit.

With that said, it's clear that, for both the U.S. and Canada, the outlook for cross-country skiing, in particular, has improved markedly in the past decade, with a few Americans finding their way to the medal stand in World Cup events. Those are the first baby steps that often foretell Olympic success.

Will it come in the Vancouver Games of 2010, where both Americans and Canadians can feel the rare pleasure of doing their thing before a hometown audience comprising more than just blood relatives?

One thing is for sure: This time, if history is made, one of us will be there to see it. The men's 15-kilometer kicks off on February 15. And some of us are already queuing up for the bus.

SPECTATOR'S GUIDE: CROSS-COUNTRY SKIING

Cross-country skiers compete on what amounts to snow-covered trails, although the trails are nothing you'd encounter on your own out in the woods: They're carefully groomed by snowcats and measured to within the millimeter for distance.

Field of Play

Cross-country courses range from 1,500 meters to 50 kilometers. Each course must have equal parts ascending, descending, and flat ground, with the easiest part near the start and the most difficult near the midpoint. Courses less than 30 kilometers long must have a total elevation gain between 600 and

900 meters (just under 2,000 and 3,000 feet) for women, 900 and 1,200 meters (3,000 and 4,000 feet) for men.

As in alpine skiing, courses differ greatly according to topography, altitude, snow condition, and other factors. Unlike alpine skiing, the distance traveled is always the same within one race specialty, that is, a 10K race is always 10 kilometers, but the amount of elevation lost and gained can vary substantially from one course to another.

Format, Rules, and Strategy

The first thing that usually trips up the casual observer of Olympic cross-country skiing is the fact that it has two distinct disciplines: classical, where skiers take straight strides in preset parallel tracks (the common kick, pole, glide stride), and freestyle, in which skiers use a skating stride (think of a speed-skating motion on skis), pushing off on the insides of their skis, across a broader, flat track with no preset grooves. Courses for the two disciplines are the same; the snow is simply groomed differently. Skaters use a broad, flat snow surface; classical skiers keep their skis in the preformed grooves, except while passing. The skating style used in freestyle is significantly faster—about 8 percent faster in course tests—than classical and was first allowed at the Olympics in 1988. Since then, individual races have alternated between classical and freestyle, from one Olympics cycle to the next. Vancouver's individual races will be in classical style, although races such as team relays and pursuits combine both styles.

The men's events for the 2010 Olympics are the 1,500-meter sprint and team sprint, 15-kilometer individual start, 30-kilometer combined pursuit; 50-kilometer mass start, and 4x10-kilometer relay. The women's races will be the 1,500-meter sprint and team sprint, 10-kilometer individual start, 15-kilometer combined pursuit, 30-kilometer mass start, and 4x5-kilometer relay.

Unless a race is designated as having a mass start, the start order is determined by a drawing. Skiers leave at 30-second intervals and, in all races except sprints and relays, race against the clock. If a field of competitors is particularly large, some races will launch skiers two at a time, in dual tracks, at 30-second intervals. When faster skiers overtake slower ones, the slower skier must yield

Biathletes traverse the course at Soldier Hollow, Utah, site of the 2002 Winter Games biathlon and cross-country ski races.

the right of way if an approaching skier yells "Track!" from behind.

The race formats:

Mass-start races begin with skiers lined up across the start line, in rows. The first one across the finish line wins.

Individual-start races begin with skiers released at 15- or 30-second intervals. The fastest time wins.

Sprints are a single-elimination tournament. Skiers start at 15-second intervals, and time trials narrow the initial field down to 16 skiers, who are grouped into four heats. The top two finishers in each heat advance. In the final, four semifinalists compete against one another for the three medals. Sprints were added to the Olympics in 2002.

Team sprints consist of semifinals and final rounds. In the semifinals, 10 or more teams of two skiers (skier A and skier B) alternate to race the relay three times each. The fastest five teams qualify for the final and race to the finish line. This event debuted at the Olympics in 2006.

The *combined pursuit,* as the name implies, combines a classical and freestyle race. The classical race—usually 10 or 15 kilometers—is first. Skiers stop at the midpoint and change into skating boots and skis. They're then restarted for the freestyle race—also usually 10 or 15 kilometers—in a staggered start according to their finish times in the classical race. Example: A skier with a 10-second lead at the end of the first race begins with a 10-second head start in the second, hence the "pursuit." This allows the first skier across the finish line in the second race to be the overall winner, making the race a much more fan-friendly event, especially in the case of close finishes. Note: In the early Olympic years for this race, 1992–1998, the combined pursuit was run on separate days. It then morphed in 2002 into two races on the same day, with a substantial gap in the middle. By the 2006 Turin Games, it had changed to

two races run consecutively, with only a short break.

Relay races are similar to track and field relays. One skier finishes and tags the next with his or her hand to send them on their way. The relay has a mass start. The first two stages are skied classical, the last two freestyle.

Race strategy is all about timing, and knowing when to expend energy and when to conserve. Cross-country skiing is a grueling sport, the most aerobically challenging of any in the world. Pacing is the key to longer events, while fast starts and impeccable technique are crucial to sprint races. In longer races, drafting behind competitors until an optimal passing time occurs is a strategy often employed by savvier competitors.

Training and Equipment

Cross-country skiers, particularly the distance racers, are widely considered the world's best-conditioned athletes. The sport requires incredible endurance, a combination of upper and lower body strength, and abnormal aerobic capacity. Because skiers use their upper bodies in harmony with their legs, they consume far greater quantities of oxygen than, for example, marathon runners or even track sprinters. And there's another requirement: a substantial and unusual tolerance for pain.

Training usually consists of daily running, cycling, roller skiing, snow skiing, weight lifting, and other endurance, aerobic activities.

The "skinny skis" of cross-country racing are extremely lightweight, usually constructed of a combination of wood and carbon fiber. The skis used for the classical style of cross-country are rigid, with more camber than skate skis, and have a more sharply upturned tip. Freestyle or skate skis have a wider shovel and generally are significantly shorter. In both cases, boots are attached to ski bindings only at the tip, allowing a full striding motion. Classical-style boots are shorter, allowing better ankle movement. Freestyle boots have higher ankle cuffs usually surrounded by a rigid exoskeleton to provide better torsional strength to accommodate the skating motion used in this style of skiing.

Ski racers wear one-piece bodysuits, lightweight hats, and gloves, and use poles made of graphite and/or Kevlar. Skate-skiing poles are typically stronger than classical ones, due to the greater amount of weight placed on them during push-off.

The key to the entire system, however, is something you'll never see: wax. For classical skiing, technicians apply glide wax to the underside of the tips and tails and a grip wax below the binding. This allows the ski to bite into the snow when the skier places his or her weight on the center of the ski while pushing off. For skate skis, glide wax is applied to the entire ski, because the skier pushes off the edges of the ski, not the flat center of the base.

Just which wax to use under what conditions is the challenge. Many a great ski racer has seen his or her race—and his or her Olympic career—go down the tubes due to a bad wax choice. Once you've started, there's no time to switch, and rules prevent doing so even if you could. The world's top ski teams protect their wax additives and application rules like closely guarded national secrets. In a sense, they truly are.

SPECTATOR'S GUIDE: BIATHLON

Biathlon combines cross-country skiing and target shooting in a unique combination of raw physical strength and fine motor skills.

Field of Play

Courses for biathlon, skied predominantly in the freestyle fashion, are very similar to cross-country courses. In fact, many of the courses are shared. The difference, obviously, is that biathlon courses, instead of looping through a grandstand area with an open oval during the middle of the race, enter a shooting range where the skier must stop, remove his or her rifle from a sling, and fire shots from standing and prone positions.

As in cross-country racing, biathlons are broken into individual starts, group starts, sprints, relays, and pursuits. Men's events at the 2010 Games are the 10-kilometer sprint, 12.5-kilometer pursuit, 15-kilometer mass start, 20-kilometer individual, and 4x7.5-kilometer relay. Women's events are the 7.5-kilometer sprint, 10-kilometer pursuit, 15-kilometer individual, 12.5-kilometer mass start, and 4x5-kilometer relay.

Format, Rules, and Strategy

In the shooting portions of biathlon races, athletes alternate between standing and lying chest down on the ground to shoot a small-bore rifle at targets 50 meters away. For standing shots, targets—round black dots—are about the size of a compact disc. For prone shots, they're about the size of a silver dollar. Biathletes know instantly when they've hit one, because the black surface turns white.

For every shot that misses the target, a distance or time penalty is assessed (usually one minute or once around a 150-meter penalty loop near the shooting range). The biathlete with the lowest ski time, start to finish, is the winner.

The challenge is obvious: It's difficult enough to hit small targets, given difficulties such as temperature, wind, and light conditions, in outdoor shooting ranges when rested. But biathletes enter the shooting range breathing extremely heavily, and they must slow their heart rate and chest contractions enough to shoot at small targets half a football field away. The sport, a throwback to ancient hunting techniques and military training, allows athletes to shave time by taking fewer breaths between rifle shots. But doing so risks missing the target, which leads to penalty laps.

LEGEND OF THE SPORT
BJØRN DÆHLIE, NORWAY, CROSS-COUNTRY SKIING

Born: 19 June 1967, Elverum, Norway
Olympics: Albertville, Lillehammer, Nagano
Medals: 8 gold, 4 silver

You could call him the Michael Jordan of cross-country skiing, but that would be a bit of an insult. Somehow, the notion of any basketball player doing what Bjørn Dæhlie did—excel at grueling cross-country races ranging from short sprints to 30-mile death marches over a two-week period against the best athletes in the world—seems laughable.

A nine-time world champion, Dæhlie virtually owned the sport in the 1990s, winning 12 Olympic medals, eight of them gold. He is the most decorated athlete in the history of the Winter Games—a feat made even more remarkable because his Olympic career was a relatively short six years. He retired in 2001 at the age of 33.

But he will live on in Olympic lore, not just for all that hardware but for the valor he displayed in acquiring it. Few of Dæhlie's trips to the medal stand came easily, and

Norwegian cross-country ski legend Bjørn Dæhlie won eight gold medals in Olympic Games from 1992 to 1998.

some came as the result of classic battles that will go down in Games history.

His medal haul began at the Albertville Games of 1992, when he and teammate Vegard Ulvang broke a 16-year Norwegian medal drought, each winning three gold medals and one silver for a full Norwegian sweep of the men's events. With the Lillehammer Games looming only two years away, Dæhlie and Ulvang, training partners who considered themselves brothers, were megacelebrities in Norway.

They didn't dominate on their home snow the way they had in France. But Dæhlie didn't disappoint. Ulvang, fighting injuries and depressed after the recent death of his brother, won only a silver in the relay. But Dæhlie again raced all five events, winning two gold and two silver medals.

A highlight of those Games was the relay, in which Norway's team, led by Dæhlie and Ulvang, engaged in an epic battle with Italy in front of a crowd of more than 100,000 screaming fans. The final leg was skated by Dæhlie and Italy's Silvio Fauner, who drafted close behind the Norwegian legend for much of the distance. With neither skier wanting to take the lead into the finish area, both nearly stopped at one point. As they exited the final turn, Fauner finally passed, and the two raced hip to hip for the final 100 meters, with Fauner winning by four tenths of a second—about one ski length. The massive Norwegian crowd couldn't help but applaud what is considered to be one of the great cross-country races of all time.

That battle, incredibly, was revisited four years later in Nagano, where Dæhlie and Norway came looking for revenge. Both teams started poorly, but Italy had moved into first by the halfway point, with Norway trailing by 12 seconds. Dæhlie, skiing third, erased that deficit and put Norway into the lead for the final leg, skied by Thomas Alsgaard. Italy's Fauner, again skiing the anchor leg, pulled into the lead late in the race, but this time it was Alsgaard who would pass at the last moment, winning by the tip of a ski (officially, three tenths of a second) to give Dæhlie his seventh gold medal.

The other races at Nagano were a struggle for the Norwegian. He chose the wrong wax for the 30 kilometers, finishing 20th. He came back to win the 10 kilometers, then took a silver in the pursuit before racing the relay. His final Olympic race would prove to be his most difficult: In the 50 kilometers, later described by Dæhlie as the most difficult of his life, he hung on to win by 8.1 seconds, with a time of 2 hours, 5 minutes, and 8.2 seconds. At the finish line, he collapsed and was unable to stand for 5 minutes as the second-place finisher, Niklas Jonsson, collapsed next to him.

Lying there, Jonsson was seen whispering something to the Norwegian great. Jonsson later said he had asked Dæhlie, "Why didn't you go 9 seconds slower?"

Dæhlie's eight gold medals, 12 total medals, and ninth medal in an individual event all stand as Olympic records. He is tied with speedskater Lydia Skoblikova of Russia with six gold medals in an individual event.

Similarly, biathletes often attempt to slow their heart rates by slowing down and "easing in" to the shooting range (they shoot two to four times, depending on the race distance), which typically improves marksmanship. But if they slow down too much, they risk being left behind in total cumulative time.

It's a fine balance, and biathlon is one of the few sports that utilizes both the aerobic-churning power of large muscle groups and the fine-motor skills of the hands and eyes. Psychological toughness comes into play as well: Skiers who miss targets during the shooting phase leave for their next arduous ski lap feeling bummed out. It's tough to rally from a poor rifle performance.

This is clearly not a sport for the faint of heart, which explains why many modern biathletes are active members of the military with special training regimens.

Training and Equipment

Biathletes' training is similar to that for cross-country skiers, but they face the added obstacle of having to adjust their heart rates at regular intervals along the course. Athletes thus focus on speed of recovery after skiing prescribed distances—a goal that can be carefully measured in a sports lab using treadmills and heart-rate monitors.

Biathletes use the same skis, poles, and suits as freestyle cross-country ski racers. Skis have to be at least as tall as the athlete minus 4 centimeters. Poles must not be longer than the athlete's height.

The .22 caliber rifle is lightweight and usually uses a five-bullet magazine. It's carried in a long sling over the skier's back.

HISTORY'S HITS AND MISSES

Here's a shocker: Cross-country skiing, or Nordic skiing, began up in those cold Nordic nations, where people had to slog through the snow to get anywhere and needed a simple, efficient way to do so.

Those Viking types have been doing it since at least 3000 B.C., maybe longer. That's a lot of practice time, particularly if you're competing against newbies from places like America and Canada. (And when the final race results are tallied, it usually shows.)

Cross-country skiing evolved from these ancient roots to become a popular competition among Norwegian military members as far back as 1767. But ski racing among civilians didn't get rolling until the 1840s, and even then it was usually part of a combined contest with ski jumping. Norway's noted Holmenkollen ski festival dates to 1892. The first year a stand-alone cross-country race was held there was 1900.

Cross-country racing was placed under the purview of the International Ski Federation in 1924 and debuted at the inaugural Chamonix Games. It's one of seven sports that have continued from the first Games to modern times. Women's cross-country events were added beginning with the 1952 Oslo Games.

Biathlon was derived from ancient hunting techniques, which later were adopted as part of military training in northern European nations—not surprisingly, the nations that largely dominate the sport.

The first biathlon races likely took place in 1767, pitting bored border guards from Norway and Sweden against one another as they stood watch—for caribou?—on their long, shared national border. Biathlon was a demonstration sport at the inaugural 1924 Chamonix Games. The first world championships, however, weren't held until 1958, and biathlon became a medal sport at the 1960 Squaw Valley Games. At that time, biathlon was the exclusive province of military members. Rule changes in 1978 switched the rifles to .22 caliber and moved the targets closer, to 50 meters, making the sport more accessible for civilians. Women competed for the first time at the 1992 Albertville Olympics.

A biathlete shoulders his rifle in the target area on the biathlon course at Whistler Olympic Park.

The Hakulinen-Jernberg Era

Given the sport's origins, it's no surprise that early cross-country races were dominated by Scandinavians. But two of them, Veikko Hakulinen of Finland and Sixten Jernberg of Sweden, stand out so prominently in the record books that they have their own historical period named after them.

For the record, the "Hakulinen-Jernberg era" lasted from 1952 to 1964. Although Hakulinen skied in the Oslo Olympics of 1952, before Jernberg arrived on the scene, the two often competed against one another in a rivalry played out at Cortina d'Ampezzo and Squaw Valley in 1956 and 1960. The result? You'd have to call it a draw.

In head-to-head competition, each man finished with two gold medals, three silvers, and one bronze. Jernberg, who competed in the 1964 Innsbruck Games after Hakulinen's retirement, finished his Olympic career with four golds, three silvers, and two bronze medals.

Koch: An American Original

Bill Koch's contributions to his sport go far beyond the Olympic Games in which he competed, and far beyond his national borders. After retiring from international competition, Koch helped refine a new skiing technique—skating, or pushing off the inside edges of the weight-bearing ski. He didn't actually invent it—credit for that usually goes to Gerhard Grimmer of East Germany, who pulled it out of his bag of tricks one day in 1971 at the famed Holmenkollen race in Norway, winning by a large margin.

Others experimented with the technique, but Koch had the vision—and the name—to popularize it throughout the sport. A ban on skate skiing in international competition quickly eroded, and the technique, known as freestyle at the Olympics, was integrated into the lineup of the 1988 Calgary Games and has been there ever since.

Koch, in retirement, invented and continues to try to popularize a new sport, sand skiing, in Hawaii.

A Swede, Inspired by an American?

A true testament to the greatness of Bill Koch was that he served as an athletic inspiration for Gunde Svan, who hails from Sweden, always a dominant force in Nordic skiing. Svan and Koch became friends as young teenagers, and the Swede credited Koch's heart on the race course for teaching him about competitive mettle.

He needed it in the 1988 Calgary Games, which Svan entered with a reputation already well established, having dominated the 1984 Sarajevo Olympics, where he won a medal in each of four races he entered. But Calgary's course seemed to get the better of him. Svan finished 10th, his worst Olympic performance ever, in the 30-kilometer individual. Four days later, he finished 12th as the defending champion in the 15 kilometers.

But he regained his strength and stride during the 4x10-kilometer relay. Skiing the third leg, Svan put the Swedes ahead of the rival Soviet team by 27 seconds. His teammate, Torgny Mogren, held on to the lead, winning by 13 seconds. Five days later, a reinvigorated Svan, back from cross-country's grave, started 69th among 70 skiers in the 50 kilometers but soon pulled to a huge lead on the scoreboard clock. He seemed to get only stronger, and at 40 kilometers led the field by a minute and a half. He beat Maurilio de Zolt of Italy by a minute and 6 seconds.

Someone Forgot to Tell Him It Was a Gimmick

The 10-kilometer classical race at Nagano in 1998 will long be remembered as the event that made Norway's Bjørn Dæhlie the first man to win eight gold medals in the Winter Olympics. But even the Swedish superstar couldn't help admiring the grit of the last-place finisher, Philip Boit of Kenya.

Boit and countryman Henry Bitok, both Kenyan runners, were recruited and subsidized by shoe giant Nike to race in cross-country skiing in the Olympics. It was largely a publicity stunt, but Boit, once he got used to the cold, took the task to heart. When he came across the finish line in 92nd place, 20 minutes behind the winner, he stumbled and was caught by none other than Dæhlie, who had returned to shake his hand—while the world waited for the medal ceremony to commence.

Boit, moved by that generosity, named one of his sons after Dæhlie—and he stuck with the sport. Dropped by Nike, he competed in sprints at the Salt Lake Games, where he finished 64th—ahead of three competitors. He returned to the course in Turin in 2006 and finished 92nd in the 15-kilometer classical, this time beating five competitors.

In 2008, Boit began training in the Methow Valley of Washington State, with the hope of competing in the nearby 2010 Olympics in Vancouver.

Bad Luck—and Uncommon Grace

Next time you hear a weekend winter warrior bemoaning bad luck in a race of some sort, remind him or her of the tale of Juha Mieto of Finland—a man who overcame some of the worst luck ever to befall an Olympian to become a legend in his own right.

Mieto, a 6-foot-5, 250-pound bear of a man with a build rarely seen in his sport, was known for his sheer toughness and tenacity. With his hulking frame, a wild, flowing beard often caked with snow, and bare hands—he had trouble finding ski gloves big enough to fit—Mieto was a mythical figure on the ski track.

He was also a walking symbol of bad luck. In the 1972 Sapporo Games, Mieto missed a bronze medal by six-hundredths of a second in the

15-kilometer race. He finished 10th in the event at Innsbruck in 1976 and came to Lake Placid in 1980 determined to finally claim the 15 kilometers, in spite of an exceptionally hilly course on Mount Van Hoevenberg. Mieto, skiing 54th, had a lead of 36 seconds when he finished. He then watched in disbelief as Thomas Wassberg of Sweden, who had started 4 minutes after Mieto in the staggered start, crossed the line one hundredth of a second faster.

Final score: 41 minutes, 57.63 seconds to 41 minutes, 57.64 seconds.

The result—made possible by a 1972 ski federation decision to switch cross-country race timing from one to two decimal places—stood, giving the gold to Wassberg. The Swede was embarrassed over the smallest margin of victory in Olympic history, saying the race should have been a tie, the medal should be sawed in half, and that both men should stand on top of the podium. Mieto, in a memorable display of sportsmanship, disagreed, saying Wassberg had won fair and square. "A gold medal," he said, "should not be split in half."

But the result, described as "inhuman" in subsequent press accounts, spurred another rule change: Beginning in 1988, races reverted to being timed in tenths of seconds. It was too late for Mieto. Had that been the case in Lake Placid, Mieto and Wassberg would have tied—and both won gold.

On the last day of the Lake Placid Games, Mieto returned to the Mount Van Hoevenberg track and won silver in the 50 kilometers. Thankfully, this time he was more than 3 minutes behind the leader.

A Giant Push From Behind

The giant Finn shows up in Olympic history on another occasion most Olympic fans don't know about—and again is noted for his grace. American skier Bill Koch is always remembered for his 1976 bronze medal. But he told Olympic filmmaker/

historian Bud Greenspan that his fondest Olympic memory will always be the 50-kilometer race that took place several days later.

Koch was leading after the first 30 kilometers, at which point his body began to give out. He thought about dropping out as skiers began passing him left and right. "With 5 kilometers to go, I could barely move, and there was a hill in front of me," Koch recalls in Greenspan's *Frozen in Time: The Greatest Moments at the Winter Olympics*. "I started up but was feeling faint."

Just at that moment, "I felt a big hand on my shoulder; I was being pushed."

He turned to find the hand connected to his skiing idol, Juha Mieto, who was risking disqualification by assisting.

"He showed me what sportsmanship and character truly are. He pushed me all the way to the top of the hill, and once there, I got renewed spirit and energy. I went on to finish 13th. I'll never forget that. Never."

Mieto retired after the Sarajevo Games of 1984 with five Olympic medals. In 2007, he was overwhelmingly elected to the Finnish Parliament.

More Bad Luck, More Uncommon Grace

When they talk about the "spirit of fair play" in the Olympics, Bjornar Hakensmoen of Norway should be Exhibit A.

Hakensmoen, 36, a cross-country ski coach, happened to be standing nearby as Canada's Sara Renner, racing in the lead on the third leg of a six-leg race, snapped a pole in the team sprint competition at the Turin Olympics, dropping her from first to fourth as a Swede, a Finn, and a Norwegian skied past. Hakensmoen never thought twice before doing what any gentleman—and sportsman—would do: He instinctively handed her one of his own.

Renner, two poles back in hand, put on a charge

to overtake the skiers who had just passed her. Thanks to a frantic final charge by fellow Albertan Beckie Scott, Canada won the silver medal. And Norway's team finished fourth, out of medal contention.

Hakensmoen unhesitatingly told reporters he'd do the same thing again.

"Winning is not everything in sport," he told the *Washington Post.* "What win is that, if you achieve your goal but don't help somebody when you should have helped them? I was just helping

At the Whistler Olympic Park site for 2010 Winter Games events, cross-country skier Beckie Scott of Canada meets with reporters near a photograph of herself in action.

a girl who was in big trouble. If you saw her, you would do the same."

He said he was shocked anyone would be surprised.

"Some countries don't give poles to their opposition. That is bullshit," Hakensmoen told Canada's Canoe.ca. "We have lots of ski poles," he said. "But tell her she owes me a great big hug."

He got the hug—as well as a grateful phone call from Canadian Prime Minister Stephen Harper. And 800 liters of maple syrup from a maple-sugar farmer in New Brunswick, shipped to the Norwegian Olympic Committee. And offers for a free two-week stay at a hotel in Banff, Alberta. Canadians proceeded to cover the front steps of the Norwegian Embassy in Ottawa with flowers and letters.

Even more surprising, Hakensmoen, in his final year of coaching, said he received nary a single complaint from his home nation, the cradle of cross-country skiing.

Some Norwegians reportedly were thankful to have a chance to rectify the karma scoreboard: Some years before, a Norwegian had been in a position to help a Swede with a broken pole. To the shame of the country, no help was forthcoming.

Renner will always cherish the moment. She kept the pole briefly, but had her coach return it, and left Hakensmoen a fine bottle of Italian Barolo, and a thank-you note.

"It's a men's pole and it's really long," she said. "But it got the job done."

Justice Delayed—Twice— for Beckie Scott

Many eyes were on Vermilion, Alberta, native Beckie Scott during the combined pursuit at the 2002 Salt Lake Games. The Canadian, skiing on the course at Soldier Hollow, trailed leaders Olga Danilova and Larissa Lazutina of Russia by a wide margin in the first, classical stage of the race. But her mere presence in the medal hunt was a story: Scott had never won a major international race before (her best finish in Nagano had been 45th), but she was locked in a tight battle with World Cup points leader Katerina Neumannova of the Czech Republic. She managed to hold Neumannova off, nipping her by one tenth of a second to win the bronze.

Or so she thought. Rumors swirling around the Russian leaders proved true when, more than a year after the race, silver medalist Lazutina was disqualified for testing positive for darbepoetin, a performance-enhancing drug. Two months after that, Danilova also tested positive. Both skiers were stripped of their medals, and Scott, almost two years after charging for that bronze, was awarded the gold medal.

Scott thus became not only the first North American woman to win a cross-country skiing medal, but certainly the first to grasp, at one time or another, all three medals for the same event.

Now retired, Scott remains a vigorous ambassador for Olympic sport, serving as a UNICEF volunteer, a member of the World Doping Agency's athletes' committee, an athlete member of the IOC, and a member of the board of directors for the Vancouver 2010 organizing committee. She and her husband, U.S. cross-country coach Justin Wadsworth, live in Panorama, British Columbia, and Bend, Oregon.

RECORD BOOK: CROSS-COUNTRY

It all began with two Norwegians, **Thorleif Haug** and **Johan Grøttumsbråten,** and a Finn, **Tapani Niku,** winning the first-ever cross-country ski medals, in an 18-kilometer race at Chamonix in 1924. And it's gone pretty much that way ever since.

Providing, of course, that you throw in a hefty box of medals for both the Soviet Union/Russia and Sweden, and a small box for Italy. There's your cross-country Olympic record book.

Norway, where the sport was invented, first organized, and competed with the most gusto, leads the all-time cross-country medal chart with 87—30 of them gold. But if you combine the medals won by Russia and its big, bad Soviet incarnation, the Russians actually have won more—92 total medals, 37 of them gold. The other contenders: Sweden, with 56 medals (24 gold); Finland, with 71 total medals (19 gold), and Italy, with 33 total medals (nine gold).

East and West Germany have combined for 13 medals, and Czechoslovakia/Czech Republic has 12. But no other nation has even hit the double-digit mark. Estonia six, Austria five, Kazakhstan and Switzerland each four, and Canada three. The United States is down there with Poland, France, and Bulgaria—all members of the one-medal club.

For the United States, that one medal came courtesy of **Bill Koch,** the Vermont native who won a silver in the 30 kilometers at the 1976 Innsbruck Games.

Canadian medalists in the sport are all women: **Beckie Scott** took gold, Canada's first, in the 5-kilometer combined pursuit at the 2002 Salt Lake Games—albeit long after the event, in which the first- and second-place finishers were disqualified for doping. Alberta native **Chandra Crawford,** a converted biathlete, took gold in the 1.1-kilometer sprint at the 2006 Turin Games, where **Scott** and **Sara Renner** of Golden, B.C., also combined to win silver in the team sprint in the now-famous "broken pole" race.

A handful of outstanding athletes from other nations have compiled some of the most impressive medal records of all Winter Games participants. Among them:

Norway's **Bjørn Dæhlie,** universally accepted as the greatest cross-country skier of all time, bowed to receive the gold medal eight times and the silver four, in the Games of Albertville (three gold, one silver), Lillehammer (two gold, two silver), and Nagano (three gold, one silver). His 12 overall medals are the most of any athlete in the Winter Olympics.

Sixten Jernberg of Sweden, a distance specialist, won nine medals (four gold, three silver, two bronze) at the Cortina d'Ampezzo, Squaw Valley, and Innsbruck Games. **Vladimir Smirnov** of Russia collected seven overall medals from 1988 to 1998. **Eero Mäntyranta** and **Veikko Hakulinen,** both of Finland, also captured seven medals each.

In women's cross-country, dominant performers include Russian great **Raisa Petrovna Smetanina,** the first woman in history to win 10 Winter Games medals. Smetanina won four golds, five silvers, and a bronze while representing the USSR and the Unified Team at five Olympics between 1976 and 1992. But that feat was equaled by Italy's **Stefania Belmondo,** who won 10 medals (two gold, three silver, five bronze) at four Olympics from 1992 to 2002. Belmondo was given the honor of lighting the cauldron at the opening ceremony for the 2006 Winter Games of Turin, in her homeland of Piedmont, Italy.

One of Belmondo's contemporaries, **Lyubov Yegorova** of Russia, won nine overall medals (six gold, three silver) at the Albertville and Lillehammer Games. Throughout her remarkable two-Olympic run, even her own teammates marveled at her strength, given that she underwent the same training regimen as they did. Or maybe not: Yegorova, who grew up in Siberia and was well on her way to becoming the most decorated female Winter Olympian of all time, saw her career end in 1997 when she tested positive for bromantan, a masking agent for steroids, at the world championships in Trondheim, Norway.

Another Russian, **Galina Kulakova,** won eight medals (four gold, two silver, two bronze) at four Olympics from 1972 to 1980. Finland's **Marja-Liisa Kirvesniemi,** Italy's **Manuela Di Centa,** and Russia's **Larissa Lazutina** and **Yelena Välbe** all won seven medals apiece. Lazutina, however, later would be disgraced by testing positive for banned substances after winning the combined pursuit in Salt Lake City—a race in which her teammate and would-be silver medalist, Olga Danilova, also was disqualified for substance abuse.

RECORD BOOK: BIATHLON

Norway's **Ole Einar Bjørndalen** is the standard bearer in biathlon, with nine overall medals (five gold, three silver, one bronze) won over the three Olympics from 1998 to 2006. Germans **Sven Fischer** (four gold, two silver, two bronze; 1994–2006) and **Ricco Gross** (four gold, three silver, one bronze; 1992–2006) own eight medals apiece.

Among women, **Uschi Disl** of Germany has garnered nine medals (two gold, four silver, three bronze) from 1992 to 2006.

Worthy of note is a rare North American bright spot in the Nordic pursuits: **Myriam Bédard** of Canada, a Royal Canadian army cadet who would go on to win a bronze medal in the 15-kilometer individual at the 1992 Albertville Games, and then gold medals in the 7.5-kilometer sprint and 15-kilometer individual at the 1994 Lillehammer Games. (Amazingly, she won the 7.5 kilometers in spite of discovering early in the race that she was wearing mismatched skis.)

NEXT STOP: WHISTLER OLYMPIC PARK

Location:	Callaghan Valley, west of Whistler, B.C.
Spectator capacity:	12,000 in each of three finishing areas
Elevation:	850 meters (2,788 feet) at the base; 910 meters (2,985 feet) at the top
Other events:	Ski jumping, Nordic combined, Paralympic biathlon/cross-country skiing
Medal ceremonies:	Whistler Village Celebration Plaza

Whistler, B.C., the cross-country and alpine ski venue for the 2010 Games, didn't have much of a cross-country skiing tradition before the Games bid was awarded to Vancouver.

It does now, thanks to the swift construction of Whistler Olympic Park, a sprawling network of cross-country and biathlon ski trails and Nordic ski jumps in the Callaghan Valley, about 12.8 kilometers (8 miles) west of Whistler. The park, plopped into the middle of a previously undisturbed (except for the occasional snowmobile trail) high plateau of first- and second-growth forest and steep, rocky foothills, is in a stunning natural location. It offers views of British Columbia Coast Range peaks, including the picturesque Black Tusk, from many points inside the park.

The Olympic Park has 35 kilometers of newly cut cross-country/biathlon trails—about 14 kilometers for competition and another 20 kilometers for recreational skiing—all of which wind through the forest. Because of that, most of the races will play out beyond the sight of spectators—unlike those in the Salt Lake Games of 2002, where trails in the cross-country venue at Soldier Hollow wound through a mostly treeless area.

At the center of the park are three separate "stadiums"—finish areas for cross-country races, biathlon, and ski jumping/Nordic combined. Each will seat approximately 12,000 fans. All access to the site will be by bus; there's little parking at the venue itself, and it lies at the end of a two-lane road constructed specifically for the Olympics.

As of this writing, no World Cup-level competitions have been held on the Whistler Olympic Park trails, although racers who participated in the Canadian national championships in the spring of 2008 had good things to say about the courses.

"Everybody is enthusiastic about the layout," said U.S. skier Torin Koos. "They're really skiable. You would think that'd be something you need in a cross-country course. But sometimes they just throw in ridiculous steep hills that are too steep to ski. Like, Nagano was known for that."

The courses were set by John Aalberg, a former U.S. skier.

"You can tell a skier laid it out," Koos said. "It's going to take really good skiing to win here; not just running up hills, where it's a matter of who has the best engine. It's going to come down to who's the best skier."

Snow should not be a problem here; it's ample in the Callaghan Valley in late February. In 2008, during the very week in which the Games will begin, about 9 feet of snow lay on the valley floor. The conditions, however, could get tricky. The Olympic Park sits at only 3,000 feet above sea level, making it easily the lowest-elevation Nordic venue in the history of the Winter Games. Skiers might have to bone up on the fine art of waxing for wetter, warmer snow than they're accustomed to on the World Cup circuit, most of which is played out in the high mountains of the Alps.

Another factor to watch for: Because organizers sought to minimize logging, most of the competition tracks for both cross-country and biathlon are contained within a zone of about 1.2 square kilometers (0.75 square mile). This means that the trails curve more than usual, creating some surprisingly sharp corners. In early races at the venue, pileups have occurred on some of these. Fans of long, straight tracks probably won't find much to their liking in the 2010 Games.

After the Olympics, the Whistler Olympic Park will remain open as a competition venue, international training venue, World Cup race venue, and recreational ski facility (it's already serving in all those capacities now, after opening in the winter of 2007–2008). Very few permanent buildings were erected here; the seating will be in portable grandstands, all to be removed after the Games. The park

The alpine views from Whistler Olympic Park will provide a stunning backdrop for the 2010 Winter Games, assuming weather cooperates.

will have full-service ski and snowshoe rentals and repairs, a day lodge, and other amenities. Trails are groomed daily for classic and skate skiing, and the venue even has a night-ski loop. It should serve as a worthy addition—and pleasant, quieter

counterbalance—to Whistler's full lineup of alpine ski facilities.

It also has something of interest to canine lovers: a designated snow park where skiers and snowshoers can take Fido out for a romp in the white stuff.

Cross-Country 2010 Schedule

February 15: Men's 15-kilometer individual; women's 10-kilometer individual

February 17: Men's and women's 1,500-meter sprint

February 19: Women's 7.5-kilometer x 2 pursuit

February 20: Men's 15-kilometer x 2 pursuit

February 22: Men's and women's team sprint

February 24: Men's 4x10-kilometer relay

February 25: Women's 4x5-kilometer relay

February 27: Women's 30-kilometer mass start

February 28: Men's 50-kilometer mass start

Biathlon 2010 Schedule

February 13: Women's 7.5-kilometer sprint

February 14: Men's 10-kilometer sprint

February 16: Men's 12.5-kilometer pursuit; women's 10-kilometer pursuit

February 18: Men's 20-kilometer individual; women's 15-kilometer individual

February 21: Men's 15-kilometer mass start; women's 12.5-kilometer mass start

February 23: Women's 4x6-kilometer relay

February 26: Men's 4x7.5-kilometer relay

Opposite: A cross-country skier makes tracks at Whistler Olympic Park.

FREESTYLE SKIING

❋ ❋ ❋ ❋ ❋

When your middle name is "Big Air," you might as well go with the big air.

That's what Jonny "Big Air" Moseley ultimately decided that day in Park City, standing at the top of a sprawling bump run on a glorious Utah day, with the whole world looking on.

For weeks, Moseley, a Puerto Rico native and the defending gold medalist in the moguls—an event he won in Nagano in 1998 by completing a skateboard-inspired 360 mute grab, which includes grasping one ski and staring, while briefly suspended in midair, at the adoring crowd—had faced an internal dilemma: Should he go with what he knew would win, or follow his heart and let it all out?

It was more than a philosophical dilemma. Moseley, who had hit the celebrity circuit fairly hard to cash in on his Nagano fame, hadn't really intended to come back to the '06 Olympics. And then after he did decide to return, he couldn't find a way to qualify.

Remaining, he believed, true to the sport of freestyle skiing, where competitors are not just athletes but also innovators and entertainers—artists, if you're disposed to use the word so freely—Mosely had been working on expanding his art form.

A bit of background will help here: Moguls skiers bop down a steep hill of large snow bumps before taking flight, literally, off of two ski jumps. Although speeds vary among competitors, most skiers run the bumps in a very similar fashion. It's your time in the air on those two mandatory jumps that allows you to spread your wings and separate yourself from the flock.

In a sport where the judges' impressions account for 70 percent of your score, it's that air time that puts you in the big time.

Moseley's new trick, which he dubbed the "dinner roll," was a 720-degree roll, with one roll completed on the horizontal axis and the other on the vertical. When he did it, his rolling body was laid out sideways as it sailed, seemingly in slow motion, down the mountain. He had developed the trick for the 1999 X Games, but had only now begun to perfect it to the point that he could complete the roll more often than not.

He decided to unfurl the trick for qualifying

events for the '06 Olympics, but it seemed only to dig him into a hole of deepening dimensions.

The few times Moseley, then 26, actually landed the trick in competition, judges didn't like it. They considered it dangerous, and some officials called it illegal. Moguls, unlike the more free-form aerials skiing, another freestyle pursuit, is a right-side-up sport. Your skis are never supposed to go above your head, and on Moseley's dinner roll, they come as close as you can get.

Weeks before the Salt Lake Games, Moseley, in his final attempt to qualify to compete in Salt Lake, finally relented and played it safe. He left the dinner roll in the breadbox and performed more traditional jumps, winning the contest and earning a spot on the Olympic team.

In the run-up to the Games, Moseley—who has always maintained that in a sport as free-form and fast-changing as moguls, the judges inevitably and invariably will be behind the curve—lobbied and

America's Jonny Moseley gets horizontal during his controversial "dinner roll" maneuver at the 2002 Salt Lake Winter Games.

received permission from technical officials to try out the dinner roll during Olympic competition.

"What I was doing was so much harder than what everybody else was doing," he said. "It was just night and day."

But it also risked getting the results it had received in earlier competition—scores that would make it impossible for Moseley to win a medal.

And so, standing there atop the slope at Deer Valley, he knew there was really no choice. Launching himself down the mountain, Moseley did a traditional jump off the first ramp, then hit the second and let it fly—a perfect, textbook dinner roll, as smooth and spectacular as any he'd ever completed.

The crowd went nuts. The judges frowned.

Moseley, whose speed score had not been among the leaders, stood in third place after his run. He wouldn't stay there for long. The last skier, a U.S. teammate, Travis Mayer, 19, who had shot from nowhere to earn a spot on the Olympic team, became the answer to an all-time trivia question by skiing the run of his life to win a silver medal, pushing Moseley to fourth.

The crowd was incensed. Moseley took it all in stride. "I was trying to change the sport and do something unique," he said later. "Maybe I was being stupid. But the truth is, I was trying to win."

His sport, he believed, had simply not caught up with him yet. And he was probably right. Such is the allure of freestyle skiing, undoubtedly the most creative snow sport on the Winter Games docket.

Skiers in the mainstream freestyle events, moguls and aerials, are as much performers as they are competitors. Because both sports are judged, à la figure skating, dramatic impact is everything—especially when the crowd, whipped to a frenzy by thumping rock music and enthusiastic announcers, is rarely satisfied with something they've already seen.

The event—known for decades as "hot-dog skiing"—has carved its own niche in the modern Olympics, attracting large numbers of thrill-sport junkies raised on the X Games and other made-for-TV sporting events. Thus, it's been warmly embraced by IOC officials looking to put some pizzazz in Winter Games television ratings.

At the 2010 Vancouver Games, they'll reach for even a bit more, introducing to the Olympic world the new sport of ski cross, a thrilling, crash-ridden gang race inspired by another new fan favorite, snowboard cross.

That event is a bit more traditional in the sense that the first one across the line wins. No judging to mess things up.

Then again, no props from the crowd for slipping the surly bonds of earth, either. Jonny Moseley peaked and retired before ski cross came along. And it's probably just as well.

Did he make the right call that day at Deer Valley? In a sport that rewards free spirit and innovation above medal counts, absolutely. Moseley retired from Olympic competition with only one chunk of gold, but with a reputation for being true to himself, and his sport, that will live on long after the medal counts are forgotten.

SPECTATOR'S GUIDE

Freestyle skiing venues are the most manmade of all sites for snow-sports events, with ski jumps constructed of wood and steel and then covered with snow, or deep moguls carved by machine and shovel into hillsides. But the results are spectacular, with enough big-air thrills—always set to rock music—to make the event a fan favorite at every Olympics.

Field of Play

In *aerials,* athletes ski down a short, steep slope, reaching speeds of 25 to 30 mph (40 to 48 kilometers per hour) before skiing off steeply banked jumps. The jumps propel skiers 12 to 15 meters (40 to 50 feet) into the air, where they perform multiple acrobatic maneuvers all the way back down to the snow below, landing, it is hoped, on their skis.

The landing hill is at a pitch of 34 to 39 degrees and is about 30 meters (100 feet) long. Top male aerials jumpers can perform triple backflips with as many as five twists built in. Quadruple backflips have been attempted and landed by a handful of skiers but to date are not legal in competition on the World Cup or at the Olympics.

Moguls skiers, performing to raucous music of their own choosing, make their way down a steep slope studded with deep moguls, or bumps interspersed between troughs, and two manmade ski jumps. With their knees pistoning at blinding speeds and their hips pivoting from side to side, they essentially bounce off the tops of the moguls, their upper bodies appearing to travel straight down the fall line, with nary a bounce or jiggle.

When they hit one of the course's prescribed jumps, they launch into the air and typically perform an aerial maneuver like a somersault or flip with one or more twists, then land on their skis and ski the next line of bumps to the next jump, until reaching the bottom—all as a rule in less than 30 seconds of frenetic activity.

The event itself is something like a cross between a rock concert and an elementary school field day, with blaring music and a party atmosphere.

"There's always a lot of energy flowing at our events," U.S. aerialist Trace Worthington told the *Washington Post.* "We are kind of a beach volleyball of the wintertime."

In *ski cross,* racers break out of a starting gate like horses and ski, in a pack of four, down a course with sharp curves, fast straightaways, and a series of whoop-de-do bumps that send them flying skyward. Good starts are crucial; it's difficult, although by no means impossible, to pass other skiers on the course. Wipeouts are fairly common, making ski cross an exciting visual spectacle.

The sport, which originated with the action-oriented Winter X Games, has been likened to motocross on skis. Racers can reach speeds exceeding 50 mph (80 kilometers per hour), and while bodily contact is prohibited, accidental bumping is not unusual.

All three disciplines are now skied in the Olympics by both men and women, with ski cross debuting at the 2010 Games at Cypress Mountain, on the outskirts of Vancouver.

Format, Rules, and Strategy

All freestyle skiing events except the newest, ski cross, have a scoring system.

In aerials, competitors are judged on jump takeoff style (20 percent), jump technique and form (50 percent), and the landing (30 percent). As in other sports such as platform diving, a degree-of-difficulty factor is then applied to determine a total score. Aerials competitions are split into two categories: upright, in which the skier's feet can't go over his or her head, and inverted, which opens the door to the most complicated flips, turns, and spins.

In moguls skiing, racers are judged on mogul turns (50 percent), jump quality (25 percent), and speed (25 percent) by seven judges. The high and low scores are tossed out. The full field skis one run, with the top 16 advancing to a second round, which is either a single ski run or a dual run, in which competitors race side by side.

In ski cross, the first skier across the finish line—barring disqualifications or penalties—is the winner. In preliminary rounds, the first two skiers typically advance. In the final round, the top four race in a winner-take-all.

Training and Equipment

Aerials and moguls skiers use short, lightweight skis and generally wear typical ski clothing—not skintight bodysuits. Because speed is not as crucial

here, the aerodynamic properties of garments are not a major issue.

Most first-time observers marveling at the graceful aerial ballet conducted by aerials and moguls skiers wonder how the skier took that first leap into a complicated jump without killing himself or herself. The answer is simple: off-snow training. All freestyle skiers begin by practicing their jumps into water, usually a large swimming pool.

The in-run ramp is made of wood covered with a specialized plastic mat lubricated with sprinklers. A skier's splashdown is softened by a burst of air bubbles from the bottom of the pool, which breaks up the surface of the water. Freestyle skiers also train in the summer on trampolines, diving boards, and gymnastic equipment, as well as the full range of conditioning equipment.

HISTORY'S HITS AND MISSES

Freestyle skiing dates to the 1930s in—once again—Norway, where hot-dogging skiers began doing tricks while training for alpine or cross-country racing. Norwegian alpine gold medalist Stein Eriksen, now the unelected mayor of Deer Valley, Utah, is the godfather of aerials, introducing the technique somewhere around 1950. He became known for front and back flips at ski demonstrations in Vermont and Colorado.

The sport existed on the ski world's fringes through the 1960s and '70s, with many alpine and Nordic skiers insisting to this day that freestyle skiing is a hot-dogger's pursuit akin to skateboarding, not real skiing.

But the august International Ski Federation recognized freestyle as a sport in 1979, introducing new rules designed to make the endeavor more fair and less dangerous. The sport got its own World Cup circuit in 1980. The first world championship

Opposite: A freestyle aerialist practices by jumping into a swimming pool in Lake Placid, New York

took place in France in 1986. Freestyle debuted as a demonstration sport in the Calgary Games of 1988, with aerials, moguls, and (God forbid) acro skiing, a sort of ski-tip ballet that looks for all the world like a sport conjured by Monty Python alums after a day of heavy drinking.

Freestyle managed to survive that inauspicious debut, and moguls became a medal sport at the 1992 Albertville Games. Aerials were added to the category for the Lillehammer Games of 1994. Acro has yet to raise its head again.

And it might not, now that ski cross has been added to the medals menu. Ski cross has been competed on the World Cup level since November 2003. It's one of a series of "new school" freestyle ski disciplines that include snowboard-inspired events such as halfpipe, big air contests, and slopestyle—rail-sliding and jumping down a course in a manmade terrain park. All are conducted on skis with twin tips for frontward and backward skiing, a design that revolutionized trick skiing beginning in the late 1990s.

Making a Visible Splash

Moguls skier extraordinaire Jean-Luc Brassard, a native of Valleyfield, Quebec, put the hot dog in hot-dogging. Never a very fast skier, Brassard was known as a showman and a stickler for perfect form in his jumps and tricks off the ramps. He also claimed fame as the first skier to popularize the wearing of flaming-bright-colored knee pads, which made it look, at least, as though his legs were moving faster over those bumps.

Not everyone was enchanted with his showboat style. Brassard's chief nemesis during his heyday was Edgar Grospiron of France, who won the first-ever moguls gold at Albertville and famously referred to Brassard's jumping style as "crap."

The Canadian got his revenge in Lillehammer, winning the gold medal while Grospiron settled for the bronze. Brassard continued to be a strong World

Freestyle Tami Bradley of Canada gets fast and loose on the Deer Park course at the 2002 Winter Games.

Cup performer up to the 1998 Nagano Games. There he served as his nation's flag bearer in the opening ceremony but ultimately was bumped off the moguls medal stand by American Jonny Moseley's memorable gold medal performance. He left the sport for a time after a knee injury in 2000, but returned to place 21st in moguls at the Salt Lake Olympics.

Throw Another Injury on the Barbie

As one might imagine, gold medals in the Winter Olympics don't come bouncing along every day for Australians. But Planet Oz—still on an Olympic high after its wildly successful hosting of the 2000 Sydney Summer Games—had its hopes up for the 2002 Salt Lake City Games for a very good reason: Jacqui Cooper.

In the three-year run-up to the 2002 Games, Cooper had dominated her sport, aerials, on the World Cup circuit. But luck wasn't with her in Utah: A week before the games, she blew out the anterior cruciate ligament in her knee during training.

The only competitor left in the event for the Aussies was Alisa Camplin, 19, of Melbourne, an ex-gymnast and talented sailor, but a relative newbie to freestyle skiing. Camplin, in fact, was best known for being something of a klutz on skis.

She had good excuses: She had never even seen snow until she was in high school, and she practiced in a jumping pond in Wandin that she described as perilously scummy. Even so, she proved uncommonly reckless on the slopes, suffering a string of injuries that included a broken collarbone, a separated shoulder, a broken hand, a torn Achilles tendon, various knee injuries, and an alarming nine concussions.

She arrived in Salt Lake a little banged up. Okay, make that a lot. In a training crash the week before, she had injured both legs—suffering what she thought were just bruises. In Utah, doctors discovered that she actually had two broken ankles.

Given all that, Aussie fans could be forgiven for hoping only that Camplin, who insisted on competing, would survive the event at Deer Valley. She did that, and plenty more. Camplin completed a pair of triple-twist, double-backflip jumps to win the gold medal. She credited speedskater Steven Bradbury's earlier gold medal for taking some of the pressure off.

She became, not surprisingly, a hero in Australia and had her smiling face, grasping her gold medal, emblazoned on a 45-cent postage stamp. Four years later, in Turin, she rose to the occasion once more, overcoming a complete knee reconstruction shortly before the Olympics to win a bronze medal. She served as her nation's flag bearer at the Games' opening ceremony. She retired in 2006 and now runs ski tours in Colorado.

RECORD BOOK: FREESTYLE SKIING

Freestyle skiing is one of the few winter sports that has long been dominated by North Americans—certainly at the World Cup level. The Nations Cup, the top trophy for team freestyle performance, has been won by America and Canada nearly every year since its inception. But Canada and the United States have by no means owned the freestyle slopes in the Olympics.

Men's Freestyle Record Book

In men's moguls, two Frenchmen, **Edgar Grospiron** and **Olivier Allamand,** won gold and silver at the first competition in Albertville, 1992. America's **Nelson Carmichael** took the bronze. In 1994 at Lillehammer, Canada's **Jean-Luc Brassard** won gold, followed in 1998 at Nagano by America's **Jonny Moseley. Travis Mayer** of the United States took a silver medal at Salt Lake City in 2002; countryman **Toby Dawson** won bronze at 2006 in Turin.

In men's aerials, **Andreas Schönbächler** of Switzerland claimed the first gold, at Lillehammer in 1994, beating out Canadians **Philippe LaRoche** and **Lloyd Langlois,** who took silver and bronze, respectively. In 1998, Montana native **Eric Bergoust** won gold for America; **Joe Pack** won a silver in 2002 at Salt Lake. The 2006 Turin Games saw the first Chinese skiing medalist, **Han Xiapeng,** followed by **Dmitri Dashinski** of Belarus and **Vladimir Lebedev** of Russia.

Women's Freestyle Record Book

In women's moguls, America's **Donna Weinbrecht** took the first gold at Albertville in 1992. **Elizabeth McIntyre** kept the United States on the medal stand with a silver at Lillehammer, and **Shannon Bahrke** ended a U.S. women's medal drought by nabbing a silver at Salt Lake—the first American medal awarded at the 2002 Games. Canada's **Jennifer Heil** got her nation on the medals board with a gold medal at Turin in 2006.

OLYMPIC FLASHBACK
SALT LAKE CITY GAMES

Feb. 10, 2002

Reported by Ron C. Judd for The Seattle Times

PARK CITY, Utah—When moguls skiers go to sleep at night, this is the dream they see:

Park City streets, Deer Valley Lodge, and 13,000 fanatical fans below. Blue sky above. And nothing but 15 feet of sweet, clean air and about

America's Shannon Bahrke reacts after winning the first U.S. medal, a silver, in moguls at the 2002 Salt Lake Winter Olympics.

50 more moguls separating you from a rock 'n' roll bump run straight to the medal stand.

Shannon Bahrke lived it yesterday, nailing a 360-degree "heli iron cross" jump at the top of her second run to snare America's first medal on the opening day of competition at the XIX Winter Games.

The medal, a surprise silver in a competition dominated by reigning freestyle moguls queen Kari Traa of Norway, was a message for the rest of America's Olympians, an ebullient Bahrke said at the finish.

"To me, this is something special, after September 11," the 21-year-old Tahoe City, California, resident said, pausing as her voice broke.

At the opening ceremonies on Friday night, she met President Bush, cyclist Lance Armstrong ("my idol," she said), and members of the New York City police and fire departments who accompanied the World Trade Center flag to Utah.

"I just think it gave me a little bit of extra fire," she said. "Now that I have the first medal . . . I hope it makes America proud. And I hope all the others in all of our sports can continue that."

Bahrke to Team USA: Follow my tracks. Don't hide the emotion. Dwell on it. Feed on it. Use it.

It's hard not to in a setting like this. Moguls skiing in general is one of the great spectator sports. Unlike alpine skiing, where much of the course is high on the mountain, far from the crowds, every knee-crunching bump and big-air flight of a moguls skier is in full view of the crowd.

On a perfect winter day at the Winter Games, Utah never looked better, and Deer Valley—normally one of the more relaxed, polite, and posh ski venues in North America, was never more electric.

On a day when U.S. favorites Hannah Hardaway (fifth) and Ann Battelle (seventh) faltered, all the deafening cheers were saved for Bahrke, who pounced from a fifth-place position after the morning's first run to grab America's first spot on a medal stand. She had barely come to a complete stop at the bottom before the news was zipping, digitally, all around the shores of Lake Tahoe.

"Shannon's got a medal!" Bahrke's aunt, Mary Ellen Courtney, was screaming into a cell phone at the finish line. "It's spreading all over Tahoe City!"

Pandemonium reigned as Team Shannon—50 friends, relatives, and Tahoe supporters decked out in red, white, and blue fleece caps made by Bahrke's mother—hugged and danced and stomped and pointed at their girl's name up in lights on the Deer Valley scoreboard.

Bahrke, who claimed her first three World Cup podiums this season, was down and almost out of freestyle skiing two years ago, when a staph infection weakened her body to the point she considered dropping the sport. She fought back, regaining her form and winning the U.S. moguls championship last season.

It wasn't until this fall that she began to share big air with the likes of Traa, the reigning World Cup champion and 1998 Nagano bronze medalist. The only loss this season for Traa, in fact, was her second to Bahrke in Oberstdorf, Germany, earlier this season.

That boosted her confidence. And here, Bahrke took full advantage of the same home course she smoked to qualify for the Olympic team by winning a Gold Cup competition here New Year's Day.

As the Olympics crept closer, Bahrke's focus sharpened visibly, said a teammate, Emiko Torito, who was a course forerunner at Deer Valley.

"You can see it just in the way she carries herself," Torito said. "You can tell she's got it on straight."

Especially when it counted most. At the top of that second run, in fifth place, with the weight of a host nation on her shoulders and her grandparents, for the first time ever, in the stands, Shannon Bahrke gripped her poles, crouched—and smiled.

"I'm not really known to smile (in competition)," said Bahrke, glitter dust on her cheeks and red, white, and blue ribbons in her braided pigtails. "That was really odd. I just felt like it was my time to do well. I had to relax. The only way I know how to do that is to smile."

She knew she was first up in America's hit parade. And she did what American skiers do at the Olympics: sucked it up and went for it.

"She said earlier that it almost seemed like an anticlimax," Torito said. "After all that buildup, it was like, 'You mean all I have to do now is go ski?'"

That was all.

An hour from now, a week from now, a year from now, a lifetime from now, Shannon Bahrke will close her eyes and go back to the apex of that heli cross, high on a hill above Park City, at the dawn of the Salt Lake Games. She'll feel the crisp air, hear the roar, remember the thrill, and float there, suspended in time, lost in the moment.

Forgive her if she never comes down.

Warm-weather spells at Cypress Mountain could melt medal hopes for anxious competitors.

In women's aerials, **Lina Cheryazova** of Uzbekistan was the first gold medalist in Lillehammer, 1994. America's **Nikki Stone** took the honor in Nagano in 1998, followed by Australia's **Alisa Camplin** in 2002 at Salt Lake, where Canada's

Veronica Brenner and **Deidra Dionne** occupied the other two rungs of the medal stand.

For those of you keeping score at home, that's 10 U.S. medals (four gold), six for Canada (two gold). Next best: Norway and France with six each, Finland with four, and many other nations with three.

NEXT STOP: CYPRESS MOUNTAIN

Location: West Vancouver, B.C.
Spectator capacity: 12,000 in each of two temporary stadiums
Elevation: 915 meters (3,020 feet) at the base; 1240 meters (3,940 feet) at the top
Other events: Snowboarding
Medal ceremonies: B.C. Place Stadium

All of the "thrill sports" of the 2010 Games will share a common address: Cypress Mountain, a popular ski area contained in a large provincial park above West Vancouver, which will host snowboarding and freestyle skiing competitions. With a seating capacity of 12,000 in each of two temporary stadiums, the mountain will carve out courses for some of the Winter Games' more spectacular spectator events, including snowboarding's halfpipe contest and snowboard cross races and freestyle skiing's high-flying moguls and aerials contests, plus the new event of ski cross.

Add spectacular views of the city of Vancouver and its harbor from the top of Cypress, and you've got a venue that'll make producers from NBC and CBC drool. Fans should love the venue as well. It's rare to have a snow-sports venue so close to a major host city.

There's one worry about Cypress, shared by organizers and competitors alike, and it's a significant one: wet, foggy, or just plain warm weather at the venue. A test event in February 2008 revealed how bad it can get: A men's World Cup moguls event was placed on hold in the middle of the first run when fog and rain rolled in. Spectators huddled under tents at the base area couldn't even see up to the midpoint of the course, so thick was the fog.

By midday, things hadn't improved. Melting snow around the base area formed into small ponds, which turned into small streams, leaving volunteers scurrying to release the backed-up floodwaters by scooping shovelfuls of brown water with snow shovels. A day later, conditions were basically the same, and an aerials event scheduled for that day was canceled.

Good weather or bad, look for this to be a hopping venue during the 2010 Games, and one frequented by a younger crowd. Its proximity to the largest metropolitan city ever to host a Winter Olympics ensures that tens of thousands of youthful, pumped fans will be on hand for the Games' hippest and newest sports.

After the Games, the area will revert to its former use—a popular day-ski area for Vancouverites in the winter and hiking area in the summer months.

Freestyle Skiing 2010 Schedule

February 13: Women's moguls
February 14: Men's moguls
February 20: Women's aerials, qualifying
February 21: Men's ski cross
February 22: Men's aerials, qualifying
February 23: Women's ski cross
February 24: Women's aerials, finals
February 25: Men's aerials, finals

SKI JUMPING AND NORDIC COMBINED

❋ ❋ ❋ ❋ ❋

His name is Vinko Bogataj, and you know him.

Oh yes, you do.

Maybe not by name, but certainly by body: Limbs flailing, torso twisting, full weight landing on the snow like a giant sack of spuds, hat and goggles flying off, body tumbling, tumbling, tumbling into a snowy oblivion—and television history.

Bogataj is a former Slovenian ski jumper whose spectacular takeoff crash on ABC's *Wide World of Sports* opening montage has been forever lodged into the brains of entire generations of North Americans, and other fans of sport worldwide.

He's the "agony of defeat" guy.

And that tells you something about his passionate pursuit, ski jumping. What other Olympic sport—or sport of any kind, for that matter, outside perhaps auto racing—is best known for a notably spectacular failure by one of its participants?

Bogataj (pronounced "BOH-ga-tie") came about all this purely by chance. Competing in the ski-flying world championships in Oberstdorf, Germany, on March 21, 1970, he attempted his third jump of the competition in heavy snow—having

already fallen on his previous attempt. About half-way down the launch ramp, the Slovenian seemed to realize he was going too fast. Subsequent frantic attempts to put on the brakes—there are no brakes in ski jumping, hence the NASCAR, can't-look-away quality—only threw him further off balance.

At the crucial moment, his feet seemed to draw back beneath him, as though he was searching for a save-me-Lord fetal position. No dice.

Out of control, Bogataj went sailing off the side of the end of the ramp very much like . . . well, like you or I would go sailing off the side of the end of the ramp, dropping 20 feet or so and then smashing and crashing and mashing himself down the slope, breaking through a retaining fence and landing in a lump down below.

From that moment on, Bogataj, who was scooped into a body sled and pulled away by ski patrollers, became a symbol for every human being who's ever screwed the pooch in a profound and utterly unforgettable way. The limp, deflated man in a nylon suit was every one of us who has ever posted a new low on the bar exam or forgotten to pick up the kids from summer camp. He is us, and we are him, and we are all lying there together, roundly defeated, with a mild concussion.

That, in fact, was the fate of Bogataj, who was *so* fortunate that ABC happened to be there filming that day, ensuring that his epic crash would be seen, over and over and over and over and over and over again, by tens of millions of people, and their children, and their children, and so on. Close your eyes, and you can still hear Jim McKay's opening melodrama:

Spanning the globe to bring you the constant variety of sport! The thrill of victory . . . and the agony of defeat! The human drama of athletic competition! This is ABC's Wide World of Sports!

Over the decades that the show ran, the producers would occasionally get bored and tinker with the opening montage, subbing in new bits of film to run behind McKay's "thrill of victory" phrase. But Bogataj's blunder was simply too good to replace. He was stuck in the "agony of defeat" slot forever— the bad spot on the apple that wouldn't go away for three decades. He was, in fact, so bad that nobody ever came along later who was worse.

Bogataj actually returned to the sport for a year or two after that thermonuclear flop—"Never with the daring that he had before," McKay would insist. He went on to serve as an instructor and factory worker. Living behind the Iron Curtain, he was blissfully unaware of his faceless-celebrity status in North America—until he was invited to a *Wide World of Sports* 30th anniversary bash in 1991, and Muhammad Ali asked for his autograph.

At last report, the man with a career-best 57th place finish in the noted Four Hills Tournament in Austria lived in Slovenia with a wife and two daughters.

In an upside-down-and-backwards way, he actually did help bring his sport—wildly popular in North America in the late 19th and early 20th centuries, before alpine skiing came along to tempt all the daredevils—back into the public spotlight, at least in a small way.

His skullbuster on ABC, coupled with some spectacular Olympic performances over the years, made ski jumping a once-every-four-years television tradition for millions of Olympic fans. People appreciate the apparently high-risk sport (actually, accidents are quite rare) not only for its historic significance—ski jumpers have competed at every Olympics since the opening Winter Games at Chamonix in 1924—but for its graceful symbolism: Little man against big, bad, steep, and slippery nature.

Indeed, few sights scream "Winter Olympics" more than a ski jumper racing down a precipitous ramp, uncoiling like a snake at the lip of the jump and sailing, nose over tips, into the cold, thin air of the Alps or Rockies or British Columbian Coast Range, skis slapping down with a perfect, telemark-style THWAP that echoes off the ridges and back through the ages.

Of course, not everyone sees it that way. Ski jumping, it also could be argued, is far from an accessible pursuit and, in that sense, is fairly contrary to the Olympic ideal of inclusion. Most people don't have access to a ski jump—and would have the good sense to stay away from one if they did.

Even from a spectator's viewpoint, it's easy to find flaws with the pursuit. Up close, the sport really isn't beautiful, iconic—or even interesting, argues Whet Moser, a columnist for Slate.com: "Ski jumping," he wrote, "combines the Winter Olympics' most distinct qualities: the looming shadow of crippling physical trauma, highly specialized and otherwise useless equipment, and subtleties that are virtually invisible to the naked eye and incomprehensible to the layman."

Well, not completely incomprehensible, as we hope the information contained herein will convey.

But it's true that being a skilled observer of ski jumping takes a little practice, a little patience—and a healthy sense of humor.

Even Vinko Bogataj appreciated the folly inherent in what he was doing.

The *Los Angeles Times* recounts a day in 2002 when Bogataj, in Los Angeles to be interviewed by an ABC reporter, got into a minor car accident on the way to the studio. All he could do was shrug his shoulders.

"Every time I'm on ABC," he said, "I crash."

SPECTATOR'S GUIDE

Ski jumping is one of the great spectacles in all of winter sport—and always a hot ticket at the Olympics, for obvious reasons.

Field of Play

Modern ski jumpers compete on jumps of two different sizes: the "normal" hill and the "large" hill. Just what defines "normal" and "large" in terms of distance has steadily evolved over the years. But trust me, when you stand on top of one, there's nothing at all normal about a "normal" hill. To the neophyte, they're all big, tall, and frightening, although the sport, in truth, is not really as dangerous as it looks. Although skiers are flying more than 140 meters (450-plus feet) on the large hills, once they get past that gut-clenching drop from the lip of the jump, they are usually no more than about 10 feet (3 meters) off the ground, thanks to the contours of the landing hill below them. It's a bit of an optical illusion—and a grand one at that.

The hill's upper portions are actually large jumping ramps, called the in-run. These structures are built of concrete or wood and covered with snow. Their height depends on the terrain; jumps built into hillsides have shorter towers. At the end of the ramp is the takeoff table, a zone that has a defined grade of 11 percent. Below is a landing hill, contoured to mimic the line of a ski jumper's flight as he or she descends down the mountain, allowing for a smooth landing with, it is hoped, little impact.

Each hill has a landing target known as the calculation point, or critical point, or K point, which is the average distance, or par, in golf terms, for the jumper to shoot for. This point, about two-thirds of the way down the landing hill, is identified on the landing strip by the K line. In the K90 (normal) competition, the line is 70 to 90 meters (230–295 feet) from the start. Skiers can fly for distances up to and beyond 110 meters (360 feet) on these jumps. In the K120 (large) competitions, the line is 90 to 120 meters (295–394 feet) away from the start. Skiers can reach distances of 145 meters (475 feet) or more. (The numbers, contrary to common misperception, do not reflect the height of the jump ramp.)

In ski flying, another version of the sport not included in the Olympics, the K line is at 185 meters (607 feet). World record holder Björn Einar Romören sailed 239 meters (784 feet) on such a hill in 2005.

Below the K line is the braking area, where the downhill pitch lessens. The flat area at the bottom of the hill is called the outrun. It's where the jumper comes to a complete stop.

Format, Rules, and Strategy
Ski Jumping

In the Olympics, each jumper gets a training jump and two scored jumps. Team competitions, conducted on the large hill, give four team members two jumps each. (Teams are winnowed to the top eight after the first jump.) The highest aggregate team score wins.

The scoring system combines distance with style points. Skiers get an automatic 60 points per jump if they land on the K line. Points (2 per meter

Opposite: A skier takes flight on the jumping hill for summer training at Lake Placid, New York

on the normal hill, 1.8 per meter on the large hill) are deducted and/or added for landings that are short of, or beyond, this line. Note that a skier's overall distance is still reliant on human eyesight; a group of judges line the course on both sides of the K point. The one nearest the space between the jumper's feet upon landing raises a flag to mark the spot.

Style also comes into play. Five judges in a tower on the side of the landing zone rate each jump, awarding up to 20 points for style, as measured by steadiness of the skis during flight, balance, body position, and the landing.

The final score is a composite of the distance score plus the style score from three of the five judges (the highs and lows are thrown out). The jumper with the highest point score from his or her two jumps is the winner.

Just what constitutes proper ski-jumping "form" in the minds of judges is something that has evolved over the years. For a century after its invention, ski jumping involved a classic form known as the Kongsberger technique: forward leaning, arms forward, skis parallel. Fine-tuned in Norway by jumpers Sigmund Ruud and Jacob Tullin Thams after World War I, this style was the norm for many years. It was modified in the 1950s by Germans who experimented with placing the arms farther back, toward the hips, to emphasize the forward lean. The style is now considered something of a relic.

The new form, the V-style, was developed by Jan Boklöv of Sweden in 1985. It's the form we're familiar with today: body leaning dramatically forward, arms tight at the sides, back straight, with the nose almost in a line with the tips of skis that are splayed in a dramatic V shape. The new style allows jumpers to ride the air longer, adding about 10 percent to jumps.

Landings are done in the traditional telemark style, with one ski slightly ahead of the other, knees bent, arms held out to the sides.

Aerodynamics is key to the sport, so contestants are keenly aware of wind speed and direction, snow speed on the takeoff ramp, and other natural factors. Proper technique includes a tight tuck on the takeoff ramp; a carefully timed uncoiling of the legs and midsection at a precise point at the end of the takeoff ramp; smooth, clean body lines in the air while sailing down the mountain; and a precise, confident, well-balanced landing.

Even neophytes can spot a good jump when they see one: The skier seems to sail forever down the mountain (actually, it's usually only 4 to 5 seconds), wringing the very last ounce of air out of a jump before letting gravity pull him back to earth. Performed correctly, the sport is visually stunning and is usually one of the more popular spectator events at most Olympics.

Nordic Combined

Nordic combined is actually two very different sports in one: ski jumping and cross-country skiing. Because the two pursuits involve completely different techniques, muscle groups, training, and physical skills, the sport is one of the most difficult to master. It is, quite simply, twice the work.

These days, the standard event, called the Individual Gundersen, starts with two jumps on the normal hill and finishes with a 15-kilometer cross-country race. In the sport's early years, results from the cross-country race, started in intervals and timed, were converted to points, which were added to the jump points to get an overall score. The highest combined point total won. That changed in 1988, with the switch to the more fan-friendly Gundersen method. Jumping scores now determine the start intervals for a pursuit race, so whoever crosses the finish line first in the cross-country event is the overall event winner.

A team event was added for the 1988 Games, and a 7.5-kilometer sprint was added in 2002. Both events use the large (120-meter) hill.

In team competition, teams of four jumpers take two jumps each, with the eight jumps resulting in a score that determines the start for a relay race. The team whose final skier crosses the finish line first is the winner.

In the sprint, jumpers get one crack at the large hill to determine the cross-country race start intervals. Skiers then compete in a 7.5-kilometer race, with the first across the finish line winning the event.

Both ski jumping and Nordic combined are limited at this time, at least in the Olympics, to men. But women have begun jumping on the World Cup circuit and, in training, on the ski jumps at Whistler Olympic Park. A petition to add women's ski jumping to the 2010 schedule was rejected in 2006 by the International Olympic Committee, on the grounds that the sport has too few competitors in too few nations. But women will jump in the November 2009 FIS Nordic World ski championships in the Czech Republic, and pressure to add women's jumping as a medal sport is likely to persist.

Training and Equipment

Lower leg strength is paramount for springing off the jumps and for landing, so leg conditioning drills are common and run the gamut: running, weight lifting, and cardio machines. But one of the most reliable forms of training is also one of the oldest: walking back up that seemingly endless row of stairs after each jump. Thanks to wetted plastic coatings on ski jumps, skiers are now able to train safely all year around.

Jumping skis are extremely long—up to 270 centimeters—and one and a half to two times as wide as alpine skis. (The maximum length is 80 centimeters more than a skier's height.) Skis have no metal edges, and most have grooves running along the bottom to keep them tracking straight on the in-run. Wax is applied in certain conditions.

Boots are ankle high and flexible, with ankle stiffeners. Boots need to be flexible enough to allow a proper amount of lean but bulky enough to withstand landings, when jumpers hit the ground with a force about three times their weight. Boots are attached to the ski only at the toe, telemark style. Ski jumpers don't use poles.

Jumpers wear one-piece bodysuits like those worn in other sports, with two major exceptions— they're lined with foam, and they're not skintight. Extra fabric, in fact, can create lift in ski jumping, as can the degree of air that passes through one's suit fabric. As a result, suits are carefully regulated for "permeability." Jumpers also wear crash helmets and goggles, in the event of that "agony of defeat" spill.

HISTORY'S HITS AND MISSES

Ski jumping originated in—where else?—Norway, the Nordic sports capital of the world. No doubt due to the lack of cable TV and other factors, people have been jumping there—or watching jumpers—for entertainment for centuries. But the first organized competition took place in 1862. A better-known tourney, the Husebyrennene, took off in Oslo in 1879. In 1892, the event moved to Holmenkollen, the cradle of Nordic sport, where it has remained ever since.

Norway's Love Affair With Ski Jumping

One indication of just how popular ski jumping remains in Norway: Oslo's Holmenkollen jump has a seating capacity of 50,000 people. The jump has been renovated and expanded dozens of times; its takeoff tower is now an impressive, artful landmark, offering sweeping views of Oslo and the Oslo fjord. The complex is undergoing further renovation and expansion for the 2011 world ski jumping championships.

Other notable ski jumping hotbeds are Germany,

The stone inukshuk *emblem for the 2010 Winter Games guards the entrance to the ski jumps at Whistler Olympic Park.*

where the Four Hills tournament is a popular annual event in Bavaria and Austria; and Finland, which shares the Nordic Tournament with Norway.

Olympic History

Ski jumping was an inaugural event at the 1924 Chamonix Games. The large-hill contest was added to the schedule for the 1964 Innsbruck Olympics and has remained there ever since. Large-hill team jumping was added in 1988.

Ski Jumping, American-Style

Ski jumping, brought to the United States in the late 19th century by Scandinavian immigrants, was one of America's first "adventure sports" and became the primary pursuit of hotshot skiers until the late 1930s. Back then, ski jump competitions, which began in Minnesota, Wisconsin, and Michigan and spread to mountain ranges on the East and West Coasts, routinely drew tens of thousands of fans.

One of the oldest and most active advocates of

the sport was the Norge Ski Club in Chicago, which set up temporary jumps on more than one occasion at Soldier Field, now home to the Chicago Bears. Other portable jumps were built in locations as unlikely as Los Angeles. The sport faded quickly in America beginning with the advent of lift-assisted, modern downhill skiing in the post-World War II period.

Mr. Excitement, Matti Nykänen

Back in the 1980s, he was the most famous person in Finland. Today, he's still right up there, but for different reasons. Matti Nykänen ruled the sport of ski jumping in the 1980s, winning a total of five medals (four gold) at the 1984 Sarajevo and 1988 Calgary Games.

But he always seemed to take the most pothole-filled road to the medal stand. After his standout performance in Sarajevo, winning gold in the 90 meters and silver in the 70 meters, he was an early favorite to win both events at Calgary. But in between events, his behavior—fueled by alcohol—got in the way. Nykänen was thrown off his national ski jumping team twice.

Still, he got it together before the 1988 Games and won the opening event, the 70 meters, handily. After several weather delays, he also dominated the 90 meters, becoming the first ski jumper to win three gold medals. But he wasn't finished. Nykänen also led his team to victory in the team jumping competition, a new event, giving him a fourth gold.

After his career dimmed, the nine-time world championship medalist became an even greater celebrity—in bad ways and good. He was accused multiple times of crimes such as domestic violence and then, in 2004, of attempted manslaughter, the result of stabbing a family friend. He was convicted of aggravated assault and served nearly a year in jail.

Nykänen also is known in Finland for his many marriages (five at last count), his cornball singing career, and various commercial gigs. In 2007, he returned to ski jumping, winning the International Masters championship in February 2008. His biography was published in 2006. Its title: *Greetings From Hell.*

Soaring Like an Eagle

Perhaps the best-known ski jumper of all time was never very good at it. Eddie "the Eagle" Edwards, the first man to represent Great Britain and Northern Ireland in ski jumping, was the only contestant who applied for the British Olympic ski jumping team for the 1988 Calgary Games.

It hadn't been easy to get there. Edwards, ranked 55th in the world entering the Olympics, did most of his training at the ski jump in Lake Placid, New York, with used or borrowed equipment. He had a few things working against him: Edwards weighed more than 180 pounds—at least 20 pounds more than the average competitor. He was also nearsighted, requiring him to jump with glasses that often fogged up, and his ski jumping campaign was completely self-financed. His qualifying jump for the Games, 77 meters, had been made in Australia.

As expected, Edwards finished last in Calgary. But his nonchalant lack of success made him an even more popular figure, and his every move was watched in Calgary by a smirking press corps that nicknamed him Mr. Magoo because of his thick glasses and owlish face.

Fellow ski jumpers were not amused. After the Calgary Games, entrance requirements were made much stricter, specifically to weed out "tourist" Olympians like Edwards. Ironically, the rule ensures that his fame will live on: The 1990 rule, drafted by the IOC, requires Olympians to compete on international circuits and place in the top 30 percent or the top 50 competitors, whichever is less. It will forever be known as the "Eddie the Eagle Rule."

Edwards tried but failed to qualify for the next three Olympic Games. In his retirement, the Eagle wrote a book and released a single, "Fly Eddie Fly," that cracked the Top 50 in Britain.

"I think what my Olympic participation shows is that you don't have to be the best in the world to be popular," he told Outside Online.

At last report, he was working as a snowboard instructor at a Colorado ski resort.

A Japanese Sweep

The 1972 Sapporo Olympics, the first Winter Games in Asia, brought the most dramatic moment in ski jumping's Olympic history. Japan, stung by the failure to win many medals at the 1964 Tokyo Games, reportedly feared a second humiliation at the Winter Games—its best finish to date had been silver in alpine skiing in 1956.

But three Japanese jumpers, led by national hero Yukio Kasay, buried that legacy for good on February 6, when 100,000 screaming fans saw Kasay win the gold medal in the 70-meter jump with the performance of his life. That would have been plenty, but his teammates rose to the occasion as well. Countryman Akitsugu Konno shocked the world by winning the silver. Teammate Seiji Aochi claimed the bronze.

The subsequent celebration was one of the most joyful locals-make-good parties in Olympic history: All three men had grown up on Hokkaido, the island home of Sapporo.

Japan Rises Once More

The spirit of those 1972 heroes clearly lived in the memories of their successors at Japan's next Winter Games, at Nagano in 1998. There, Kazuyoshi Funaki, the winner of the famous Four Hills jumping contest

Japanese ski jumper Kazuyoshi Funaki celebrates the gold medal at the 1998 Nagano Games.

in Austria and Bavaria before the Games, claimed the gold medal in the 120-meter jump before adoring hometown fans in the Japanese Alps. He also took the silver medal in the 90 meters, then joined teammates Masahiko Harada, Hiroya Saito, and Takanobu Okabe to claim the team jumping medal, one of the Games' emotional highlights.

It was particularly sweet vindication for Harada, a 1993 world champion who had mistimed a jump to cost his team the team gold medal at the 1994 Lillehammer Games. His first jump in the team competition at Nagano had been nearly as bad—it was so short that it actually led to a subtraction in points for Japan.

Going into the second round of jumps at Hakuba, Japan trailed Austria. Harada's teammates placed solid jumps to retake the lead, leaving the event in the once-disgraced jumper's hands. This time, he nailed it, flying 137 meters and sending the crowd, on a snowy day, into hysterics. The jump had strengthened Japan's lead, and Funaki put the finishing touches on the victory with a masterful leap of 125 meters.

Arriving as it did at the end of the Games, the team jumping gold made the Nagano Olympics for Japan.

A Slight, 50-Year Delay

One of the most fascinating medal stories in Winter Olympic history involved Anders Haugen, who spent most of his life in the Lake Tahoe area teaching skiing—and not knowing he was the only American ever to win a ski-jumping Olympic medal.

The story began in 1924 at Chamonix, where Haugen, then 36, competed in the 70-meter ski jump for America. He finished fourth behind Norwegian skiing and jumping legend Thorleif Haug—or so he thought. Even at the time, the decision was hotly disputed.

Americans on the scene pointed out that Haugen's combined distance for his two jumps was greater than

Haug's. But judges said Haugen's unorthodox style—far ahead of his time in aerodynamics, Haugen leaned far out over the tips of his skis—had cost him too many style points to earn the medal.

He lived with the decision for 50 years, until a chance event in Norway changed history. At a 1974 gathering marking the half-century reunion of Norwegian athletes from the Chamonix Games, athlete Thoralf Strömstad, who had finished second to Haug in the Nordic combined, sat down with historian Jakob Vaage and discovered an error in the computation of scores that had gone unnoticed for half a century.

The final score sheet showed Haug with 18.00 points, compared to Haugen's 17.916. But the math on Haug's score was wrong; the actual score should have been Haugen, 17.916, Haug, 17.821. The finding was reported to the IOC, which officially reversed the medal standings.

Norwegians didn't protest. Haug had his own handful of medals from those Games. In addition to the falsely awarded bronze, Haug, then 29, had won gold in the Nordic combined as well as in the 50-kilometer and 18-kilometer and cross-country ski races. (The latter race result was combined with the ski jump for the Nordic combined medal.)

So it was that in September 1974, Haugen, a three-time U.S. champion who was born in Norway and emigrated to the United States in 1908, was invited to the legendary ski jump at Holmenkollen in Oslo and at long last presented his bronze medal. It was awarded by Haug's daughter, Anna Marie Magnussen, who had kept her father's medals for 40 years after his death.

On that day, Anders Haugen, who had paid his own way to the Chamonix Games, was 85 years old—no doubt the oldest man ever to dip his head to receive an Olympic medal. When he died at age 95, he was the only American to ever earn one in ski jumping. He still is.

LEGEND OF THE SPORT
BIRGER RUUD, NORWAY, SKI JUMPING

Born: 23 August 1911, Kongsberg, Norway
Died: 13 June 1998
Olympics: Lake Placid (1932); Garmisch-Partenkirchen; St. Moritz (1948)
Medals: 2 gold, 1 silver

Norway's Birger Ruud will go down in history as one of those rare athletes whose bravery and accomplishments away from the sport overshadow his triumphs within it.

Ruud, a ski jumper who would be remembered as one of the Winter Games' most diversified athletes, earned his first gold medal at Lake Placid in 1932, winning the large-hill individual ski jump competition in an extremely tight race over his boyhood friend, Hans Beck. Both Ruud and Beck had grown up in a small Norwegian mining town, Kongsberg, southwest of Oslo.

Friendly competition among elite athletes, in fact, was something Ruud grew up with. His brothers, Sigmund and Asbjørn, were also accomplished jumpers. The trio dominated international jumping in the 1930s, winning world championships in 1931, 1935, and 1937.

At the 1936 Garmisch-Partenkirchen Games, Ruud attempted an unprecedented double, entering both the traditional ski jumping competition and the Games' newest sport, alpine skiing. It seemed a natural fit: He was a talented, all-mountain skier who had won a world championship in the alpine combined in 1935. As it happened, the Games' first alpine event was an alpine combined downhill/slalom. He almost won it: Ruud led the downhill race by 4.4 seconds, but he missed a gate in the slalom and took a 6-second penalty that dropped him to fourth. A week later, he won the gold medal in ski jumping.

Ruud's fame spread around the globe as he traveled for competition. A February 28, 1938, *Time* magazine article recounts Ruud's appearance at a ski jumping contest in Vermont—while on his honeymoon:

At the age when the average U. S. moppet is getting a tricycle from Santa Claus, the average Norwegian child is getting a pair of skis. In Norway children start to ski when they are 4, can usually jump 60 ft. when they are 8 and 150 ft. when they

A life-size, bronze sculpture of ski-jumping legend Birger Ruud flies over Kongsberg, Norway.

are 12. To encourage the sport, the Norwegian Ski Association each year gives 5,000 pairs of skis to children who cannot afford to buy them.

So it is not surprising that the best ski jumpers in the world are developed in Norway. Last week, when 9,000 ski enthusiasts gathered in the little town of Brattleboro, Vt. to witness the ski-jumping championship of the U. S., the entry list looked like an Oslo telephone directory. Sprinkled among the Class A competitors were a few native Americans but the majority were Norwegians sojourning in the U. S. A dozen or so were topflight, but the performer the crowd had really come to see was Birger Ruud, the No. 1 product of Norway's extraordinary ski-training system.

The crowd was not disappointed. With gaping mouths it watched jumper after jumper slant through the air—eight with leaps of over 200 ft.—but it was 130-lb. Birger Ruud who made the spectators gasp with his prodigious and perfect jump of 216 ft., a whizzing arc ending with the wood slapping evenly on the hard snow.

It broke the hill record by 19 ft. and clinched the championship with a total of 229.8 points (based on best distance and form in two jumps). Six out of the first ten placed were Ruud's countrymen.

Like all other athletes, Ruud, by now a Norwegian hero, had to sit on the sidelines as Olympics were canceled in 1940 and 1944 because of World War II. But he didn't sit around and mope. After the German occupation of Norway, Ruud defied the Nazis at every turn, hosting his own ski jump competitions to raise money for the Resistance. He was arrested in 1943 and served 18 months in Grini prison camp. Upon his release, he joined the Norwegian resistance and—traveling on skis, of course—helped locate and stash ammo dumped from British planes.

In 1948, with Europe finally freed, Ruud returned to the Olympic Games at St. Moritz as a coach but then decided to enter the ski jump event, and once more did himself and Norway proud. He won a silver medal in the ski jump, behind countryman Petter Hugsted, who also hailed from Ruud's hometown of Kongsberg.

Ruud retired from the sport but remained a heroic figure to Olympic fans and Norwegians. He was cofounder of the Kongsberg Skiing Museum, and in 1994, at 82, he helped carry the Olympic flag into the opening ceremony for the Lillehammer Games. He reportedly had been asked to light the Olympic Cauldron but had to pass because of a heart condition.

A life-size, bronze sculpture of Ruud flying through the air on jumping skis is now a prominent feature in Kongsberg's city center.

Who Are You Calling a Coward?

The winner of the ski-jump contest at Chamonix that inaugural Olympic year was Norway's Jacob Tullin Thams, who edged out countryman Narve Bonna. Nobody knew it at the time, but he would go on to make history once more, in his own way.

Thams, seeking to defend his title in 1928 at St. Moritz, was one of many Norwegian jumpers who told the Swiss hosts, after their first jumps, that the starting point for the jumps was too high, giving an advantage to lesser-skilled jumpers. The Swiss, decidedly not neutral in this case, essentially responded by calling the Norwegians pansies.

Thams, enraged, took to the hill and jumped so far—73 meters, at that time unprecedented—that he sailed beyond the landing area, into the flat below, according to IOC historical accounts. And there, he fell on the landing. He was promptly docked so heavily on style points that he dropped from 5th place to 28th.

He got his revenge, sort of, in 1938, at the Berlin Summer Olympics, where he won a silver medal in 8-meter class yachting. Thams thus became one of only five athletes to have medaled in both the Summer and Winter Olympics.

Germany's Nordic Combined God

No Olympian dominated the incredibly challenging sport of Nordic combined like Germany's Ulrich Wehling, one of the most versatile athletes ever to compete in the Olympics. Aside from ski jumping and cross-country, Wehling excelled at cycling, running, tennis, and track. At his first Winter Games—Sapporo in 1972—Wehling, 19, was third in the ski race and fourth in the jump, with his combined score earning the gold medal.

He repeated the feat at Innsbruck in 1976, winning the jump contest and finishing 13th in the ski race, despite an eye infection that left his vision impaired. In Lake Placid in 1980, Wehling was on top of the medal stand again, becoming the third athlete—along with figure skaters Sonja Henie and Gillis Grafström—to win three successive gold medals in the same Winter Olympics event.

RECORD BOOK: SKI JUMPING AND NORDIC COMBINED

Ski jumping is yet another Nordic sport ruled by the Nordic nations, particularly Finland and Norway. The flying Finns lead in gold medals, with 10 of their 22 overall medals being gold. The Norwegians, however, have 28 overall medals, nine of them gold. Not far behind is Austria, with 20 medals, five of them gold. Japan has fared unusually well for a nation its size, with nine overall medals, three of them gold.

Norwegian dominance has manifested itself both early and late in Games history. They captured every gold medal from 1924 to 1952. Then the sport briefly left them behind, as the advent of large-hill jumping brought more medals to Austria, Germany, and Italy. By 1964, they were back on top of the medal stand, and they often wind up there today, although Japan also has risen as a major ski jumping power.

Ski jumping has never been kind to North Americans. The United States has a single medal, a bronze awarded 50 years after the fact to **Anders Haugen.** Canada has never won an Olympic Games ski jumping medal.

In Nordic combined, the results are similar. Norway leads with 26 total medals, 11 gold, followed by Finland (14 medals, four gold), East Germany (seven medals, three gold), and Austria (10 medals, two gold). Neither America nor Canada has won a medal in Nordic combined.

Individual medalists of note: Norway's **Birger Ruud** won the Olympic gold medal in both 1932 and 1936 and, amazingly, returned to the postwar Olympics to capture another silver medal in the

1948 Games, at age 36. Finland's **Matti Nykänen** is the all-time individual leader, with five medals, four of them gold, split between the 1984 Sarajevo and 1988 Calgary Games.

NEXT STOP: WHISTLER OLYMPIC PARK

Location: Callaghan Valley, west of Whistler, B.C.

Spectator capacity: 12,000 in each of three finishing areas

Elevation: 850 meters (2,788 feet) at the base; 910 meters (2,985 feet) at the top

Other events: Cross-country skiing, biathlon, Paralympic biathlon/cross-country skiing

Medals ceremonies: Whistler Village Celebration Plaza

The landmarks—some would say scars—left behind by a Winter Olympic Games are many, but none so prominent as the ski jumps. Most of the earlier jumps, even those built on the sides of mountains, are enormous structures, with giant concrete towers jutting into the sky and massive steel or wood super-structures supporting the skier launch ramp.

Depending on one's taste in architecture, they're either cool historical relics or garish exer-cises in lack of foresight. In some places, such as Lake Placid, New York, a tiny village in the midst of hundreds of thousands of acres of green forestland, they look decidedly out of place. In others, such as the wide-open country around Calgary, Alberta, they are visible for dozens of miles.

At Whistler Olympic Park, the opposite is true. No visitor to Whistler, the bustling, international-destination ski village 120 kilometers (75 miles) north of Vancouver, will ever see the ski jumps

A snow groomer smooths the finish area beneath the ski jumps at Whistler Olympic Park.

unless he or she goes looking for them. The Olympic Park, home to the ski jumps, the biathlon range, and cross-country ski trails, is hidden in the woods, 12.8 kilometers (8 miles) west of Whistler proper (if there is such a thing). And the ski jumps themselves are almost hidden from view inside the Olympic Park, because of their low-profile construction.

The architects, seeking a minimalist approach that didn't detract from the "wilderness" nature of the site, which previously was completely undeveloped, made effective use of existing topography. Both ski jumps are carved into existing hillsides, eliminating the need for a giant tower. The result is a pair of gracefully curved jump ramps that seem to be sprouting from the side of the hill itself. It's a grand setting, overall, with first- and second-growth forest surrounding the jumps on three sides.

Temporary bleacher seats will put spectators very close to the landing area and then will be removed post-Games, when the entire Olympic Park will revert to a training facility and day-use Nordic area for recreational skiers.

Ski Jumping and Nordic Combined 2010 Schedule

February 12: Normal-hill qualifying, individual men's

February 13: Normal-hill final, individual men's

February 14: Nordic combined, normal-hill individual men's

February 19: Large-hill qualifying, individual men's

February 20: Large-hill final, individual men's

February 22: Large-hill team, men's

February 23: Nordic combined team large hill

February 25: Nordic combined large-hill sprint, men's

SNOWBOARDING

❄ ❄ ❄ ❄ ❄

The irony was almost too rich. And we'd all been complicit in the setup.

In the days before the 1998 Nagano Olympics—way before anyone outside Whistler, B.C., had heard the name Ross Rebagliati—a lot of us journos were cranking out stories about the new kids on the Winter Olympics block: snowboarders.

The inclusion of mountain-sports bad kids—at least by reputation—was revolutionary at the time. One, because it showed the International Olympic Committee actually taking progressive steps to keep its sports offerings fresh and in tune with a younger audience perceived as more interested in spending a few TV hours watching the X Games than the men's downhill. And two, because those IOC folks, in this regard, were even a bit ahead of the snowboarders themselves, who hadn't campaigned to make their sport medal-worthy.

That flew in the face of history. Generally, new sports undergo years of organizing, begging, pleading, cajoling, and even, in the old days, very likely bribing to be considered by the IOC. Not snowboarding, which the IOC actively courted, going so far as to help nudge the staid ski federation, the FIS, into taking the board sport under its wing and stealing it away, in essence, from an existing snowboard governing body.

That set off something of a moral dilemma among the world's top snowboarders. There was no question that their sport was athletically suitable for Olympic competition: Top-level snowboarders are every bit as talented as elite skiers, for instance. But there was ample question about whether the loose, laid-back world of snow riding—which thrived on a contrarian, free-spirited ethic more akin to surfing than to opening ceremonies—would fit comfortably within the Olympic framework.

Many boarders, amped at the chance to win an Olympic medal, quickly got over this. But some didn't. Norway's Terje Haakonsen, at the time widely considered the world's premier snowboarder, announced that he wouldn't ride in the Olympics—not this one, not any one. But tellingly, no other elite-level riders followed suit.

In America, from Mount Baker, Washington, to Stratton Mountain, Vermont, the dual-coast birthplaces of modern snowboarding, riders instead geared up for what most of them—and many of us—assumed would be an easy medal grab for Americans. We did, after all, invent the sport, which ought to count for something, right?

But on the ground in Nagano, the first snowboard competitions proved to be far from a sensation. Giant slalom racing, which kicked off the events, took place at Mount Yakebitai at Shiga Kogen—notably, a ski resort that, like a few holdouts in the United States, still banned snowboarding, right up until the lighting of the flame.

Weather conditions were atrocious, with heavy snow, rain, and fog fouling early schedules. But when the riding did begin, an unheralded Canadian rider named Ross Rebagliati smoked his second run, coming from far back in the pack to beat favorites that included America's Chris Klug. Rebagliati, a free-spirited rider from Whistler, B.C., grabbed snowboarding's first gold. After his race, he dedicated it to a friend who had recently been killed in an avalanche.

The IOC beamed proudly, suggesting that these ne'er-do-wells really did fit in nicely with the whole notion of Olympic spirit.

The announcement came three days later, and most of us in the main press center in Nagano didn't know whether to laugh, cry, or run for our laptops: Rebagliati had tested positive for marijuana.

Standing on the cusp of history, we all wrote the next day, only a snowboarder would find a way to get disqualified for using a performance-*impeding* drug. Pot, after all, doesn't exactly enhance your performance at anything, except maybe snacking or playing jazz riffs.

When the smirking subsided, the arguing began. The IOC stripped Rebagliati of his medal; the Canadian Olympic committee filed an appeal with the Court of Arbitration for Sport. Rebagliati, for his part, wondered if he'd get out of Japan in one piece, given the nation's strict drug laws. He was, in fact, grilled by police about the matter.

He claimed he hadn't smoked dope for nearly a year. How, then, to explain the positive test? He'd attended a pre-Olympics party, he said, in Whistler, where the typical B.C. bud marijuana is four or five times more potent than normal. His positive reading was the result of second-hand smoke ingestion.

More smirking and teasing commenced, and fellow snowboarders were either horrified or howling. But the matter was more significant than it appeared on its face: It forced the IOC to look, for the first time, at the relevance of positive marijuana tests at the Olympics.

Ultimately, the arbitrator ruled that no legal basis existed to strip Rebagliati's medal because of marijuana use, because the ski federation and IOC hadn't listed it as a prohibited substance.

Rebagliati was allowed to keep his medal, which in fact he had never physically relinquished. And no one should be surprised that he became a national hero in Canada, where marijuana laws are, well, relaxed by many other nations' standards. Rebagliati, a local celebrity in Whistler, which named a city park after him, was among the dignitaries and honored athletes at Canada Hockey Place when Whistler learned via satellite of its successful Olympic bid.

For years, he enjoyed a lucrative sponsorship deal with Roots, then the Canadian Olympic Committee's primary sportswear sponsor. He's even threatened to make a comeback for the Vancouver Games.

Good luck to him there. From that rough, foggy, scandal-plagued start in the mountains of Japan, Olympic snowboarding has grown by leaps and bounds, in both quality and fan attention.

When organizers increased the size of the pipe, the Games' halfpipe contest grew, both in big air and fan appreciation. In the Salt Lake 2002 Games,

Rosey Fletcher competes in the parallel giant slalom at the 1998 Nagano Games.

the halfpipe contest—swept by Americans, in the men's division—stood as a highlight, in terms of both crowd response and television ratings.

The sport has come a long way since Ross Rebagliati clung to his gold in a Nagano police station. In the end, they couldn't take it away from him. Nor will they ever take away his legacy as the first-ever snowboard gold medalist.

It's safe to say that no rider alive, past, present, or future, will ever leave a smoke trail like Ross.

SPECTATOR'S GUIDE

Because of its fast-paced action, soaring jumps, and spectacular wipeouts, snowboarding has quickly grown from a stepchild Olympic sport to a true fan favorite.

Field of Play

Snowboarding is contested on slopes with heavy degrees of human shaping. The *halfpipe,* where freestyle snowboarding takes place, is a carved snow trough, about 110 meters (360 feet) long and 13 to 17 meters (42 to 56 feet) wide, with walls about 3.5 meters (11.5 feet) high. The *parallel giant slalom* course is much like those used in alpine skiing for a giant slalom: A set of gates set 7 to 15 meters (23 to 50 feet) apart over a vertical drop of 120 to 250 meters (394 to 800 feet) so racers can compete side to side, making turns all the way down the course. *Snowboard cross* courses are long, undulating trails—just barely wide enough if all four competitors were to run side by side—with a series of whoop-de-do jumps.

Format, Rules, and Strategy

Snowboarding at the Olympics has evolved since its first inclusion as a medal sport in Nagano in 1998. That year, the *giant slalom* was just that: a single rider running a course of gates. To add more excitement, particularly for TV, the event morphed into the *parallel giant slalom* for the Salt Lake 2002 Winter Games. Under the new format, racers run on side-by side courses. Timed qualifying runs narrow the field to 16 competitors, who enter a single-elimination tournament. The elimination matches actually consist of two races: One run is taken and

Ross "The Boss" Powers catches big air in the halfpipe at the 2002 Salt Lake Winter Games.

then the racers switch sides. Double winners move on; if there's a split, the combined times of the two runs decides it.

The *halfpipe* competition has remained the same. The scoring is an arbitrary judging system, not unlike figure skating, in which riders are awarded points for tricks and jumps. Rest assured, snowboarding is the only sport in which competitors earn a separate score for "amplitude," or the speed and height of the move, coupled with the "energy" of the rider. Other scoring factors include difficulty, variety, execution of tricks, and the overall flow of the run. Deductions are made for falls. In the finals, six riders take two runs each, with only the best score of the two counting.

In 2006, Turin Games organizers, in a deft move, added *snowboard cross,* a bow to the X Games generation of television snow sports watchers. In this event, riders race in a pack of four down a course with big-air jumps; sharp, banked corners; and other obstacles. It's gripping action, with plenty of body contact and occasional come-from-behind victories at the finish line.

A series of knockout heats are conducted, with the first two finishers moving on to the next round, until a final in which the only four remaining duel head-to-head. Some contact is allowed, but outright interference is verboten. The format proved so popular that Vancouver organizers added the similar *ski cross* event for the 2010 Games.

Training and Equipment

Most snowboarders train primarily by riding. Off-slope work includes using muscle-toning equipment, flexibility training, trampoline exercises, and balancing exercises on a Swiss ball.

Even though the sport of snowboarding is only about three decades old, the modern competition snowboard is a far cry from early versions. Freestyle boards, used in the halfpipe and other trick-riding events, are between 134 and 160 centimeters long (depending on the size and riding style of the rider) and about 24 centimeters wide. The boards are twin-tipped, allowing them to land and slide both frontward and backward.

Alpine boards, used for slalom racing and snowboard cross, are designed for speed. They range from 145 to 175 centimeters long and about 18 to 20 centimeters wide. They have a distinctly squared tail, which aids in carving longer-radius turns. Alpine riders wear hard-shelled plastic boots, similar to alpine ski boots, for direct transmission of body weight to board edge. Freestyle riders wear soft, flexible boots, which create more subtle pressure on the edges of the board.

Alpine riders wear crash helmets, goggles, and bodysuits built for racing. Freestyle riders typically wear baggy clothing and soft hats.

HISTORY'S HITS AND MISSES

Unlike most Winter Games sports, whose roots stretch back centuries, snowboarding is a relatively recent phenomenon—less than 40 years old at the dawn of the 2010 Games.

Several people lay claim to having produced the first snowboard, as it were—a single board with dual foot mountings designed to mimic the motion of surfing on snow. The first crude board to be mass-manufactured, the Snurfer, was based on a 1960s design by Sherman Poppen, a Michigan engineer who built the device for his daughter.

An early adopter and experimenter with that product was Vermont's Jake Burton Carpenter, who refined the idea into something most closely resembling a modern snowboard, launching in 1977 a company that would dominate the industry up to the present day. Other experimenters were developing competing products around the same time, notably Dimitrije Milovich's Swallowtail, the precursor to the Winterstick line, debuting in 1976. Another

early pioneer, California's Tom Sims, was making snowboards in his garage the same year Burton's company got off the ground, teaming with collaborator Bob Weber to develop the Skiboard. Burton and Sims became competitors in a gear race that continues to this day.

With that gear in hand, early riders began to make tentative first tracks at U.S. ski areas in the early 1980s. At first, they were banned from most ski resorts, so they had to seek refuge in more far-flung corners. Stowe in Vermont and Mount Baker Ski Area in northwest Washington were the first traditional ski resorts to develop active—and skilled—snowboard communities. They spread like wildfire.

By 1990, resort operators, recognizing snowboarding as a key to their survival, allowed the sport at most ski resorts. Today, only a couple of holdouts remain.

Boarders, Meet Your Bureaucracy

Snowboarding got its own World Cup competition in 1987, and its future as an international, perhaps even Olympic medal, sport became clear. A long and often counterproductive argument ensued within the snowboard community: Should a freeform, maverick sport such as snowboarding be subject to the rules of an international federation? If so, which one?

By 1998, the debate was over. Snowboarding, the International Olympic Committee decided, would fall under the auspices of the International Ski Federation, or FIS. It was quickly added as a medal event, with halfpipe and giant slalom, for the 1998 Nagano Games.

The decision wasn't without controversy, which

Opposite: Danny Kass, Ross Powers, and J.J. Thomas on the medal stand in Salt Lake, where the U.S. swept the men's halfpipe competition.

has faded but still burns in the hearts of some snowboard pioneers. Placing the sport within the structure of the International Ski Federation put it in the hands of the chief proponents of skiing, the very sport snowboarders had revolted against. And it was a snub to the International Snowboarding Federation, a snowboarders' group that had been sanctioning international competitions since the early 1990s.

One result of that rift had a substantial impact on the Nagano Games: Norwegian snowboard legend Terje Haakonsen announced that he would never attend an Olympics, a vow he has kept.

Since that time, most snowboarders have accepted the FIS oversight, under which the sport has thrived, particularly after its popularity at the Salt Lake Olympics of 2002.

Home Snow Advantage

American snowboard fans had waited through two Olympic cycles for the expected dominance in a sport invented in the United States. At the 2002 Salt Lake Winter Games, they finally saw it in Park City. With a raucous crowd of more than 16,000 looking on, America's Ross Powers, Danny Kass, and J. J. Thomas stole the show, winning gold, bronze, and silver. It was the first time any nation had swept a snowboard event and was America's first Winter Games sweep since men's figure skating in 1956.

Powers, a Vermont native who had turned 23 the day before, popped off the most memorable halfpipe run in Olympic history, catching huge, hospital air and pulling off seven textbook twists and grabs. Coming a day after teammate Kelly Clark grabbed the gold medal in the women's contest, the sweep put America firmly in the halfpipe driver's seat—a precedent that would be upheld four years later in Turin, where newcomers Shaun White and Hannah Teter claimed gold, while Kass and Gretchen Bleiler won silver.

OLYMPIC FLASHBACK
NAGANO GAMES

Feb. 4, 1998

Reported by Ron C. Judd for The Seattle Times

Author's note: One of the things we Olympic writers get paid to do before every Games is prognosticate. That's always risky business, but it's even more so when the sport in question has never been competed before in the Olympics. Such was the case with snowboarding, which, when it debuted in Nagano in 1998, was widely considered to be a set of gimme medals for the Americans — who, after all, had invented and largely perfected the sport. It turned out quite differently, and the sport preview I wrote in advance of those Games is interesting today because of that as well as the early questions about whether snowboarders going to the Olympics constituted a sellout. Today, that question has largely been answered by the snowboard world: No.

Phil Mahre and Bonnie Blair keep theirs in trophy cases.

Todd Richards has other plans for the Olympic gold medal he expects to bring home from Nagano, Japan.

"I want to win a medal and wear it out to some bars," the U.S. Olympian said recently. "It's going to be the goofiest damn thing. . . . The whole attitude of all this organized baloney just makes me laugh."

Welcome to the wonderful world of Winter Olympic snowboarding.

Richards, a favorite in the Olympics' first snowboard halfpipe competition Feb. 12, was telling *Transworld Snowboarding* magazine two things the rest of the snowboard world already knows: The five rings are about to get a coat of duct tape. And nobody is sure whether that will be good or bad for one of America's fastest-growing winter sports.

Snowboarders will compete for medals in both halfpipe and giant slalom competitions, reflecting the two general disciplines (trick and free riding) in a renegade sport that grew simultaneously from early 1980s roots at Mount Baker, Washington, and Stratton Mountain, Vermont.

Predicting medal outcomes is a crapshoot. Not only is the event new, other intangibles loom — such as whether athletes from the U.S. and elsewhere will agree to wear team uniforms.

The mere notion of pouring a snowboarder — someone who considers riding more a lifestyle, or even religion, than a team sport — into a red, white, and blue monkey suit makes some of the sport's founders cringe. Snowboarding, after all, was launched by renegades, for renegades, and accepting the standards of the stodgy International Olympic Committee ranks right up there with litter patrol on most riders' wish lists.

Some of them, most notably snowboard superstar Terje Haakonsen of Norway, have chosen to forsake the Games altogether, leaving it to patriotic posers.

But the jury in the foothills of the Cascades remains decidedly out on the merits of Olympic snowboarding.

"It seems like the majority is kind of undecided; they're waiting to see what happens," said Marcella Dobis, a former World Cup rider and current proprietor of Mount Baker Snowboard Shop in Glacier, Whatcom County.

Some riders see it as legitimization of the physical rigors of the sport they love, she said. But others view it as a pure sellout, a cheap commercialization of their lifestyle. Even those willing to give Olympic snowboarding a chance, such as Dobis, are angry at the way the U.S. Ski and Snowboard Association has chosen to market the U.S. team. The team's official mascot, for example, is "Animal," a Jim Henson cartoon character.

"That's a complete misrepresentation of what snowboarding's all about," Dobis said. "It's this little animal that's broken out of jail, with chains around its wrist and neck. He looks crazed, absolutely crazed. It almost made me cry.

"This is how our federation is portraying snowboarding? The feeling you receive for snowboarding is pure love. Love for the mountains, love for being up there with nature."

Washington's Mike Jacoby, a favorite for a medal in the giant slalom, says it is possible to mix love and politics on the snowboard slopes. A Columbia Gorge resident, Jacoby fits the laid-back image of a Northwest free-riding snowboarder. But he's also competed on the World Cup circuit for more than 10 years, with an eye on this month's Olympics.

"There's really only one person [Haakonsen] who's not going," Jacoby said. "He's taking a stand. I'm happy he's getting his wish. Obviously, he's taking the easy way out. He's not willing to do the work.

"I'm not focusing on the people who don't want to do it. As far as us out there on the hill, we don't even care. We're having a blast. The only thing that'll happen is that more people will get into it, more will enjoy it."

Jacoby and other riders suggest all the criticism about commercialization is hypocritical. Most riders complaining about uniforms, for example, aren't doing it because they can't stand to be categorized. They're doing it because of logo conflicts with gear sponsors. In that sense, snowboarding sold itself to commercial America years ago.

So why not celebrate the sport by honoring its best athletes?

The Olympics, Jacoby said, gives kids something to strive for.

"These Olympics will create dreams," he said. "And the future is about dreams."

The present, however, is about medals, and the U.S. should bring some home in a sport invented here.

Snowboarder Chris Klug races in the parallel giant slalom at the 1998 Nagano Winter Games.

A Higher Cause

By all appearances, Aspen, Colorado's Chris Klug was living the good life in his late teens: professional snowboarder, Olympian (he finished sixth in the inaugural giant slalom in Nagano), and all the trappings of a successful life. But he could never escape the nagging fear of an illness that could eventually have killed him.

During a routine checkup, Klug was diagnosed in 1991 with primary sclerosing cholangitis, a rare degenerative bile duct condition—the same affliction that had killed Chicago Bears star Walter Payton in 1999. The only cure was a liver transplant. After waiting for years on a transplant list, he received the liver of a 13-year-old accidental shooting victim at University Hospital in Denver.

Amazingly, Klug was back on the World Cup snowboard circuit four months later. Six months after that, he claimed his first podium in Italy. And at the Salt Lake Games in 2002, Klug won a bronze medal in the parallel giant slalom at Park City, overcoming a broken boot that he patched together with duct tape at the last minute. He continues to ride and work to raise awareness of the need for transplant donors. At this writing, Klug remains the only transplantee Olympian in Games history.

She Pulled a Jacobellis

American Lindsey Jacobellis' flub in the inaugural women's snowboard cross contest at Bardonecchia during the Turin Games of 2006 was one of those moments that will live in Olympic infamy.

Leading the final run by more than 3 seconds ahead of Switzerland's Tanja Frieden, Jacobellis, 20, heavily promoted by her sponsor, Visa, before the Games, had run away from the pack, and was seconds away from victory. Clearing her second-to-last jump, she reached down and gripped her board, in a classic snowboarder, big-air stance—a backside method grab that includes a 60-degree twist.

Except she biffed, falling on her back like a sack of spuds, within sight of the finish line as Frieden blazed past for the improbable gold medal. The move, replayed a billion times on TV, became a signature moment—and led to what likely will be a lifetime correlation between her name and the unfortunate consequences of hot-dogging, as in "he pulled a Jacobellis at the finish line."

Fortunately, the biff was much more crushing for most spectators than for Jacobellis herself. The first-time Olympian from Vermont took it in stride, finally conceding that she had hot-dogged and explaining to reporters, "Snowboarding is fun. I was ahead. I wanted to share my enthusiasm with the crowd. I messed up. Oh well; it happens."

It didn't go down quite so easy with her coach, Peter Foley, who was last seen collapsing in a heap at the finish line when Jacobellis pulled her . . . well, Jacobellis.

He later lamented to the Associated Press, "She definitely styled that a little too hard."

RECORD BOOK: MEN'S SNOWBOARDING

The young sport of snowboarding has seen only one repeat champion: **Philipp Schoch** of Switzerland claimed gold in the parallel giant slalom at both Salt Lake City and Turin, beating out his older brother, **Simon**, who settled for silver at the 2006 Games.

The United States' dominating performance on home snow along the Wasatch Front at the Salt Lake Games gave it a couple of multiple medalists. **Ross Powers** of Stratton, Vermont, won bronze in the halfpipe at Nagano, then came on strong to lead a U.S. sweep of the event in 2002 at Park City, Utah. New Jersey native **Danny Kass** won the silver in the halfpipe at both Salt Lake City and Turin.

Shaun White kept the U.S. halfpipe streak alive in Turin, winning gold. And American **Seth**

Wescott won the inaugural snowboard cross competition at the same Olympics.

Canada's only men's medal was the gold garnered by **Ross "Second-Hand Smoke" Rebagliati** at the Nagano Games.

RECORD BOOK: WOMEN'S SNOWBOARDING

American women have dominated recent halfpipe competition, just as their male counterparts have. **Kelly Clark** took gold in the event at Salt Lake City; **Hannah Teter** defended the title in Turin in 2006, as teammate **Gretchen Bleiler** rode to silver. Two other medals marked success at the Turin Games: Alaska's **Rosey Fletcher** took bronze in the parallel giant slalom, and Vermont's **Lindsey Jacobellis,** in a competition that will go down in history, fell just short of the finish line while hot-dogging at the end of the inaugural women's snowboard cross, handing the gold medal to **Tanja Frieden** of Switzerland.

Canada's lone women's medal is **Dominique Maltais'** bronze in the snowboard cross in Turin.

The only woman to win two medals in snowboarding has been France's **Karine Ruby.** She took the gold in the giant slalom at Nagano and raced to bronze in the revised event, the parallel giant slalom, in Salt Lake City.

America's Lindsey Jacobellis bites it only feet from the finish line in the snowboard cross finals at the 2006 Turin Games.

NEXT STOP: CYPRESS MOUNTAIN

Location: West Vancouver, B.C.

Spectator capacity: 12,000 in each of two temporary stadiums

Elevation: 915 meters (3,020 feet) at the base; 1,240 meters (3,940 feet) at the top

Other events: Freestyle skiing

Medal ceremonies: B.C. Place Stadium

See the Freestyle Skiing chapter for a description of this venue.

Snowboarding 2010 Schedule

February 15: Men's snowboard cross

February 16: Women's snowboard cross

February 17: Men's snowboard halfpipe

February 18: Women's snowboard halfpipe

February 26: Women's snowboard parallel giant slalom

February 27: Men's snowboard parallel giant slalom

FURTHER READING

* * * * *

BOOKS

The leading narrative histories of the Winter and Summer Games are the frequently updated *The Complete Book of the Winter Olympics* (Sport Classic Books) and, published to coincide with the summer games, *The Complete Book of the Olympics* (Aurum Press Ltd.), both by Olympic historian David Wallechinsky and Jaime Loucky. These encyclopedic books list the top-eight finishers at each Olympic event throughout history, and include features about athletes and notable Olympic events. Both are indispensable references for Olympiphiles.

For the Olympic movement overall, see *The Official History of the Olympic Games and the IOC: From Athens to Beijing, 1894-2008,* by David Miller (2008; Trafalgar Square Publishing). This impressive history includes an extensive recap of every Olympics, plus appendices with medal winners and other exhaustive statistics. It's a work for serious Olympic wonks only.

More accessible and reader-friendly for the casual fan is *The Olympic Games, Athens 1896 to Athens 2004,* (2004; Dorling Kindersley), a book chock full of photographs, results, and recaps worthy of any coffee table. A wealth of Games imagery from both the Summer and Winter Olympics, the book also includes appendices with medal winners for all the Olympics.

An indispensable guide to the mechanics, rules, and strategies of all the global sports played at the Olympics, both Summer and Winter, as well as many other sports more obscure to North American fans is *Sports: The Complete Visual Reference,* by Francois Fortin (2000; Firefly Books). The book includes wonderful, color illustrations of fields of play, equipment, and other details for every sport.

A recent historical work for fans of ice skating is *Figure Skating, A History*, by James R. Hines, (2006; University of Illinois Press) a comprehensive look at the competitive past of that sport.

Now out of print but often found at used bookstores, filmmaker Bud Greenspan's *Frozen in Time: The Greatest Moments at the Winter Olympics* (1997; General Publishing Group Inc.) is a wonderful compendium of short-story versions of fabled Olympic achievements.

ONLINE

It's sometimes challenging to navigate, but the official International Olympic Committee website, www.olympic.org, is a good reference point for Olympic history, policy, and current events in the Olympic movement. The site's searchable athlete medal-winner database is a particularly useful function, although one prone to frequent jumbled-up search results that lump random sports in with those specified. Caveat emptor. A relatively new (at this writing) addition to the field is an Olympic reference site, www.sports-reference.com/olympics/, containing the exhaustive Games data collected over the years by a group of Olympic historians and statisticians calling themselves MADmen—all members of the International Society of Olympic Historians. It's a good, quick reference for medalists, records, and other Olympic hard data.

The official website for the 2010 Vancouver Winter Games is www.vancouver2010.com.

IN PERSON

Olympic fans seeking to soak up Winter Games history in person can do so by visiting almost any former host city. In North America, those are Lake Placid, New York; Squaw Valley, California; Calgary, Alberta; Salt Lake City, Utah; and now Vancouver/Whistler, British Columbia. Two-time host Lake Placid in particular works hard to keep its Olympic spirit alive, with a fine Olympic Museum and elite-level training for World Cup events at most of its Winter Venues nearly all year around.

The small World Figure Skating Hall of Fame and Museum, with much fine memorabilia and history, and currently in Colorado Springs, Colorado (there has been talk of moving it elsewhere) is a worthwhile stop if you're in the area.

True Olympiphiles at some point will want to make a pilgrimage to Lausanne, Switzerland, home of the International Olympic Committee (IOC) and The Olympic Museum, situated on lovely grounds on the shores of Lake Geneva. The museum also houses the official Olympic Archives, available to the public by arrangement. See www.Olympic.org for schedules and more information about the museum.

ACKNOWLEDGMENTS

❄ ❄ ❄ ❄ ❄

A book filled with as much history and personal experience as this one wouldn't be possible without friends, colleagues, and supporters who make the process not only bearable but unforgettable.

Major thanks are due my longtime friend and colleague, photojournalist Dean Rutz, who has redefined the term "trouper" while accompanying me on Olympic journeys around the globe, and whose fabulous work graces many of the pages of this book. I'll always be ready to "chase the torch" with Dean at any Olympics, anytime, anywhere.

Thanks also to my longtime editors, Kate Rogers of The Mountaineers Books and Cathy Henkel of *The Seattle Times*, for helping make this work possible.

Other colleagues who help keep me sane when things go bad—and they always do—while covering the Olympics as a journalist also deserve singling out: Thanks to Meri-Jo Borzilleri, my wife and fellow Olympiphile, for always being there and nodding with interest, even if feigned, at all my newly discovered trivial details of Olympic glory from 60 years ago. Thanks also to colleagues Elliott Almond and Candy Thomson, two trusted friends who "get" the magic of the Olympics but aren't afraid to laugh at its unseemly underbelly.

Thanks also to the many Olympic athletes, coaches, and officials who have offered their time and expertise over the years, and who have on occasion allowed us to come along on what truly qualifies as a magic ride. It's also worth noting that none of this work would be possible without dedicated officials who make Olympic sports accessible to journalists and, by extension, the public, especially Bob Condron, media coordinator for the U.S. Olympic Committee—and one of the world's leading connoisseurs of Dairy Queen chocolate-dipped cones.

And finally, my deepest gratitude is owed to the fans of Olympic sport who have read my work and taken the time not only to say thanks, but also to impress upon editors the need to give the Games the coverage they deserve. You make it all worthwhile.

INDEX

❋ ❋ ❋ ❋ ❋

A

Aamodt, Kjetil André, 38, 176-78
aerials, 208-09
Albertville, France, 33-34
Albright, Tenley, 97, 103-04
alpine skiing, 35-36
  downhill, 169
  field of play, 169
  format, rules, and strategy for, 169, 173
  giant slalom, 173
  great moments in, 166-69
  history of, 30, 174-75, 179-81
  legends of, 170-72, 174-81
  medalists in, 181-83
  slalom, 29, 173
  super combined, 173
  super-G, 169, 173
  training and equipment, 173-74
  Whistler Creekside, 185-87
Axel jump, 27, 96, 100

B

Bahrke, Shannon, 214-15
Bakken, Jill, 36, 66-67
Benshoof, Tony, 78
biathlon, 35-36, 39
  field of play, 193
  format, rules, and strategy for, 193, 196
  history of, 196
  legends of, 197-201
  medalists in, 202
  training and equipment, 196
  Whistler Olympic Park, 202-04
Blair, Bonnie, 144-45
bobsled, 39
  Canadians, 69-70
  field of play, 61
  format, rules, and strategy for, 61, 63
  great moments in, 68-73
  history of, 58-61, 68
  Jamaican, 71
  medalists in, 73
  sleds, 64
  training and equipment for, 63-64
  weight limits, 64
  word origin of, 65
Bodine, Geoff, 70
Bogataj, Vinko, 218-20
Boit, Philip, 198
Boitano, Brian, 103
Bradbury, Steven, 152-53, 160
Brassard, Jean-Luc, 211-12
Button, Dick, 27, 92-95, 100

C

Calgary, Alberta, 33, 43
Camplin, Alisa, 213
Canada Hockey Place, 126-27
Chamonix, France, 18, 21, 23
Christian, Bill, 119
Christian, Roger, 119
Cortina d'Ampezzo, Italy, 27
cross-country skiing
    field of play, 190-91
    format, rules, and strategy for, 191-92
    great moments in, 188-90
    history of, 196
    legends of, 194-95, 197-201
    medalists in, 201-02
    race formats, 192
    training and equipment, 192-93
    Whistler Olympic Park, 202-04
curling
    field of play, 81-82
    format, rules, and strategy for, 82
    history of, 79-80, 83
    legends of, 84
    medalists in, 85
    participants in, 83-85
    stones used in, 83
    training and equipment for, 82
    Vancouver Olympic Centre, 85-86
Cypress Mountain, 45, 47, 216-17, 244

D

Dæhlie, Bjørn, 34-35, 194-95, 198, 201-02
Davis, Shani, 141-42, 161-62
doubles luge, 76

E

Edwards, Eddie, 225-26

F

figure skating, 35-36
    Axel jump, 27, 96, 100
    field of play, 89
    format, rules, and strategy for, 90-91, 96
    history of, 26, 28, 97, 101-04, 106
    ice dancing, 30, 96-97, 108
    jumps, 27, 90, 96
    legends of, 92-95
    medalists in, 106-08

    men's, 106
    Pacific Coliseum, 109
    pairs, 96, 107-08
    popularity of, 87-89
    scandals in, 101-02
    scoring, 90-91
    training and equipment, 97
    at Turin Games, 98-99
    women's, 106-07
Fiske, Billy, 68-69
freestyle skiing
    aerials, 208-09
    Cypress Mountain, 216-17
    field of play, 208-9
    format, rules, and strategy for, 209
    history of, 211
    legends of, 206-08, 211-13
    medalists in, 213, 216
    moguls, 209
    ski cross, 209
    training and equipment, 209, 211
Funaki, Kazuyoshi, 226

G

Garmisch-Partenkirchen, Germany, 26
giant slalom, 173
Grafström, Gillis, 23-25
Greene, Nancy, 180
Grenoble, France, 29

H

Hackl, Georg, 35, 73-75
Hakensmoen, Bjornar, 199-200
Hakulinen, Veikko, 197
halfpipe, 235-37
Harada, Mashahiko, 227
Harding, Tonya, 35, 100-01
Haugen, Anders, 227
Heiden, Eric, 32, 135-37, 140
Henie, Sonja, 23, 26, 100
history, 18-39
hockey. *See* ice hockey

I

ice dancing, 30, 96-97, 108
ice hockey, 35
    in Canada, 117-20
    Canada Hockey Place, 126-27

description of, 110-13
field of play, 113
format, rules, and strategy for, 115-16
history of, 24, 35, 116-20
legends of, 122-23
medalists in, 120-21
men's, 120-21
"Miracle on Ice" team, 30, 32, 111-12, 118-19
at Nagano Games, 124-25
penalties, 116
training and equipment, 116
UBC Thunderbird Arena, 126-27
women's, 120, 126
Individual Gundersen, 222
Innsbruck, Austria, 28-30
International Olympic Committee, 21-22
International Ski Federation, 26, 239

J

Jacobellis, Lindsey, 242-43
Jacoby, Mike, 241
Jaffee, Irving, 138-39
Jansen, Dan, 33, 140-41
Jernberg, Sixten, 197, 202
Johnson, Bill, 32, 179, 181
journalism, 9-11

K

K line, 220
Kerrigan, Nancy, 35, 101
Killy, Jean-Claude, 29, 174-75
Klammer, Franz, 30, 178-79
Klug, Chris, 242
Koch, Bill, 188-90, 197-99, 201
Koss, Johann Olav, 34, 143
Kostelić, Janica, 36, 38, 170-72
Kwan, Michelle, 35, 88-89, 104-06

L

Lake Placid
    1932 Games, 24-26
    1980 Games, 30, 32, 71, 112
Lillehammer, Norway, 34-35
Lipinski, Tara, 16, 104, 106
luge
    Americans in, 71-72
    doubles, 76
    field of play, 61

format, rules, and strategy for, 63
history of, 30, 68
legends of, 74-75
medalists in, 73, 76-77
men's, 73, 76
sleds, 65
training and equipment for, 63-64
weight limits, 64
women's, 76-77
word origin of, 65
lutz, 96

M

Mahre, Phil, 32, 179, 182
Mahre, Steve, 32, 179
Maier, Hermann, 38, 180-81
McDermott, Terry, 139
medalists
    alpine skiing, 181-83
    biathlon, 202
    bobsled, 73
    cross-country skiing, 201-02
    curling, 85
    figure skating, 106-08
    freestyle skiing, 213, 216
    ice hockey, 120-21
    luge, 73, 76-77
    nordic combined, 230-31
    short-track speedskating, 162-64
    skeleton, 77
    ski jumping, 230-31
    snowboarding, 244
    speedskating, 143, 146-48
Mieto, Juha, 198-99
Moe, Tommy, 34-35, 179, 181
moguls, 209
Monti, Eugenio, 29, 69
Moseley, Jonny, 206-08

N

Nagano, Japan, 9-10, 22, 35, 71, 124-25, 233-34, 240-41
1912 Games, 21-22
1916 Games, 22
1924 Games, 22-23
1928 Games, 23-24
1932 Games, 24-26
1936 Games, 26

1948 Games, 26-27
1952 Games, 27
1956 Games, 27
1960 Games, 27-28
1964 Games, 28-29
1968 Games, 29
1972 Games, 29-30
1976 Games, 30, 43
1980 Games, 30, 32, 71, 112
1984 Games, 32-33
1988 Games, 33, 43
1992 Games, 22, 33-34
1994 Games, 34-35
1998 Games, 35
nordic combined
    format, rules, and strategy for, 222-23
    legends of, 230
    medalists in, 230-31
    Whistler Olympic Park, 231-32
Nykänen, Matti, 225, 231

O

O'Hare, Tommy, 161
Ohno, Apolo Anton, 36, 39, 151-56, 158-61
Orser, Brian, 102-03
Oslo, Norway, 27

P

Pacific Coliseum, 109, 164
pairs figure skating, 96, 107-08
parallel giant slalom, 236
Parra, Derek, 141
professional athletes, 26, 29-30, 35

R

Rebagliati, Ross, 35, 234
Renner, Sara, 199-200
Richmond Oval, 148-50
Ruud, Birger, 228-31

S

Sailer, Toni, 27, 175, 178
Salchow, Ulrich, 21, 96
Salt Lake City, Utah, 36, 214-15
Sapporo, Japan, 29-30
Sarajevo, Yugoslavia, 32-33
scandals, 36, 101-02, 161-62
Schmirler, Sandra, 84

Scott, Beckie, 200-01
Shea, Jack, 72-73, 138
Shea, Jim, 72-73
short-track speedskating
    field of play, 156
    format, rules, and strategy for, 156-57
    great moments in, 151-56
    medalists in, 162-64
    Pacific Coliseum, 164
    scandals in, 161-62
    team relays, 157
    training and equipment, 157-58
skating. *See* figure skating; short-track speedskating;
speedskating
skeleton, 36
    field of play, 61
    format, rules, and strategy for, 63
    history of, 68
    medalists in, 77
    men's, 77
    sleds, 65
    training and equipment for, 63-64
    weight limits, 64
    women's, 77
    word origin of, 65
ski cross, 209
ski flying, 220
ski jumping
    field of play, 220
    format, rules, and strategy for, 220-22
    history of, 223-25, 230
    Japan's success in, 226-27
    legends of, 218-20, 225-30
    medalists in, 230-31
    training and equipment, 223
    Whistler Olympic Park, 231-32
skiing. *See* alpine skiing; cross-country skiing; freestyle skiing
slalom, 29, 173
snowboarding, 35
    Cypress Mountain, 244
    field of play, 235-36
    format, rules, and strategy for, 236-37
    halfpipe, 235-37
    history of, 237, 239
    medalists in, 244
    men's, 244
    at Nagano Games, 233-35, 240-41

parallel giant slalom, 236
snowboard cross, 236-37
training and equipment, 237
women's, 244
speedskating
description of, 128-31
distances, 131
field of play, 131
format, rules, and strategy for, 131-32
history of, 27-28, 32-33, 36, 38-39, 134, 138-43
inline roller skating contributions, 141
legends of, 135-37
medalists in, 143, 146-48
men's, 143, 146-47
Richmond Oval, 148-50
short-track. *see* short-track speedskating
skates used in, 132
technique, 132-34
training and equipment, 132, 134
women's, 147-48
sports coverage, 11
Squaw Valley, California, 27-28
St. Moritz, Switzerland
1928 Games, 23-24
1948 Games, 26-27
Street, Picabo, 35, 166-67, 181
super-G, 169, 173
Svan, Gunde, 198
Syers, Madge, 21

T
television broadcasting, 12, 28
Thams, Jacob Tullin, 230
Thunberg, A. Clas, 23, 25
tickets, 48-49

toe loops, 96
Tomba, Alberto, 33-34, 182
Tretiak, Vladislav, 122-23
triple Axel, 100-01
Turin, Italy, 36, 38-39, 98-99, 130
2002 Games, 36, 43, 214-16
2006 Games, 36, 38-39

U
UBC Thunderbird Arena, 51, 126-27

V
Vancouver
awarding of games to, 40-43
description of, 47, 49-51, 53-56
facts about, 53
legacy of games for, 51-53
tickets, 48-49
transportation, 51
venues, 44-46
weather, 46-47
Vancouver Olympic Centre, 85-86
Vancouver Organizing Committee, 41
V-style, 222

W
Wehling, Ulrich, 230
Whistler, 40-41, 43, 49, 51-52
Whistler Creekside, 185-87
Whistler Olympic Park, 51-52, 202-4, 231-32
Whistler Sliding Centre, 52, 77-78
Wickenheiser, Hayley, 114-15

Y
Yamaguchi, Kristi, 13

AWARD-WINNING
SPORTS COVERAGE.

*We are the in-depth sports voice
for the Northwest and your
best Olympics source.*

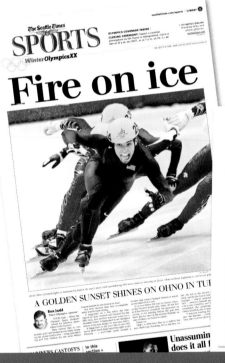

ABOUT THE AUTHOR

❄ ❄ ❄ ❄ ❄

Ron C. Judd, a veteran newspaper columnist and Olympic journalist, first grew to love the Winter Olympics by watching them on TV. A high-schooler during the unforgettable 1980 Lake Placid Winter Games, he vowed to find a way to experience the Games in person. Once it finally became clear that he would never qualify in the giant slalom—or any other athletic event, for that matter—he talked his way into an assignment covering the 1998 Winter Olympics in Nagano, Japan, for *The Seattle Times*.

He has covered all the Games since, but will always most fondly recall those of Turin, Italy, where, in his spare time, he fell in love with another Olympic journalist, Meri-Jo Borzilleri, a Lake Placid, New York native. A year later, standing on the Lake Placid Olympic Oval where Eric Heiden had won five gold medals in 1980, she agreed to become his wife, making the Olympics a true family affair.

Judd is the author of numerous other nonfiction books, including two works of humor: *The Roof Rack Chronicles* and *The Blue Tarp Bible*. As an Olympic writer and blogger for *The Seattle Times*, he looks forward to covering the 2010 Winter Olympics, which will be held less than an hour's drive from his home in Bellingham, Washington.

Keep abreast of future works, and updates to information in this book, at his website, www.ronjudd.com.

Author Ron C. Judd, Bobby Bobsledder, and Meri-Jo Borzilleri take a break from World Cup Bobsled action at Mount Van Hoevenberg, New York

THE MOUNTAINEERS, founded in 1906, is a nonprofit outdoor activity and conservation club, whose mission is "to explore, study, preserve, and enjoy the natural beauty of the outdoors...." Based in Seattle, Washington, the club is now the third-largest such organization in the United States, with seven branches throughout Washington State.

The Mountaineers sponsors both classes and year-round outdoor activities in the Pacific Northwest, which include hiking, mountain climbing, ski-touring, snowshoeing, bicycling, camping, kayaking, nature study, sailing, and adventure travel. The club's conservation division supports environmental causes through educational activities, sponsoring legislation, and presenting informational programs.

All club activities are led by skilled, experienced instructors, who are dedicated to promoting safe and responsible enjoyment and preservation of the outdoors.

If you would like to participate in these organized outdoor activities or the club's programs, consider a membership in The Mountaineers. For information and an application, write The Mountaineers, Club Headquarters, 7700 Sandpoint Way NE, Seattle, WA 98115. You can also visit the club's website at www.mountaineers.org or contact The Mountaineers via email at clubmail@mountaineers.org.

The Mountaineers Books, an active, nonprofit publishing program of the club, produces guidebooks, instructional texts, historical works, natural history guides, and works on environmental conservation. All books produced by The Mountaineers Books fulfill the club's mission.

Send or call for our catalog of more than 450 outdoor titles:

The Mountaineers Books
1001 SW Klickitat Way, Suite 201
Seattle, WA 98134
800-553-4453
mbooks@mountaineersbooks.org
www.mountaineersbooks.org